PRAISE FOR David Bach and Smart Women Finish Rich

"There's a reason why *Smart Women Finish Rich* has sold over a million copies—it works! David Bach has helped millions of women for over two decades be smarter with their money. His no-nonsense approach will inspire you to take action to live your best life."

—Jean Chatzky,
financial editor of NBC's *Today*
and host of the HerMoney podcast

"David Bach is the one financial expert to listen to when you're intimidated by your finances. His powerful and easy-to-use program will show you how to spend, save and invest your money to afford your dreams."

—Tony Robbins,
New York Times bestselling author of
Money: Master the Game

"David Bach knows how to teach when it comes to money and getting people to take action because he's done it now for over two decades. I watched him change tens of millions of people's lives when I produced a half dozen *Oprah* shows with him and his message. I also saw firsthand how his books helped our audience members and Harpo's staff (my friends and myself) take charge of our financial lives. *Smart Women Finish Rich* is my favorite guide when it comes to women and money because I know it works."

—Candi Carter,
executive producer of *The View*
and former producer of *Oprah*

"*Smart Women Finish Rich* is simply a remarkable book that is even more relevant now than when it was first published. Twenty years later, this Anniversary Edition will help a new generation of women achieve financial security and live lives of independence and purpose."

—Richard Bradley, editor in chief of *Worth* magazine

"In *Smart Women Finish Rich*, David Bach empowers us to take control of our finances and become better investors. This book is a must read for any woman who wants to make sure her money is working as hard for her as she worked to earn it."

—Randi Zuckerberg,
New York Times bestselling author of
Pick Three and *Dot Complicated*

"When I first started my career, I was deep in debt and full of shame, fear, and embarrassment about money. *Smart Women Finish Rich* helped me turn that around and create what I'd always dreamed of: real financial freedom. I've recommended this book to millions of our fans and will continue to do so. Because when women are economically empowered, the whole world wins."

—Marie Forleo,
author of *Everything Is Figureoutable*
and host of the award-winning show *MarieTV*

"*Smart Women Finish Rich* is THE definitive guide for all women seeking financial independence and a prosperous life. Seriously—get this book, read it and use it. Your older self will thank you."

—Farnoosh Torabi,
bestselling author of *When She Makes More*
and host of So Money podcast

"Straight-shooting, action-oriented tips for getting a handle on your spending and savings habits . . . presented in a straightforward, non-intimidating manner perfect for the finance newbie."

—ABCNews.com

"[David] Bach gets across complicated stuff: how to organize a portfolio, keep the taxman at bay, invest in yourself, and earn more, all of which makes this book one of the best overall."

—*Working Woman*

"The best financial writers keep it simple, and David Bach is absolutely one of the best. Bach makes it clear that financial security is a matter of understanding a few simple rules and applying them consistently. When you absorb the lessons of *Smart Women Finish Rich*, you will retire secure and in command of your retirement."

—Eric Schurenberg,
former editor of *Money* and *CBS MoneyWatch*,
and CEO of Mansueto Ventures

"David Bach set a new standard 20 years ago with *Smart Women Finish Rich*—and now the expanded and updated edition raises the bar once again. Bach takes out the intimidating jargon and speaks candidly to women about what we care about: how to earn financial freedom and live the life we choose."

—Bobbi Rebell CFP®,
former Reuters columnist, author of
How to Be a Financial Grownup,
and host of the Financial Grownup podcast

"This book will help any woman take control of her financial future and live rich. David offers sound, easy-to-follow advice for saving, investing and earning more. His book helps women create a purpose-focused financial plan that takes into account both their finances and their values."

—Jennifer Barrett,
chief education officer at Acorns
and editor in chief of *Grow.com*

"Inspires women to start planning today for a secure financial future. Every woman can benefit from this book. . . . Bach is an excellent money coach."

—John Gray, author of *Men Are from Mars, Women Are from Venus*

PRAISE FOR Smart Couples Finish Rich

"I know how hard it is to make a personal-finance book user-friendly. Bach has done it. *Smart Couples Finish Rich* picks up where *Smart Women Finish Rich* left off. . . . This is an easy, lively read filled with tips that made me smile and at least once made me laugh."

—*USA Weekend*

"David Bach offers a prescription both to avoid money conflicts and to plan a harmonious future together. . . . The bottom line is action, and Bach's chatty writing style helps motivate you to that end."

—*Businessweek*

"*Smart Couples Finish Rich* teaches women and men to work together as a team when it comes to money. Bach's nine steps are powerful, yet easy to understand and fun to implement. The entire family can benefit from this great book."

—Robert T. Kiyosaki, author of *Rich Dad, Poor Dad*

"Bach specializes in commonsense advice and a clear-cut path for engaging your partner in fruitful discussions about your shared financial future. . . . His advice serves to free you and your beloved from the stress of never being quite sure of exactly where you stand financially. You'll probably be surprised by how big a difference Bach's strategy can make in your relationship."

—*Better Investing*

"Bach does a great job convincing couples to think about money, talk about money, get a financial plan in order—and yes, spend less and save more."

—*American Way*

Also by David Bach

The Automatic Millionaire®

Smart Couples Finish Rich®

Start Late, Finish Rich

Start Over, Finish Rich

The Finish Rich Dictionary

The Finish Rich Workbook

The Automatic Millionaire Homeowner

The Automatic Millionaire Workbook

Debt Free For Life

Fight for Your Money

Go Green, Live Rich

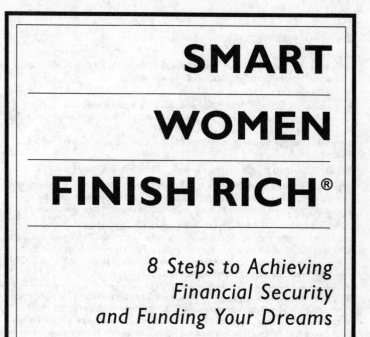

SMART

WOMEN

FINISH RICH®

*8 Steps to Achieving
Financial Security
and Funding Your Dreams*

DAVID BACH

CURRENCY
NEW YORK

Originally published in hardcover in the United States in 1998, and subsequently in a
revised trade paperback edition in the United States in 2002 by Broadway Books, an
imprint of the Crown Publishing Group, a division of Penguin Random House LLC.

Currency books are available at special discounts for bulk purchases for sales
promotions or corporate use. Special editions, including personalized covers, excerpts
of existing books, or books with corporate logos, can be created in large quantities
for special needs. For more information, contact Premium Sales at (212) 572-2232 or
e-mail specialmarkets@penguinrandomhouse.com.

Library of Congress Cataloging-in-Publication data is available upon request.

ISBN 978-0-525-57304-3
Ebook ISBN 978-0-525-57305-0

Printed in the United States of America

Cover design: Jennifer Carrow
Cover photograph: tycoon751/iStock/Getty Images

16 15 14 13 12 11 10 9

Second Revised Edition

To my beloved grandmother Rose Bach,
who taught me the importance of living life to its fullest.
You will forever be with me in thought and spirit.
I miss you.

CONTENTS

Step Seven
Raising Smart Kids to Finish Rich 298

Step Eight
Follow the 12 Commandments of Attracting
Greater Wealth 326

Bonus Chapter
8 New Tax Changes You Need to Know About
for 2018 and Beyond 359

PREFACE TO THE 20TH-ANNIVERSARY EDITION

A PERSONAL MESSAGE FROM DAVID BACH

THANK YOU for being here. If you're a returning reader, welcome back! If you're a new reader, welcome home, as I always like to say.

You're now holding in your hand (or reading on your device) the completely revised and updated edition of *Smart Women Finish Rich*. The original edition first appeared in print some twenty years ago. Looking back, with over seven million copies of my books now in print, it's hard for me to believe that the book that started it all—*this* book—might easily have never happened. Not everyone believed in this book.

In fact, many agents and publishers passed on *Smart Women Finish Rich* when I first set out to try to find a home for it back in 1997. And even the ones who didn't pass didn't have much faith in it. One publisher told me that even though he was willing to put out the book, he thought it would never sell more than 10,000 copies. "David," she said, "women don't buy investment books." Needless to say, I didn't sell the book to that publisher.

Thinking back on that, I have to laugh. Fortunately, I found a publisher who did believe. The team thought the book could sell 30,000 copies and ultimately become what they called an "evergreen." Being a new author, I had no idea what that meant, but I loved that they believed in my mission. "I don't care what they offer, sell it to them," I told my agent. Then I asked her what exactly does "evergreen" mean? My agent explained that an evergreen was a book that could sell for years, sometimes for as long as a decade. Wow, I thought, a decade! Seriously? That would be amazing.

In retrospect, we all underestimated what this book could do and how many people it would help.

So here we are, two decades down the road, and I'm thrilled to welcome you to the 20th-Anniversary Edition of *Smart Women Finish Rich*. To date, this book has sold more than one million copies. More important, it's helped millions of women around the world take control of their financial futures—and it has been shared from generation to generation, friend to friend.

What accounts for this success? To be honest, I think a lot of the credit has to go to my grandma Rose Bach. My Grandma Rose helped me buy my first stock when I was seven years old, and she inspired me not just to be an investor but to dream big. She had this wonderful saying: "If you can dream it, you can see it, and if you believe it, you can achieve it." I'm not sure she invented the saying, but the way she always said it made it stick with me. And so, more than 20 years ago, inspired by Grandma Rose Bach—a woman who started with nothing and became a self-made millionaire—I set out to write my very first book, *Smart Women Finish Rich*.

My goal was to help a million women take charge of their financial futures quickly and easily. At the time, I thought this was an extremely challenging goal, but I had a big dream. So, excitedly, with the support of an enthusiastic publisher, I set out to do it. It started slowly.

Smart Women Finish Rich came out in 1998. It got zero national media attention. That was disappointing, but I was determined to spread the book's message by myself, if necessary, and that's exactly what I did. In those first weeks and months, I drove myself to dozens of bookstores throughout Northern California to do readings and book signings. At the beginning, I could often count on the fingers of one hand the number of people who showed up to hear me. But over time the audiences started to grow. And then one day I looked up and *Smart Women Finish Rich* was a regional bestseller in Northern California. I kept on pushing and about a year later the book had made the national bestseller lists not only in *The New York Times* and *The Wall Street Journal* but also in *Business Week*, *USA Today,* the *San Francisco Chronicle, The Boston Globe*, and *The Washington Post.*

And I kept pushing. Bookstore after bookstore. City after city. Speech after speech—I toured the entire country with the message of *Smart Women Finish Rich.* Eventually, I did a PBS special called *Smart Women Finish Rich* and we launched our *Smart Women Finish Rich®* seminars throughout North America. Now millions of women were hearing about the book, reading it, and sharing it with their friends.

By 2004, I was appearing regularly on *Oprah*, talking about how women could and should take control of their financial lives, and then *Business Week* ranked *Smart Women Finish Rich* as the #2 business book of the year—five years after it was first published.

As word of the book and its message spread, I began to receive what would ultimately amount to thousands of e-mails and social media posts from readers around the world letting me know how *Smart Women Finish Rich* had helped them take charge of their financial lives. Truly, the book has had an amazing impact. So why update it? The reason is simple. Learning about money is a never-ending process. The world is constantly changing, and for women the changes over the past two decades have been especially dramatic. When I first wrote this book, I had to champion the idea that women should take charge of their financial lives. Today, for women, taking charge of their financial lives is a given! And the #MeToo movement will continue to accelerate women's desire to control their financial destinies. The only real question is, what's the best way to go about it?

Answering this question—providing you with a road map to financial security—is the mission of *Smart Women Finish Rich.* To accomplish this, the book has been painstakingly refreshed and updated from beginning to end. The timeless principles I have taught for 25 years have remained, because they continue to work. With that said pretty much everything else in the book has been revised to take into account how much the entire world of investing has changed over the last 20 years (not to mention what's happened to technology). From retirement accounts and insurance to financial apps and resources, to health care and entrepreneurship, even teaching your kids about money—it's all been revised to reflect the latest developments in these areas. The good news about everything that has happened in the world is that investing has become easier than ever—to the point where most of you today can manage your finances from your phones.

Finally, one of the most important changes in our financial lives that this new edition covers is the impact of the big tax reform bill passed by Congress in 2017. The Tax Cut and Jobs Act of 2017 is the most sweeping tax and pension reform in decades, and I have included in this Anniversary Edition the changes you need to know about everything it has changed, from retirement accounts to mortgage deductions. I have also included a new bonus chapter at the back of the book called "8 New Tax Changes You Need to Know About for 2018 and Beyond." The fact is, these new tax-law changes are a big deal. If you intend to live smart and finish rich, you've got to keep abreast of them.

One thing has not changed in this updated edition; the book's primary goal remains the same. *Smart Women Finish Rich* is still about the simple idea that if you take the right kind of action now, you can truly live and finish rich. Living rich to me is the most important message in this book, This book shares the simple idea that any woman—regardless of income, age, race, or marital status— has the power to experience a future of fulfillment, independence, and true financial security and freedom based on her values. If I've learned one thing about women and money over the past 20 years, it's this: *Once a woman learns how to take charge of her finances, there is no stopping her.* There is no stopping you. Today there are more women college graduates, business owners, CEOs, congresswomen and senators, entrepreneurs, and homeowners than ever before. Clearly, the growing financial empowerment of women is the new reality in the households of America, and it is going to change our destiny as a nation.

So let's get started.

I hope you enjoy this 20th Anniversary Edition. If you have any suggestions for a future edition—whether they concern something I may have missed or something I didn't explain fully enough—please let me know. Since the original *Smart Women Finish Rich came out,* I've published eleven other books. All of them were written as a result of your questions and suggestions. So take the time to browse the back pages and visit our website at **www.davidbach.com** to learn more.

Once again, to all of you who helped make the original *Smart Women Finish Rich* the success it's been, THANK YOU.

If you are a returning reader, welcome back. If you're here for the first time—welcome and enjoy.

Your journey begins today.

David Bach
New York
May 2018

FREE! SPECIAL BONUSES FOR READING THIS BOOK

Over the years, many of you have asked if you could get the worksheets in this book in the form of downloadable PDFs. Well, you can now download them at **www.davidbach.com**. Visit the book section on the website and then click on Resources. You can also register on the website to receive our popular and free *3 Minute Sunday* newsletter. Enjoy.

WHY SMART WOMEN ARE TAKING CONTROL OF THEIR FINANCIAL FUTURES

I'll never forget the moment I asked my mom, "What really makes the world go round—money or love?" I was only about five at the time. She looked me straight in the eyes and said, "David, love is what makes life special . . . but without money you are in deep trouble!" Actually, "deep trouble" are my words. What my mom really said can't be repeated. I had never heard my mom use an "adult" swear word before, so even at age five I knew then and there that not having money could be really painful. The obvious next question that came to my five-year-old mind was "Are we rich, Mom?" That question took a little longer for her to answer (I think she eventually made me go play with my toys), but the thought of money has stayed with me ever since. If not having money is so bad, why don't more people figure out how to get and keep it? It can't be that hard. Or can it?

More than 45 years later, I feel privileged to have personally taught thousands of people—mostly women—how to invest and manage their money and then to have gone on to coach millions more through my bestselling books, coaching program, and media appearances. And I'm happy to report that when you strip away all the baloney, learning how to handle your own finances turns out to be relatively easy. Indeed, through my Smart Women Finish Rich® seminars alone I've helped hundreds of thousands of women travel the same road to financial independence you are going to take in this book. They have learned—as you will—the three keys to smart money management that enable a woman to gain control over her own financial destiny . . . and, yes, finish rich:

- How to use both your head and your heart in making financial decisions.
- How what I call "the Latte Factor®" can transform even the most modest wage earner into a significant investor.
- How my "three-basket" approach to financial planning can assure you of not only long-term security but the ability to realize your lifelong dreams.

As you will discover, my approach to personal money management involves some powerful and exciting techniques. And all of them are pretty easy to master. Before we get started, however, it might be a good idea for me to address a question that often comes up at this point—namely . . .

WHO AM I TO HELP YOU FINISH RICH?

One way to answer this question is to tell you that for more than 25 years, I have spent my career dedicated to women's financial empowerment. My experience started as a financial advisor at Morgan

Stanley, where in my twenties I was a partner in The Bach Group, which managed more than a half billion dollars of people's money. Most of my hundreds of clients were women who came to me after attending one of my investment seminars or through referrals from other women. Today, I am a co-founder and Director of Investor Education of AE Wealth Management, one of the country's fastest-growing Registered Investment Advisors (RIAs).

But what you probably really want to know is why a man (and, yes, I admit it—I can't hide the fact that I am a man) is so driven to teach and empower women in particular to take control of their finances.

Well, the answer has mainly to do with my grandmother. Her name was Rose Bach, and she was unlike any other grandmother I ever met.

MY GRANDMA, THE INVESTOR

The head buyer for wigs at Gimbel's (back when Gimbel's was one of America's leading department stores), Grandma Bach was a working woman at a time when most women weren't. Now, my grandparents were never wealthy; in fact, they never even owned their own home. Nonetheless, my grandmother decided at a very early age that she wanted to be an investor. Acting on her own, she took her earnings and put as much as she could afford into stocks and bonds. Over time, and without any advice from her husband, she built up a high-quality portfolio. When she passed away in 1997, at the age of 86, her investments were worth close to $1 million—this, from a woman whose first job paid only $10 a week!

There were many things my Grandma Bach taught me, but for our purposes, there's one lesson that deserves to be singled out:

You don't have to be rich to be an investor!

Of course, by becoming an investor, if you do it wisely like my Grandma Bach, you will almost certainly get rich!

It was Grandma Bach who helped me make my first stock purchase. I was seven years old, and my favorite restaurant in the world was McDonald's. So whenever I spent time with my grandmother, she would take me there for lunch. One day, at her prompting, instead of asking for catsup for my fries when I marched up to the counter, I looked at the woman on the other side and asked, "Is this company public?"

The counter lady looked back at me as if I were nuts, then called over the manager. Yes, he told me, McDonald's was a publicly traded company. After a little persuasion from Grandma Bach (and a lot of vacuuming and dishwashing), I saved my allowance for three months and managed to accumulate enough money to buy three shares of McDonald's Inc.

That was more than 45 years ago. Since then, McDonald's stock has gone up in value and split so many times that those original three shares of mine have multiplied into more than 360 shares. If I'd had enough money to purchase 100 shares of the company back then (an investment of around $10,000 at the time), my McDonald's holdings today would be worth more than $2 million! (I often give my parents a hard time for not having loaned me the additional money.) And all I had done was go out to lunch with my grandmother when I was a little kid and put my allowance into a company whose hamburgers I liked.

EVERY WOMAN CAN BE WEALTHY

Because Grandma Bach was my biggest inspiration as a child, I grew up thinking every woman was like her—aware of the importance of investing and pretty darn good at it too. So it came as something of a shock to me, when I followed my father into the investment business, to discover that, if anything, the opposite was true. Most women never receive even a basic education in finance until it's too late—which is to say, after they get divorced or are widowed and suddenly find themselves forced to deal with everything at the worst possible moment. The result, all too often, is financial devastation.

I wanted to help. I wanted every woman to have the information, the education, and the tools to take care of herself financially no matter what the circumstances. So I designed an investment seminar called "Smart Women Finish Rich!" in which I did two important things. One, I addressed the heart as well as the head, recognizing that financial planning is as much an emotional issue as it is an intellectual one. And two, I laid out a simple but effective pathway that any woman could follow to achieve financial security and freedom.

The response was immediate and incredible. First dozens, then hundreds of women signed up for my classes, and over the years I've personally given speeches for rooms of hundreds of women to as many as 5,000. Additionally, thousands of financial advisors in more than 1,500 cities have taught Smart Women Finish Rich® seminars from coast to coast with thousands of women attending every month. Why the huge response? In a word, necessity. As one student told me, "Growing up, no one taught me about money, not my father, not my mother, not my school—so I realized it was time to teach myself." Explained another student: "Nobody is going to take care of me. I have to take the responsibility myself." Added a third: "We'd be in deep trouble if we left everything up to our husbands. We need to know about our finances so we can be independent and take care of ourselves."

Though my students come from all walks of life—rich, poor, old, young, married, single—virtually all of them believe in the empowering importance of education. As a working mother of two from Walnut Creek, California, put it after taking my course, "Understanding your own finances is as important as knowing about your health. You can't make financial decisions if you're not educated."

What *I've* learned from my seminars is that women *want* to be responsible for their financial futures. The problem is, most of them just don't know how to get started. Or if they've taken steps in certain areas, they've neglected others. I can't tell you how gratifying it's been for me to see the thousands of women who've been through my seminars taking control of their financial destinies, making better decisions about their financial futures, and feeling great about their financial well-being as a result.

WELCOME TO THE CLUB!

And now you are going to join their ranks.

Congratulations are in order, for you've just taken a very important step toward achieving financial security and independence. The fact that you've picked up this book shows that you've decided to take control of your financial future. You may not believe it, but in making that decision and acting on it, you've just completed the hardest part of the process.

Congratulations, too, because this is your time. There is more wealth in women's hands today than ever before. Much more! According to the Boston Consulting Group, $39.6 trillion of the world's wealth is now controlled by women. Fidelity estimates that women now control 30 percent of global private wealth. This is up 25 percent in just five years. Furthermore, it is estimated that women's wealth will grow by 7 percent annually, to reach $72 trillion globally by 2020. Why is this happening? The answer is that women are earning more; they are acquiring more wealth through inheritance, death of a spouse, and divorce; and, most important, they are becoming entrepreneurs.

Today's entrepreneur is, in fact, a woman. Women are now opening businesses at a rate three times that of male entrepreneurs. According to the American Express annual report "State of Women-Owned Businesses," as of 2017 there are an estimated 11.6 million women-owned businesses in the United States. What's more, between 1997 and 2017, the number of women-owned firms grew by 114 percent compared to a 44 percent increase in all businesses—a growth rate more than 2.5 times the national average. These women-owned businesses now employ nearly 9 million people and generate more than $1.7 trillion in revenue.

According to the Bureau of Labor Statistics, there are now 73.5 million women in the U.S. workforce compared to just 18.4 million working women in 1950.

What all this is leading to today is record levels of wealth for women. The percentage of women who have at least $1 million in their 401(k) accounts has doubled in the past decade, climbing from 10 percent of female 401(k) holders in 2005 to 20 percent as of 2017, according to Fidelity. In addition, according to the American College of Financial Services, women make up 45 percent of all American millionaires. Finally, it is estimated that women will inherit 70 percent of all assets that are passed down during the next 20 years.

SOMETHING MEN MAY NOT WANT TO HEAR . . .

Having worked as a financial planner and advisor with literally thousands of women over the years, there's something else I can tell you about women and money: As a rule, women make better investors than men. When women become investors, they generally devise a plan, and then they stick to it. In a word, they "commit." Men, on the other hand . . . well, we've all heard that dreaded phrase "fear of commitment," haven't we? Rather than stay with a great, solid investment, men often get bored and start looking around for the next "hot thing."

My experience is that women simply do not do this. As a rule, women who invest tend to be wary of so-called hot tips. Not many men. Time after time I have had male clients phone me with orders to buy 1,000 shares of stock merely because they heard a "hot tip" at the gym or on the golf course. Often these requests to make a stock purchase involve no research, just brazen bravado.

And this is not just my opinion. The statistics bear me out. According to a 2016 Fidelity analysis of more than 8 million clients, women generated investment returns that were higher by 40 basis points, or about half a percent. Just a fluke? Hardly. According to a 1995 study by the National Association of Investors Corporation (now known as **BetterInvesting.org**), women's investment clubs outperformed men's clubs by 11 percent per year and coed clubs by 5 percent . . . and did so for 10 of the 12 years included in the study! In fact, the lifetime earning rate for women's groups was significantly better than for men—10.5 percent to 9.7 percent.

Do you find that surprising? Many of us do. That's because we've unthinkingly accepted the stereotype that money management is a man's "game"—one that women simply aren't suited to play. Why? It may have something to do with the fact that most of us grew up watching our fathers manage the family money. Certainly, many women have told me that was the reason it never dawned on them to take an active role in shaping their financial futures. Whatever the cause, however, far too many women decide early on that when it comes to money, they'd prefer to stay on the sidelines. They say things like, "Well, I'm not good with money," or "I'm not driven by money," or "I'm not materialistic," or "Money doesn't make you happy," or "Why bother—the more you make, the more the government will take," and on and on, trying to justify their fear of dealing with their financial situation.

A "GAME" YOU CAN'T *AFFORD* TO SIT OUT

I think that is a mistake. As a woman today, you've got to stop watching and start participating. Even more important, you've got to start calling the shots for yourself. There's no getting around it: This so-called money game (a misnomer if ever there was one) has very real, very serious consequences for all of us. People who say they've decided not to play the money game are only fooling themselves. After all, how we handle our money colors every aspect of our lives—the education of our children, the sort of home we provide our families, the type of contribution we make to our communities (not to mention all those mundane things like the kind of food we eat, the clothing we wear, and the vacations we take).

The fact is, none of us really has a choice: We are all playing the money game whether we want to or not. The only question is: Are we winning?

Most people, unfortunately, are not. Why? Because no one ever taught them the rules. Think about it. How could you possibly ever win a game—or even do well at it—if you didn't know the rules? You couldn't. Maybe every once in a while you'd luck out—but that's all it would be: luck. You couldn't depend on it; you certainly wouldn't want to risk your bank account, your retirement income, or your dream of homeownership on it.

So what we need in order to take control of our financial destiny is a copy of the rules. An instruction manual. A road map.

MORE GOOD NEWS FOR WOMEN

That's what this book is: It's a financial road map that will show you how to get from where you are right now to where you want to be. The good news here is that women tend to be pretty good about using road maps. Certainly they're better than most men. Men generally prefer to drive around aimlessly, hoping to spot a familiar landmark, rather than admit they're lost and ask someone for directions. You know what I'm talking about. I'm sure you were once out on a date, or maybe you were in the car with your husband or your father, and suddenly you realized you had been driving for what seemed like an awfully long time with no sign of the Wayne's Kountry Kitchen you were looking for. The conversation probably went something like this.

> YOU: Honey, I think we're lost. Maybe we should stop in a gas station or something . . .
> HIM: No, we're fine. I know exactly where we are.
> YOU: But . . .
> HIM: I *said* we're fine. It's just a ways up here—I'm sure of it.

Of course, what each of you was thinking at the time was something else again.

> YOU: He doesn't have a clue where we are. If he'd just pull over and get some directions, we could figure this out and get there!
> HIM: I can't believe we're lost! I thought I knew the way. Jeez, where *are* we? I probably should stop and ask for directions, but if I do that, she'll know I don't know where we are, and so will some stranger. How much of a loser would *that* make me!

The same thing tends to happen with our money. As a rule, men feel they are supposed to know what they're doing when it comes to personal finance, so even when they don't, they often pretend that they do and resist asking for help. As a result, many men wind up making wrong turns onto bumpy back roads that strand them (and you) 100 miles from Wayne's Kountry Kitchen.

Women, on the other hand, have relatively few hang-ups about admitting it when they don't know something. That's why they can make better investors than men. It's because they don't have any trouble with the idea that they have to have an education in order to be successful. Women are comfortable not only learning and studying but also asking questions—and by asking questions, of course, they learn more. I see this in my investment seminars all the time. When women take the classes, they study, read, and ask questions. Their goal is to become educated—to learn the techniques of managing their own finances. It's not to prove to everyone else in the class that they're smarter than the instructor. (That role invariably goes to some guy sitting in the back of the room who thinks he has all the answers—but whose money is still sitting in a savings account earning a measly 0.1 percent interest.)

IT'S TIME FOR YOU TO TAKE CHARGE

The basic premise of this book is simple. I believe in my heart and soul that no matter what your age, status, or situation—whether you're in your twenties or your eighties; whether you're single, married, divorced, or widowed; whether you're a career woman or a homemaker—you are more than capable of taking charge of your finances and your financial future, and you should. All that's required is that you be given the right tools—which is where this book comes in. The fact is, you already have a great deal of financial power—specifically over spending decisions. It is estimated that women currently control 70 to 80 percent of all purchasing decisions in America. It's now time for you to control your investment power too.

A JOURNEY THAT WILL CHANGE YOUR LIFE

In the pages that follow, what we are going to do is embark on a journey—an eight-step journey that begins with education and ends with your taking action. By the time it's done, you will have learned the fundamental principles of personal financial management—principles you can use to turn your dreams of freedom, security, and independence into concrete realities.

As you will see, the eight steps that make up our journey to financial security and independence cover a considerable amount of ground. At the same time, however, they are individually quite easy. They are so easy, in fact, that not only will you be able to use them to change your life, you also will be in a position to teach them to the people you care about so they can achieve the same kind of success you have.

Specifically, each of our eight steps consists of a series of easy-to-understand, practical strategies for taking control of your financial future—specific strategies you can begin implementing before you've even finished reading. As you make your way through them, you'll learn not only what your options are, but which options might be best for you—and how to design a customized course of action tailored to your own particular situation.

In the first leg of our journey, you'll find out what you don't know—but should—about your own personal and family financial situation. After that, you'll learn how to identify your own deep-seated attitudes toward money, how to define the personal values those attitudes reflect, and how to create realistic financial goals based on those values. Once you know where you want to go, you'll be shown exactly what you need to do to get organized and how you can start building a nest egg on even the most modest income (just like my grandma Bach did). This last point is especially important, since so many women seem to think that investing and financial planning make sense only for people with high incomes and lots of money. As you'll see by the time we're finished, it's not how much you make that counts, it's how much you keep!

Finally, our program will lay out a series of simple yet powerful strategies designed to provide you with: (1) an effective plan for long-term security, (2) financial protection against the unexpected, and (3) the ability to build the kind of life you've always dreamed about. Along the way, it will explain everything you need to know about tax planning, wills, insurance, the stock market (including the ten big mistakes most investors make), retirement planning, how to buy a house, and how to hire a financial advisor.

In the end, whether you earn $25,000 a year or $25,000 a month, our eight-step journey will dramatically change the way you think about money—and by doing that, it will change your life.

BECOME ONE OF THE FINANCIAL ELITE

Individually, each of the eight steps in our journey is as powerful as it is simple. Indeed, as I suggest to the women who attend my seminars, if you manage to learn and apply just two or three of the eight steps, I am confident you will wind up in better financial shape than 90 percent of the people in the country. If you do four or five of the steps, I believe you will find yourself in the top 5 percent of the population—financially better off than 95 percent of Americans. And if you do all eight of the steps, I believe you can elevate yourself to the nation's financial elite—the top 1 percent of the population. What's more, you'll be able to bring your family and loved ones along with you.

And as you acquire the tools you'll need to control your economic destiny, our eight-step program also will help you learn to become comfortable with the idea of taking financial responsibility for yourself. This is a key point, for the psychological and emotional aspects of financial planning are enormously important. Yet, for some reason, most approaches to the subject ignore them.

The fact is, of course, that nothing brings out emotion like the topic of money. (According to marriage counselors, it is the leading cause of divorce.) Needless to say, everyone attaches different emotions to the issues of saving and investing. Some people save to create security and provide for their families; others spend to feel free or experience adventure. Whatever the case may be, the emotions we attach to money often determine whether we will live our lives in comfort or poverty. Yet people rarely know what is truly driving them emotionally when it comes to money.

THE BAG-LADY SYNDROME

Among women, the impact of emotion on their financial lives shows up clearly in what experts call "the bag-lady syndrome," in which women who are materially well off still find themselves living in daily fear of going broke and being forced to live on the street. According to a 2006 survey by Allianz Life Insurance Company, 48 percent of women who earn more than $100,000 per year are afraid they will become bag ladies. I can't tell you the number of female clients of mine with investment portfolios worth literally millions of dollars who have sat in my office and asked me, "David, if the market goes down, will I be a bag lady?" This sort of worry may be baseless, but it is real, and it can't just be dismissed. In fact, the Allianz survey found that bag-lady fears stem from a lack of confidence, as well as a perceived dependence on others.

By showing you how to understand the emotional and psychological needs that affect the way we all think about money, the program in this book will teach you how to overcome the fears that often lead to financial paralysis and, worse, shortsighted decision making and help you gain confidence in your own financial abilities. Equally important, you'll learn how to create a meaningful agenda from which you can design a long-term financial plan that will truly reflect what you are looking for in life.

HOW BEST TO USE THIS BOOK

Before we begin in earnest, I want to give you some tips on how to read this book. First, please think of this book as a tool. As I put it earlier, it's a kind of road map—your personal road map to a successful financial future. At the same time, I'd like you to think of me as your "money coach," a new friend who can offer some helpful advice on how you can get to where you want to go.

You also should understand that each of the eight steps that make up this book can be followed separately or in conjunction with the others. My recommendation is that you go through them in order, reading each chapter at least twice before you move on to the next one. Why? Because repetition is the secret of all skill, and when we read something for the first time, we don't always catch it all or retain as much as we may like.

Another suggestion: As we progress on our journey together, and as you learn lots of new things about handling money, don't get bogged down by all the stuff you suddenly feel you should have done years ago but didn't. If I bring up something you didn't know or wish you had known sooner, don't get down about it. What you are *not* doing right now is not the issue. The issue is what you *will* be doing with your newfound knowledge once you finish reading this book.

With that in mind, I'd like to share a quick story with you about a young woman who attended one of my seminars.

IT'S NEVER TOO LATE . . . OR TOO EARLY!

Lauren stood up in the class looking a little depressed. "David," she said, "I think I'm the youngest woman here and I'm not sure I belong here, but I know I need to get started planning for retirement and I don't know what to do."

As I scanned the class, I realized Lauren was right about one thing. She probably was the youngest of 100 or so women in the room. I smiled at her, then turned to her classmates and asked, "How many of you ladies here wish now that you had taken a class like this 20 years ago?"

Every hand in the room went up. I looked back at Lauren. "It looks to me," I said, "like you're in the right room at the right time." A few weeks later Lauren came into my office. It turned out she was 28, college-educated, and was pursuing a career in management consulting. Like many women her age, however, Lauren was not taking advantage of her retirement plan. In fact, even though she was earning more than $50,000 a year, she was living paycheck to paycheck. Employing the same techniques that I will show you in this book, I showed Lauren how she could get her spending under control immediately and start "maxing out" her contributions to her retirement plan. As a result, less than three years later, Lauren now has more than $20,000 in her retirement account, and at the rate she is saving, she could easily have $2 million to her name by the time she reaches her late fifties! Even more exciting, by using the tools you will learn in this book, Lauren got herself a new job and has doubled her income! Today, at age 31, she is totally in charge of her money and has a brilliant new career that pays her what she is worth.

Now, I'm not going to take credit for all of this. Lauren deserves most of the credit. She attended the class, took the advice, and (most important) acted on it.

And you can too.

Remember, this book is about moving forward and taking control of your life, not giving yourself a hard time for what you didn't know before you picked it up.

Finally, this book *is* meant to be fun. Enjoy yourself. You are about to embark on an exciting journey to the new "you"—a woman in control of her destiny who has learned how to take charge of her own financial future.

Let's get started!

LEARN THE FACTS—AND MYTHS—ABOUT YOUR MONEY

Wendy sat in my office, perched on the edge of her chair, alert, inquisitive, and a little bit embarrassed. An experienced and highly successful real estate agent, she had come to me for a financial consultation—and the facts of her situation were hardly reassuring. Although she earned well over $250,000 a year and was able to put two kids through private school at an annual cost of $15,000 each, her personal finances were a mess. A self-employed single parent, she had less than $25,000 saved for retirement, no life or disability insurance, and never bothered to write a will.

In short, this intelligent, ambitious businesswoman was completely unprotected from the unexpected and utterly unprepared for the future. When I asked Wendy why she had never done any financial planning, she shrugged and offered a response I'd heard countless *times before:* "*I've always been too busy working to focus on what to do with the money I make.*"

Looking across the restaurant table, I could see the sadness in my mother's eyes. A good friend of hers had just gone through a bitter divorce. Suddenly, after more than three decades of marriage to a wealthy surgeon, the friend now found herself living in a tiny apartment, struggling to make ends meet as a $25,000-a-year secretary. Like many formerly well-off women, she had never paid much attention to her family's finances, and as a result her estranged husband was able to run rings around her in the settlement talks. It was a terrible thing—all the more so because it could have been prevented so easily—and it made me wonder if my mother was similarly in the dark. So I asked her. "Mom," I said, "do you know where the family money is?"

I thought it would be an easy question. After all, my father was a successful financial consultant and stockbroker who taught investment classes three nights a week. My mother had to be up to speed on the family finances.

At first, however, she didn't reply. Then she squirmed slightly in her chair. "Of course I know where our money is," she finally said. "Your father manages it."

"But where is it? Do you know where he's got it invested?"

"Well, no, I don't. Your father handles all that."

"But don't you have your own accounts, your own line of credit?"

My mother laughed. "David," she said, "what do I need a line of credit for? I have the best bank in the world—your father."

The reason I've started our journey with these two stories is that I know you are a very special woman—the kind of woman who believes in herself. Specifically, you believe that you possess the abilities and the intelligence to have the kind of life you feel you deserve. (If you didn't, you would have never picked up this book in the first place.) You also believe—correctly—that money is important and that you need to learn more about accumulating and protecting it. Finally, I know that you are someone who recognizes that it takes more than a single burst of enthusiasm to improve yourself and develop new skills; it also takes commitment and education.

That is why the first step of our journey is all about getting motivated to educate yourself now and on an ongoing basis about your money and the role it plays in your life. I believe that no matter what your current situation is—whether you are already wealthy or living paycheck to paycheck—a little education combined with motivated action can go a long, long way.

I also know from working with thousands of women that, sadly, neither Wendy the real-estate agent nor my mother is at all unusual. Yes, women own a huge portion of all the financial assets in the world. Yes, most American women work and nearly half of them are their family's main income earner. Yes, the statistics about divorce and widowhood are appalling. Yet, despite all this, the sad fact is that shockingly few women know even a fraction of what they should about the state of their own personal and family finances.

By the same token, very few people know all of the fundamental principles about money that you are about to learn. And, most important, even when they think they do, they rarely follow the principles on a consistent basis. This last point is a key one, for as you will discover in the course of our journey, it is not what we learn that makes a difference in our lives but what we do with what we learn.

THE FACTS AND MYTHS ABOUT YOU
AND YOUR MONEY

What we're going to do in this chapter is familiarize you with what I call the financial facts of life. By the time you have taken in all the facts, you will understand fully why it's essential that you take charge of your own financial future. Moreover, you will be totally motivated to get started learning how to do it.

The first fact of financial life to understand is that while planning ahead is important for everyone, it's more important for women. Indeed, though in many ways we live in an age of equality, there is no question that . . .

Fair or not, women need to do more financial planning than men.

As I said in the introduction, women in the twenty-first century have more opportunities and resources available to them than their mothers, grandmothers, and great-grandmothers did, which makes this an excellent time for you to begin a journey to a secure financial future. And it's more than just a matter of economics. Because of advances in both technology and public attitudes, women are not only living longer than ever before, they are active longer. In my seminars, I often joke that today's 80-year-old women are drinking "green juice" and doing aerobics every morning. I know my grandma Bach was like that. Up to the age of 86, she hiked five miles a day and went dancing three nights a week! In her mid-eighties, my grandmother enjoyed a life that was more active, socially and physically, than mine was at 30!

But if the good news is that we live in an age in which the barriers that held women back for so long seem finally to be falling, the bad news is that there are still many obstacles to be overcome. For one thing . . .

Women still typically earn just 80 percent what men do.

And that's just the *average* pay gap between men and women. Black and Latina women earn 63 percent and 54 percent, respectively, of what men earn.

In addition, women are less likely to have a steady income stream over the course of their lifetimes. In some cases, that's due to discrimination, but it's also due to the fact that responsibilities such as child rearing and caring for elderly parents cause women to move in and out of the workforce a lot more than men do. In all, over their working lifetimes, women spend a total of 11½ years off the job on average, versus only 16 months for men.

What's more, according to a recent study by the U.S. Department of Labor . . .

Women are the ones hurt most by corporate downsizing.

That's because it takes women longer to find new work, and the replacement jobs women get are often part-time posts that offer less pay and fewer benefits.

As a result of all this, you have less money available to put away in a 401(k) or other retirement account,—which is why Vanguard reports that . . .

On average, women have accumulated 34 percent less money in their retirement accounts than men.

But it's not simply that, as a woman, you'll have a smaller retirement income to look forward to. It's also that, as a woman, you'll have to make that income go further. Specifically, you probably are going to live longer than most of your male counterparts (by an average of about seven years, according to the National Center for Health), which means that you are going to need even more retirement resources than they will. And not just for yourself. Because of your longer life expectancy, chances are that the financial burden of caring for elderly parents will fall on your shoulders.

WHAT ALL THIS ADDS UP TO
IS ONE BIG OUCH!

This, in a nutshell, is why long-term financial planning is more important for women. Compared to men, you've got to be more farsighted, start saving earlier, and stick to your plans with more discipline. Fortunately, doing all this is not only possible, it's actually relatively easy. The trick is simply recognizing that it needs to be done—which leads us to the other basic fact of financial life: Ignorance is *not* bliss. Quite the contrary . . .

It's what you don't know that can hurt you!

A wise woman once said, "It's not what you know that can hurt you but rather what you don't know." I'd like to extend that thought a bit and suggest that what generally causes the most suffering and pain is what you don't know that you don't know.

Think about that for a minute. In our everyday lives, there are really only a few categories of knowledge.

- What you know you know (e.g., how much money you earn each month).
- What you know you don't know (e.g., what the stock market will do next year).
- What you know you should know (e.g., how much it will take for you to be able to retire comfortably).
- What you don't know you don't know (e.g., that the 1097-page 2017 Tax Cuts and Jobs Act made sweeping changes to the federal tax code. Many of these changes to the tax code could directly affect how much you will be able to afford to spend on child care, college tuition, medical expenses, and your own retirement).

It's this last category, by the way, that causes the most problems in our lives. Think about it. When you find yourself in a real jam, doesn't it always seem to be the result of something you didn't know that you didn't know? (Consider the "prime" Florida real estate you bought that actually was in the middle of an alligator swamp.) That's the way life is—especially when it comes to money. Indeed, the reason most people fail financially—and, as a result, never have the kind of life they want—is almost always because of stuff they didn't know that they didn't know.

This concept is incredibly simple, but it's also tremendously powerful. Among other things, it means that if we can reduce what you don't know that you don't know about money, your chances of becoming financially successful—and, most important, staying financially successful—can be significantly increased. (It also means that the more you realize you don't know as you read this book, the happier you should be, because it shows you are already proactively learning!) So how do we apply this concept? Well, I think the best way to reduce what you don't know that you don't know about money is to learn what you need to unlearn. That is, you need to discover what you may have come to believe about money that isn't really true. Or, as I like to put it . . .

Don't fall for the most common myths about money.

Whenever I conduct one of my Smart Women Finish Rich® seminars, I generally begin the class by suggesting that the reason most people—not just women—fail financially is that they have fallen for a bunch of money myths that are simply not true. As we're learning the facts, I think it's important to spend a little time exploring these myths and learning to recognize them for what they are. The reason is simple: By doing this, you lessen the chances that you'll ever be taken in by them.

MYTH NO. I
Make more money and you'll be rich!

The most commonly held myth about personal finances is that the most important factor in determining whether you will ever be rich is how much money you make. To put it another way, ask most women what it takes to be well off, and they will invariably say, "More money."

It seems logical, right? Make more money and you'll be rich. Now, you may be thinking, "What's wrong with that? How can it be a myth?"

Well, to me, the sentence "Make more money and you'll be rich" brings to mind certain late-night TV infomercials, with their enthusiastic pitchmen and slick get-rich-quick schemes. My current favorite is the one in which a guy wearing a gold necklace smiles into the camera and says you can earn a fortune while lying on the sofa watching television. Without getting into the question of whether his particular scheme makes any business sense, let me suggest to you that the basic premise of his pitch—namely, that the key to wealth is finding some quick and easy way to boost your income— is simply not true. In fact, what determines your wealth is not how much you make but how much you keep of what you make.

I'll take that even further. I believe that most Americans who think they have an income problem actually don't. You may not believe that. It's possible you feel you have an income problem yourself.

Perhaps you're thinking right now, *David, I'm sorry. I don't care what you say—with my bills and expenses, I'm telling you I have an income problem.*

Well, I'm not saying that you might not be facing some financial challenges. But I would be willing to bet that if we were to take a good look at your situation, we'd find that the problem really isn't the size of your income. Indeed, if you're at all typical, over the course of your working life you will likely earn a phenomenal amount of money. If you find that hard to believe, take a look at the Earnings Outlook chart (see page 26).

The numbers don't lie. Over the course of their lifetimes, most Americans will earn between $1 million and $3 million!

Based on your monthly income, how much money does it look like you will earn in your lifetime? It's well into seven figures, isn't it? Don't you think you deserve to keep some of that money? I do— and I bet you do too! Unfortunately, most of us don't keep any. In fact, the average American works a total of some 90,000 hours in his or her life—and has nothing to show for it at the end! **According to a recent report by GoBankingRates, 42 percent of Americans have less than $10,000 saved for retirement!**

How do we explain that? It's simple, really.

The problem is not our income, it's what we spend!

We'll go into detail on this concept in Step Four. For now, just trust me on this one. It's not the size of your income that will determine your financial well-being over the next 20 or 30 years; it's how you handle the money you earn.

I know that sounds hard to believe, but it's true. Consider the findings in a bestselling book that I highly recommend to my students. It's called *The Millionaire Next Door*, and it was written by a man named Tom Stanley, who interviewed hundreds of millionaires and came up with some findings that surprised me and probably will surprise you.

There's a phrase Texans use to describe someone who is all show and no substance: "Big hat, no cattle." What Stanley found was that most millionaires are just the opposite. In other words . . .

EARNINGS OUTLOOK

How much money will pass through your hands during your lifetime and what will you do with it?

Monthly Income	10 Years	20 Years	30 Years	40 Years
$1,000	$120,000	$240,000	$360,000	$480,000
$1,500	180,000	360,000	540,000	720,000
$2,000	240,000	480,000	720,000	960,000
$2,500	300,000	600,000	900,000	1,200,000
$3,000	360,000	720,000	1,080,000	1,440,000
$3,500	420,000	840,000	1,260,000	1,680,000
$4,000	480,000	960,000	1,440,000	1,920,000
$4,500	540,000	1,080,000	1,620,000	2,160,000
$5,000	600,000	1,200,000	1,800,000	2,400,000
$5,500	660,000	1,320,000	1,980,000	2,640,000
$6,000	720,000	1,440,000	2,160,000	2,880,000
$6,500	780,000	1,560,000	2,340,000	3,120,000
$7,000	840,000	1,680,000	2,520,000	3,360,000
$7,500	900,000	1,800,000	2,700,000	3,600,000
$8,000	960,000	1,920,000	2,880,000	3,840,000
$8,500	1,020,000	2,040,000	3,060,000	4,080,000
$9,000	1,080,000	2,160,000	3,240,000	4,320,000
$9,500	1,140,000	2,280,000	3,420,000	4,560,000
$10,000	1,200,000	2,400,000	3,600,000	4,800,000

Source: Janet Lowe, *The Super Saver: Fundamental Strategies for Building Wealth* (Longman Financial Services Publishing, United States, 1990).

SMALL HAT, LOTS OF CATTLE

Here are some of Stanley's findings:

- The average net worth of a millionaire is $3.7 million.
- The average millionaire lives in a house that cost $320,000.
- The average millionaire's taxable income is $131,000 a year.
- For the most part, millionaires describe themselves as "tightwads" who believe that charity begins at home.
- Most millionaires drive older, American-made cars. Only a minority drive new cars or ever lease their cars.
- Fully half of the millionaires Stanley surveyed never paid more than $399 for a suit.
- Millionaires are dedicated investors—on average, investing nearly 20 percent of their total household income each year.

What amazes me about these facts is that a family with a net worth of nearly $4 million (the average net worth that Stanley surveyed) is, by most people's standards, very wealthy. I certainly feel $4 million is a rather comfortable amount to have accumulated, and I'd be willing to guess that you do too. Yet the income these people earn (an average of $131,000 a year) is really not all that high. It's certainly above average, but it is definitely not of the extraordinary magnitude we tend to associate with people who have amassed great wealth.

The fact is, what has allowed most of these people to become millionaires is not how much they've made but how little (relatively speaking) they've spent. To use a sports metaphor, while their offense was probably pretty good, the defense they've played with their money has been nothing short of brilliant.

Unfortunately, most people handle their finances in the opposite way. They are great on offense and lousy on defense. As a financial advisor, I've personally met in my office with many people who make over $100,000 a year and feel wealthy and live wealthy but in fact are not wealthy.

Here's a case in point.

BIG HAT, NO CATTLE

Nora first came to see me after attending a retirement-planning course I taught at the University of California–Berkeley Extension. The moment she entered my office it was clear I was dealing with a very successful woman. Her clothes were the current year's top of the line, she was wearing a gold Rolex watch worth at least $10,000, and I had seen her drive up in a brand-new $82,000 Mercedes-Benz (which, it turned out, she leased).

A fit and attractive 48-year-old, Nora owned and ran a company that employed ten people and grossed more than $5 million a year. But though her personal income was more than $200,000 a year and she had been pulling down a six-figure income for well over a decade, her net worth was almost zero! Nora didn't even have a retirement account started. She did have about $50,000 in equity in her home, but she also had two mortgages on the house, on which she owed a total of $400,000. To make matters worse, Nora had run up more than $35,000 in credit-card debt!

After she filled me in on her situation, I shook my head and said, "Nora, are you planning on working forever?"

She looked at me, confused. "What do you mean?" she asked.

"Well," I said, "were you planning on working for the rest of your life?"

"No," she replied. "I hope to retire by the time I turn fifty-five."

"Really?" I said. "With what?"

Nora blinked at me, not seeing what I was getting at.

"Is your business salable?" I continued.

Nora bit her lip. Her business, she explained, was built mainly on a few good relationships that probably couldn't be transferred to anyone else.

"I see," I said. "Then I suppose you have a wealthy relative who is planning to die in time for you to inherit this money when you turn fifty-five?"

Once again, Nora looked perplexed. "No," she said slowly, "I don't have any inheritance coming."

"Then I'm confused," I said. "How are you going to retire? You don't have any savings. You can't sell your business. The equity in your house is minimal."

Nora shrugged. "I make so much money," she said, "that I thought I could play catch-up."

SPEND MORE THAN YOU MAKE, AND YOU'LL HAVE A SERIOUS PROBLEM!

I'd like to tell you there was a quick fix for Nora, but there wasn't. First of all, Nora had some really bad habits—the worst of which was that she simply spent more than she made, all the time! Second, she didn't really believe me when I told her that she needed to change her ways and change them fast.

It took Nora 18 months to get around to opening a retirement account and making her first contribution. That, however, was four years ago, and these days, fortunately, Nora is a completely different person. Every two weeks now, like clockwork, she sends in a contribution to her retirement fund. Not only is she fully funding her retirement account, but she is putting away even more money in some additional tax-deferred accounts (which we will cover in Step Five). So far Nora has managed to save close to $90,000, and by slightly increasing her monthly mortgage payments, she will have her house fully paid off in 15 years instead of 30, which will save her close to $285,000! (You'll learn how you can do this for yourself in Step Six.) Equally important, she has stopped leasing brand-new luxury cars (instead, she bought a used one), and she has paid off all her credit-card debt.

Nora isn't bringing home any more money than she was before. Yet now, for the first time, she is building real wealth. What changed? The answer is her spending habits—and, most important of all, her investment habits. That's the key. Like Tom Stanley's millionaires, she saw through the income myth and learned that it's not how much you make, it's how much you keep.

One important advantage Nora did have going for her was that she realized early on that she had to take care of herself, which is one reason she started her own business. Instinctively, she understood that one of the most fundamental principles of smart money management is self-reliance—or, as I like to tell my clients . . .

> ### *Don't ever put your entire financial fate in someone else's hands.*

This brings us to the second biggest myth I see women falling prey to—what I call the Cinderella myth, otherwise known as the "My husband will take care of me" myth (or, even worse, the "Find and marry a wealthy spouse and everything will be fine" myth).

> ### MYTH NO. 2
> ## My husband (or some other man/woman/ fill in the blank) will take care of me.

Now, before I go into detail on this subject, let me say that I know it is entirely possible that you are happily married or that you have chosen to be happily single. Nonetheless, I have found from experience that this myth is worth spending a little time on, for some version of it affects nearly every woman. Indeed, over the years, hundreds of women have shared with me their painful personal stories of how their lives were nearly destroyed by the belief that some man or *someone*—if not a husband or spouse, then a parent, or a grown child, or an employer, or a financial advisor—would take care of them. And when I started to write this book, many more women implored me not to pass over this issue lightly. So here goes.

> *It's neither safe nor practical to assume that the man in your life can be counted on to take care of your finances.*

Why do I say this? Let's look at the facts. If men generally have been in charge of their families' money for the past century or so, then clearly they have not been doing a very good job. Consider this sobering statistic . . .

> *Only 45 percent of Americans have enough savings to cover at least their essential living expenses in retirement!*

But wait, the bad news gets worse. The median retirement income for Americans between the ages of 65 and 74 is just $34,285 per year—and this means that half of all Americans have incomes lower than that amount. I'm sure I don't have to tell you that in many places, $34,000 a year won't even cover basic living expenses. Would it cover yours?

The cherry on top of this bad news sundae is your expected longevity. As I noted earlier, women live longer yet tend to earn fewer pensions and other retirement benefits than men do. Thus, you are likely to be forced to make do with even less.

What all this adds up to at retirement—or, more accurately, does not add up to—is another scary statistic . . .

> *The average income for a woman over 65 is just over $18,000 a year.*

You can't live on that—not these days, not in any semblance of comfort. And quite frankly, I wouldn't want you to have to try!

But, you may ask, what about Social Security? That will help, won't it? Maybe—assuming the system will deliver on all the benefits that are currently promised to you by the time you reach retirement age. The fact is, Social Security was never intended to be a retirement plan. At most, it was designed to provide an income *supplement*.

Look at the numbers. In 2016, the latest year for which figures are available, the average retired woman's Social Security benefits totaled just $14,424 a year, or just $1,202 a month. That's not to say you should forget about Social Security. It's just that you shouldn't count on it to provide more than a small fraction of your retirement income. As it happens, there's a very simple way to find out now what your Social Security benefit ultimately will look like—and I can't emphasize enough the importance of taking advantage of it right away. This is especially crucial for women, since, as I mentioned before, women tend to work less consistently throughout their lifetimes than men—and, as a result, often their Social Security benefits turn out to be much smaller than they had been expecting.

What you want to do in order to avoid any unpleasant surprises down the road is to sign up for a "*my* Social Security" account at **www.ssa.gov/myaccount/**. This account portal shows you all of your Social Security earnings history and estimates your future benefits. It has all but replaced the paper "Personal Earnings and Benefit Estimate Statements" that the Social Security Administration used to provide, and offers you the flexibility and convenience of online access to your Social Security benefit information.

This is something you should do immediately. Today. *This very minute*. It's really quite easy, and the Social Security Administration uses multifactor authentication to make sure your information always remains secure. If, however, you prefer to receive a paper statement for any reason, you can still request one online, by visiting the Social Security Administration's website at **https://www .ssa.gov/** and filling out Form SSA-7004. It will take four to six weeks to receive your paper Social Security Statement in the mail.

When it comes to divorce, women still end up with the short end of the stick.

Yes, we all want to believe that we can count on our spouses. Unfortunately, the statistics tell a very different story. About 50 percent of all marriages end in divorce. What about alimony and child support and community property? The bleak truth is, once her husband is gone, the average divorcée sees her standard of living plummet. According to a 2009 study by Stephen Jenkins, a professor at the London School of Economics, women who worked before, during, or after their marriages see a 20 percent decline in income after a divorce. At the same time, to add insult to injury, men see their incomes rise more than 30 percent after a divorce!

These statistics are hardly news. But despite all the attention they've received over the years, apparently many women remain convinced that they will be the exception to the rule—and they are shocked when they're not. I can't tell you the number of women who've come to me for advice after being absolutely blindsided by the spouses in whose hands they'd trustingly placed their futures. Unfortunately, by then it's usually too late to do more than try to pick up the pieces.

To be fair, there are many good men out there. But even if you're fortunate enough to have wound up with one of them, that's still no guarantee of a happy and secure future. Why? Because no matter how good the man in your life is, sooner or later he is going to die—and whether it's sooner or later, it probably will be before you do. *According to WISER, 80 percent of women die widowed—versus 80 percent of men who die married.* Let that sink in for a second. Remember, the average woman lives seven years longer than the average man. Of course, no one likes to think about this. Indeed, it's terrible how many well-intentioned men who sincerely love their wives and families simply refuse to face up to this inescapable truth. The worst thing about this sort of denial is that it leads otherwise good spouses to put off dealing with disagreeable reminders of their mortality such as life insurance and wills. And that's a prescription for disaster. For try as we might to ignore it . . .

The average age of widowhood today is just 59!

Because of our unwillingness to accept this unpleasant reality, we tend to be woefully unprepared to cope with it when it comes to pass. That's why, for a woman, losing a husband is generally as devastating economically as it is emotionally. Indeed, it has been estimated that as of 2008 widows accounted for nearly half (46 percent) of all poor women over the age of 60, and 65 percent of poor women over the age of 75, according to the Census Bureau. How did they get that way? Inadequate—or, more likely, nonexistent—planning.

When I shared this notion in one of my investment seminars, a woman named Sarah stood up in tears. "David," she told the room, "everything you're saying is true. I'm 57, and my husband was a successful lawyer who owned his own practice. He passed away six months ago and now I'm almost bankrupt."

I asked Sarah how this could have happened. It turned out that though her husband specialized in trusts and wills, he had never bothered to do one for himself!

The entire group was aghast. I could see the question on everyone's face: *You mean a lawyer who wrote wills for a living didn't have a will himself?* But when I asked the class, "How many of you have a will?" less than half the people in the room answered in the affirmative. And when I asked further, "How many of you have reviewed your will in the last five years?" less than 10 percent of them raised their hands. So maybe Sarah's story shouldn't have been surprising after all.

Then I asked Sarah, "If your husband was so successful, why are you almost broke?" She replied that when her husband died she discovered that the $2 million home in which they lived carried a $1.5 million mortgage. With her husband gone and no income of her own, the massive mortgage payments were now way beyond her means. As a result, Sarah found herself forced to put the house up for sale. Unfortunately, this was at a time when the California real estate market was badly depressed, and she couldn't find a buyer. To make matters worse, not only had her husband neglected to make a will, he had never taken out life insurance. And as if that wasn't bad enough, he had used their home as collateral on loans for his law practice—which was now defunct, because his former partners had elected to start a new firm without the obligation of her husband's debts! Sarah was in big trouble, all because she had assumed her husband would take care of her, and he had not prepared for the unforeseen.

Sarah's case was extreme, but it was by no means unusual. In any case, there is an important lesson to be learned from her experience: Don't ever let the "some man will take care of you" myth become your reality. It's a recipe for disaster. There's one more myth I want to share with you.

> **MYTH NO. 3**
> **The government finally has gotten inflation under control.**

There seems to be an increasingly widespread notion that we no longer need to worry about inflation. This is a particularly dangerous myth not simply because it's untrue, but because it breeds complacency. Indeed, I can't think of anything more financially self-destructive than the idea that we don't need to worry so much about the future because the government finally has gotten inflation under control.

It certainly would be nice if that were true. Unfortunately, it's not. To the contrary . . .

Inflation is still Public Enemy Number One.

Sometimes when I teach a class, someone will raise a hand and actually try to debate this issue. "But, David," she will say, "it sure looks as if the government has control over inflation. After all, I don't see things costing a lot more today than they used to."

Well, that's not what the statistics say. What the numbers tell us is that over the past 20 years, the annual increase in the cost of living has averaged about 2.1 percent; over the past 10 years, it's averaged about 1.6 percent. The Federal Open Market Committee forecasts that inflation will run between 2 percent and 3 percent per year between 2018 and 2060.

Now, that may not sound like very much, but it is. Just remember that based on these levels of inflation, something that cost $100 in 1997 would set you back $155 in 2017, according to the Bureau of Labor Statistics. In addition, don't forget that when most people retire, they do so on a fixed income. Unfortunately, if you retire on a fixed income and inflation continues at 3 percent a year, you are going to be in deep trouble. Why? Because, at that rate, your purchasing power will be cut nearly in half within 20 years. In other words, the dollar sitting in your purse today will be worth only about 55 cents 20 years from now. In 30 years, it will be worth only about 40 cents.

There's nothing new about this phenomenon. When I talk about inflation in my seminars, one of the biggest laughs I always get is when I ask, "How many of you drove here tonight in a car that cost more than your first home?" What's amazing is that usually a third of the people in the class raise their hand. That's the power of inflation. Here's another example: The car I drive today cost more than twice what my parents paid for their first home in Oakland, California, and it was a nice five-bedroom house with three bathrooms. If you think I'm exaggerating, take a look at this chart.

CONSUMER PRICES: STICKER SHOCK SINCE 2000				
Typical Prices	2000	2010	Today	Projected in 20 Years
House	$167,000	$221,000	$384,000	$608,682
Automobile	$21,047	$24,899	$35,870	$41,569
Gasoline (10 gal.)	$15.10	$27.90	$25.95	$46.60
Stamp	$0.33	$0.44	$0.49	$0.89
Day in Hospital	$1,148	$1,910	$2,271	$7,436

Sources: (1) U.S. Department of Housing and Urban Development—average price of new homes, 4th quarter 2016; (2) Kelley Blue Book—November 2017 average new vehicle transaction price; (3) AAA National Average Gas Prices, accessed February 1, 2018; (4) U.S. Postal Service; (5) The Henry J. Kaiser Family Foundation, report: "Hospital Adjusted Expenses per Inpatient Day, 2015."

There is no denying the lesson these numbers teach us.

The future is going to be expensive.

That's why, despite all the recent talk about how inflation is no longer a problem, I still consider it to be Public Enemy Number One. Just healthcare costs and college education costs alone are reasons to worry about inflation, as each is going up at about double the current rate of inflation, according to CNN Money and *USA Today*. The good news here is that learning how to keep your nest egg growing faster than inflation isn't all that hard. But if you don't recognize inflation as a problem in the first place, chances are you won't bother to try to do anything about it—and if you don't try to do anything about it, you are going to find yourself in a world of hurt one day. So don't believe the myth about inflation being under control.

SHOW ME THE MONEY

Now that we have exposed these money myths for what they are and looked at the external realities of what we can expect in our financial futures, let's examine the facts. The place to begin is close to home, with information about your own personal financial situation. Why here? By way of explanation, let me share a personal story with you.

When I was younger, I once asked my father why so many women seemed to be so devastated financially after a divorce or the death of a husband. "David," he said, "women are not typically involved with the family finances. So when it comes time to split up the pie, they don't know how much pie there is to split up, or even where to find it."

That's it? I thought. *Women don't know where the money is?* Could it really be that basic? I doubted it.

Out of curiosity, I took my mother to lunch to see if she agreed with my dad's assessment. What followed was the scene I described at the beginning of this chapter. As I mentioned, a good friend of my mom's had just gone through a brutal and costly divorce. Quite understandably, my mother was very upset about it—not least because her friend was now in financial trouble so serious that she had been forced to take a secretarial job and move to a tiny apartment.

"But, Mom," I said, "they were living in a million-dollar house. Where did all the money go?"

"It turned out her husband had used all the equity in their house to build up his medical practice," my mother explained with a sigh. "And now, with the HMO situation, his practice isn't doing so well." As much as I hated to admit it, it looked as if my dad was right. The terrible outcome was a result of the woman's lack of knowledge about her family's finances. She had signed papers allowing her husband to take out a second mortgage without knowing or even asking about what she was signing. The result was, for her, a financial disaster. It was scary.

With that in mind, I asked my mom the test question: "Do you know where our family's money is?"

As I said, though I thought this would be an easy one for her to answer, it turned out that she had no idea. All she could tell me about our money was that my dad took care of it. And when I pressed her about her ignorance, she simply laughed at me.

I couldn't believe it. This, from a woman who was president of a million-dollar nonprofit theater group, involved in numerous charity boards, and published two professional newsletters. This brilliant, beautiful woman was the same person who, when personal computers first appeared on the market, convinced the family that we needed one—and then single-handedly taught herself to master its intricacies so completely that she was able to computerize my father's entire business! Yet she hadn't a clue as to where our money was invested.

I was horrified. If a woman as sharp and successful as my mom could be so in the dark about money, what was happening to the millions of other women in this country who weren't married to men who managed money for a living? In the years since then, of course, I've seen firsthand how widespread this sort of ignorance is and how much damage it can do. So with that in mind, I ask you now the same question I asked my mother . . .

***Do you know what's going on with your money
and your family's money?***

To help you answer this important question. I've prepared a short quiz. Take a few moments to complete it, answering true or false for each statement. The results should give you a good idea of how knowledgeable you are (or aren't) about your personal finances.

THE "SMART WOMEN FINISH RICH" FINANCIAL KNOWLEDGE QUIZ

TRUE OR FALSE:

[ ]   [ ]   I know the current value of my home, including the size of the mortgage and the amount of equity I've built.

[ ]   [ ]   I know the length of the mortgage-payment schedule and how much extra it would cost each month to pay down the mortgage in half the time. I also know the interest rate we are paying on the mortgage and if it is competitive in today's market.

[ ]   [ ]   I know how much life insurance I [and my spouse, if applicable] carry. I know how much cash value there is in the policy, and I know the rate of return my cash value is earning.

[ ]   [ ]   I know the details (including amount of coverage, cost, monthly or yearly payment, etc.) of all other insurance policies carried by myself [and my spouse, if applicable]. This includes health, disability, term life, and so on.

[ ]   [ ]   I have reviewed my life insurance policy in the past 12 to 24 months to see if the price I am paying for it is still competitive in today's marketplace.

[ ]   [ ]   If I own my own home, I know what kind of home-owner's coverage I have and what the deductibles are. If I rent, I know the amount of renter's insurance I have and what its deductible is. In either case, in the event of a fire or other catastrophic loss,

I know whether my insurance will reimburse me for the actual cash value of my property or the cost of replacing it at today's current values.

[ ]   [ ]   I have attempted to protect my family's nest egg from lawsuits by carrying an "umbrella" insurance policy that includes liability coverage.

[ ]   [ ]   I either prepared my own tax return this year or reviewed my tax situation with the person who prepared my return.

[ ]   [ ]   I know the location and amounts of all my or my family's investments, including

- cash in savings or money-market accounts
- CDs or savings bonds
- stocks and bonds
- mutual funds
- 529 college savings plans
- real estate investments (deeds, mortgages, rental agreements, etc.)
- collectibles (valuation and where items are)

[ ]   [ ]   I know the annualized return generated by each of the above investments.

[ ]   [ ]   If I or my family owns a business, I know the current valuation of the business, including how much debt it currently carries and the value of its liquid assets.

[ ]   [ ]   I know the value, location, and performance of all my retirement accounts [and those of my spouse, if applicable], including IRAs, SEP-IRAs, Solo-401(k)s, and company pension plans.

[ ]   [ ]   I know the percentage of income I am putting away for retirement and what it's being invested in [and, if applicable, how much my spouse is putting away and what he is investing in].

[ ]   [ ]   I know if I [and my spouse, if applicable] am making the maximum allowable contribution to my retirement plan at work, whether my employer is making matching contributions, and what the vesting schedule is.

[ ]   [ ]   I know how much money I [and my spouse, if applicable] will be getting from Social Security and what my [and, if applicable, his] pension benefits will be.

[ ]   [ ]   I know whether my [and my spouse's, if applicable] income is protected should I [or my spouse] become disabled because I own disability insurance. In addition, I know what the exact coverage is, when the benefits would start, and whether the benefits would be taxable.

[ ]   [ ]   I [or my family] maintain a safety deposit box, know how to gain access to it, and have reviewed its contents within the past 12 months. If I have the only key, other family members know where to find it if something should happen to me.

SCORING:

Give yourself 1 point for every time you answered "true" and 0 for every time you answered "false."

14 to 17 points: Excellent! You have a good grasp of where your money is.

9 to 13 points: You're not totally in the dark, but there are some areas in which your knowledge is less than adequate.

Under 9 points: Your chances of being hurt financially because of insufficient knowledge are enormous. You need to learn how to protect yourself from future financial disaster.

If you scored well on this test, congratulations! But don't go out and start celebrating just yet. Even among knowledgeable money managers, it's rare to find anyone, male or female, who has a handle on every aspect of their own finances and what they could and should be doing to assure themselves of a secure future. So even if you scored 12 or above, I guarantee you'll discover many secrets and ideas that will be of enormous value to you in the pages that follow.

WHAT IF I DIDN'T SCORE WELL?

If you didn't score so well, take heart—by the time you've finished this book, you'll know *exactly* what you need to take immediate charge of your financial health and invest wisely for your family's future security.

If you're like most people, you probably knew some of the answers but not all of them—and some of the questions may have struck you as awfully complicated. Trust me, none of it is really that difficult. Before long you'll be surprised by just how easy understanding your finances can be. Indeed, you'll probably wonder why you ever thought any of it was confusing. In the meantime, don't panic because you've just discovered there is all this information about your family finances that you don't know. We'll take care of it all soon enough.

At this point, what's important is simply that you realize that there's a lot you don't know—and, even more important, a lot that you now *want* to know. If that's how you feel, pat yourself on the back—you've completed Step One. You are motivated to educate yourself about how to take control of your financial future—which is what the "Smart Women Finish Rich!" journey is all about.

ENOUGH WITH THE BAD NEWS ...
LET'S GET TO THE GOOD STUFF!

It's possible that some of the myths about money that I've presented to you in this first step have struck you as being overly negative. If so, I apologize. As a rule, I make it a policy to avoid negative people, those dream stealers, as I call them, who seem to enjoy raining on other people's parades. But I started our journey this way for a reason: Because I know you purchased this book in order to make a positive change in your life, and sometimes change can be difficult. In fact, many people live their lives going nowhere and doing nothing, not because they like where they are but simply because they are afraid of change. Overcoming this fear takes real motivation. It has to hurt so much that finally you can't take it anymore and you say, "Enough is enough! I want my life to be different!"

It's in this spirit that I've offered some cautionary tales and depressing statistics. I simply want you to come to grips with the fact that if you don't take care of your financial future, no one—not the government, not your employer, not your spouse—is going to do it for you. And it definitely won't take care of itself.

But don't let the negativity get you down. Remember: Those gloomy facts and figures don't have to be your reality!

I often repeat to clients what Grandmother Bach used to tell me. "You know, David," she would say, "when I was growing up, going to work, starting my career, many people asked me why was I worrying about retirement plans. 'You'll have Social Security,' they'd say. 'You'll have a pension from your company.' But even at a young age, I didn't think it was a good idea to depend on someone else to take care of me—not my employer, not the government, not even your grandfather."

That's why, unlike most of her friends, my grandmother always made a point each time she got a paycheck of putting some money aside and buying some high-quality stocks or bonds. It's also why, unlike most of her friends, when she reached retirement age, she was able to enjoy herself in worry-free comfort.

I hope now that you've accomplished Step One, you're motivated to take control of your financial future by getting educated about your money.

Now it's time to begin Step Two, in which we take a look at what's important to you about money.

PUT YOUR MONEY WHERE YOUR VALUES ARE

As a financial advisor, I specialize in doing what we call **Purpose-Focused Financial Planning™**. What this means is that I help my clients discover (often for the first time) what their true values about money actually are.

Initially at least, talking about personal values often throws people for a loop. It's not the sort of thing most of us expect to be discussing with a financial professional. Most people assume that when they meet with a financial advisor, the conversation will focus on investments, on assets and liabilities, on taxes and how many years they have to go before retirement. Well, all that does need to be talked about, but it's not where I believe the conversation should begin. What needs to be discussed first is what is really driving you when it comes to money.

Think about it. Your attitudes about money are what define everything that matters about your personal financial situation: how much money you need, how hard you are willing to work for it, how you will feel when you finally get it. That's why I can say with total confidence that once you understand what money really means to you, you will be unstoppable. Indeed, the process I am about to share with you is probably the single most effective tool I know to help people create a life plan that will lead them to the ultimate financial security they want.

A SMART WOMEN FINISH RICH® SEMINAR IN ACTION

I gave a seminar once in my hometown of San Francisco, but it could have been anywhere. As usual, the room was filled with women of all ages and types—old, young, rich, poor, single, married, you name it. Also as usual, I began with an announcement and a question. "My name is David Bach," I said, "and I'm here to show Smart Women how to finish rich. Would that be okay with any of you?"

Virtually in unison, every woman in the room shouted out, "Yes!" That's generally the answer I get. I grinned at the crowd and continued. "Well, here's my next question, and it's the most important one I will ask you tonight. But don't worry—it's also the easiest." I looked out at them intently. "When you stop and think about it, what's really important about money to you?"

The room was totally silent. "Come on," I said. "This is easy. Think."

Still, nobody said anything.

"The reason you came here tonight is because you recognize that money is important," I persisted. "But what is really important about it? Most important, what is important about money to you?"

Finally, someone broke the silence. "No more student loans!" a young woman called out.

I turned to the big pad that had been placed on an easel behind me. Pulling out a marker pen, I wrote down what the young woman had said. "Okay," I repeated, "what's important about money to you is 'no more student loans.' What else? Who else wants to tell me what's important about money to them?"

A sixty-ish woman sitting a few rows behind the "student loan" woman was the next to answer. "Security," she said. "I want to know that if something should happen to my husband, I won't need to worry."

I nodded and wrote "security" on the pad.

Then another woman spoke up. "Freedom," she said. "What's important about money to me is freedom."

I turned to face this woman. "That's great," I said. "But 'freedom' means different things to different people. What's important about having freedom to you?"

The woman stood up and looked around the room. "I just want to know I can do what I want to do when I want to do it."

Before she could go any further, another woman jumped to her feet. "I've got one," she shouted. "I want to know that my husband can't control what I do. What's important to me is knowing I have choices."

She was joined by yet another woman who said that what was important about money to her was "feeling like I can do what the Lord meant for me to do with my life, which is to help others."

Within about ten minutes, I had filled two entire sheets with different reasons why money was important to one or another of my students. It was incredible. Money clearly meant something different to each and every woman in the room.

Then I started circling some of the words and phrases I had written down. First I circled "security," then "freedom," then "ability to have choices," "happiness," "live a life of meaning," "able to do what God wants me to do," "more time with family," "help others," "feel satisfied," and "feel happy." By the time I was done, about 80 percent of the reasons I had written down were circled. That first answer—"pay off student loans"—wasn't among them, though. Neither was "pay off credit-card debt," or "pay off mortgage," or "travel to Hawaii."

Leaving the class to wonder about this for a moment, I looked out at them and shook my head. "Once again," I said, "a group of women has proven to me how much more in touch with yourselves you are than men." I paused for a moment. "Have you noticed what almost all of you did?" I asked. "Take a close look. Every reason I circled has one thing in common."

The sea of faces staring back at me seemed stumped.

"Look closely," I repeated. "Almost all of the reasons you listed were values. Notice how only a few of the reasons I wrote down are goals, like 'pay off school loans' or 'get the mortgage paid off.' Almost everything here is an idea like security, freedom, and happiness. These are values—your values—the most important things in life. They're the stuff you will do just about anything in the world to achieve—because ultimately they are truly who you are!"

Slowly, first on just a few faces, then on more and more of them, I could see a light dawning.

"Guess what, ladies?" I continued. "What you just did was the most important part of taking control of your financial future, and you did it almost effortlessly. You see, as women you have a tremendous advantage over men: You are already in touch with your feelings and your values. For the most part, men don't get this stuff. It takes them way more time." I grinned at the class. "Pretend you're a man right now," I instructed. "What would you say if I asked you what's important about money to you?"

The room erupted. "Cars!" someone shouted. "A big house!" someone else said. "A boat!" "Football!" "Beer!" "Women!" The class couldn't stop. It was hilarious.

I laughed along with them. "Exactly," I shouted over the hubbub. "It's all goals, all stuff. No values."

Then I got serious again. "Without values, goals rarely get accomplished," I said. "Show me someone who is not reaching their full potential, and I'll show you someone who missed the importance of designing his or her life around their values. Values are the key. When you understand them correctly, they will pull you toward your dreams—which is a lot better than having to push yourself!"

WHAT'S IMPORTANT ABOUT MONEY TO YOU?

What I've just described is the way I usually start my Smart Women Finish Rich® seminars. In the pages that follow, I'm going to take you on the same personal journey that this group of women—and thousands of women like them—have taken in my classes and in my office. That is, we're going to discover what is important about money to you and in turn discover your values.

The process of understanding "what's important about money to you" is absolutely essential. Asking yourself what money means to you, after all, quickly forces you to evaluate what it is you are looking for in life. And understanding what you are looking for in life is the foundation on which all smart financial planning is based.

Think about it. How could you possibly put together an empowering financial plan unless you know what it is you really care about? Let's say what's important about money to you is the security it can provide, but your current state of financial affairs has you living from paycheck to paycheck. Well, then, something is wrong, isn't it? Clearly, your financial behavior is out of whack with your deepest values. Similarly, let's say what's important about money to you is the freedom it can bring you, but in actuality you are tied to a job working 60 hours a week to pay a mortgage on a large home—wishing all the while that you were traveling more. Once again, your financial life is in conflict with what you are really all about.

Money is not an end in itself. It is merely a tool to help us achieve some particular goal. If the way we handle our money conflicts with our personal values, we are not going to wind up living happy and fulfilled lives.

So how do you figure out what you are looking for in life and how to use money as a tool to get it? Well, fortunately, you don't have to go to Tibet and meet with a guru on a mountaintop. All you need to do is get clear about what your values are. Once you've done that, it will be easy to develop your financial goals (which we will do in Step Three).

What's great about this process is that it is one of the most powerful legs of your journey to financial security as well as one of the least complicated. What makes it so simple is the fact that you already know what your values are. They are not something you have to study for years to learn. The fact is, most of us have a pretty good sense of who we are and what's important about money to us. These things may not be immediately apparent, but with just a little bit of digging some amazing realizations will pop to the surface.

So let's eavesdrop right now on some values conversations I've had over the years. By listening in, you should begin to see how the process works. Specifically, what you are about to learn is how to put your values down on paper and build what I call a *values ladder*.[1] This simple but highly effective tool will help you clarify what's pulling you toward (or keeping you from) taking control over your own financial situation. Once you understand how the process

---

[1] The values conversation and values ladder are concepts derived from Bill Bachrach/Bachrach & Associates, Inc. (**www.billbachrach.com**), and have been included here with permission.

works, we can apply it to your situation and life and make sure that from this day forward, your values are clear so that you are pulled only toward your financial goals.

ONE WOMAN'S VALUES EXERCISE

Here's an example of a conversation that worked really well and helped a client of mine greatly. Jessica was a successful 33-year-old computer salesperson who met with me in my office after taking one of my investment classes. She was married (to her college sweetheart) and had an eight-year-old daughter, Ginny, and a dog named Teddy.

Jessica seemed very focused the day she came to see me, and we got right down to business. Having already attended my seminar, she knew exactly what I was trying to get at when I asked her to tell me what was most important to her about money.

"Well, David," she said, "I guess when I think about money what's really important to me is security."

"That's great," I said. "Of course, security means different things to different people. Help me to understand what's important about security to you."

Jessica didn't hesitate. "Having security lets me feel that I'm free to do what I want, when I want," she replied.

"And what does that feeling of being able to do what you want mean to you?" I asked.

"I guess it means having a sense of freedom. Not feeling constrained by the duties of life."

"I see. So what would not having these constraints in your life and having this freedom mean to you?"

Jessica thought for a moment. "It would mean that I'd have more time to be with my daughter, who is growing up so fast that she's going to be in college before I know it," she said. "And I could spend more time with my husband and my friends, who I rarely see now because I'm always so busy."

"Okay," I nodded. "Let's assume for a moment that you have security, and that as a result you have the freedom to spend more time with your daughter and your husband and your friends. What's important about being in that position to you?"

"Well, I guess it would make me feel calmer and happier," Jessica responded. "Definitely happier. Right now I feel burned out all the time. I'd like to not be tired for a change."

"And what's important to you about that?" I asked her.

Jessica smiled wearily. "I just spend so much time rushing around now trying to do everything—working, being a wife and a mother, keeping the house and bills in order—that I don't feel like I have a life. Some days I don't even remember what it feels like to not be exhausted."

"So it's important for you to not rush around and to feel you have a life again," I said.

Once again Jessica did not hesitate. "Yes, definitely," she said firmly. "I want my life back."

When I asked Jessica what she would do if she had her life back, she said she'd start taking better care of herself, exercising and eating better. When I pressed her on why she wanted to do that, she said her aim was to live longer and be a better example to her daughter.

"Okay," I continued, "so now that you are going to live longer and be an example to your daughter, what else would you do with your life?"

Jessica frowned for a moment, lost in thought. "That's a tough one to answer," she said finally. "I'm not sure."

I wasn't about to let her off the hook. "I know you're not sure," I persisted, "but if you were sure, what do you think you would say?"

"Well," she said slowly, "I guess if I really had my life together the way I wanted it, I would focus on getting more involved with charity groups in my community."

In response to my follow-up questions, Jessica explained that "making a difference and giving something back" was really important to her.

"Is there anything more important to you than making a difference and helping others?" I asked.

Jessica looked me in the eye. "I just want to know that when I go, I'll have lived a full life, loved, been a good example to my daughter and my family, and really made a difference." She blushed self-consciously. "That's all," she said.

That, of course, was a lot—a lot to think about, and a lot to remember when it came time to construct a financial plan. Fortunately, as Jessica and I talked, we kept a record of the values that were important to her, in the order that she had come up with them. On page 55, you'll see Jessica's values ladder. As you can see, at the bottom of the ladder is Jessica's **first value**, security. Above it, each successive rung contains the next value that Jessica told me was important to her.

Take a moment and reread the conversation. Notice how quickly Jessica and I were able to build her values ladder.

DOES YOUR FINANCIAL BEHAVIOR MATCH YOUR VALUES?

What Jessica and I learned from our values conversation was that there was nothing more important to her than having more time to devote to her family and community. As things stood, most of her time (and energy) was going to her job. With that in mind, the next thing we did was look at Jessica's financial situation and habits to see how they stacked up against her values ladder.

As a computer salesperson, Jessica earned about $75,000 a year. That's a solid income by any measure, yet for some reason she was still living from paycheck to paycheck. Hence, the pressure she felt to spend so much time at work.

JESSICA'S VALUES LADDER

making a difference
helping others

WIA living longer &
example to daughter **TY?**

WIA not rushing/feeling
like I have a life **TY?**

WIA feeling calmer
and happier **TY?**

WIA more time with
daughter/husband **TY?**

WIA freedom/no duty
constraints **TY?**

WIA security **TY?**

WIA = What's important about   **TY** = to you

(ALWAYS START WITH)
"What's important about money to you?"

Why was Jessica so strapped for cash? We looked at her spending patterns and found that she was spending a lot of money on what were clearly nonessential items: more than $300 a month on clothes, $100 on an unlimited data plan for her iPhone, $350 on restaurants, $150 on dry cleaning, $525 on a leased car, and on and on. In all, she was spending more than $2,000 a month—well over half her take-home pay—*on things that had absolutely nothing to do with what was most important to her:* namely, having more time to devote to her family and community.

When I pointed this out to her—that she was spending more than four hours of every eight-hour workday toiling to pay for luxuries that did nothing to give her the life she really wanted—Jessica was shocked. But, fortunately, she was also motivated to change her ways. Once she realized how much time and energy she was, in essence, wasting, she worked out a plan under which she was able to start saving money for the first time (and thus stop living from paycheck to paycheck) while slowly cutting back the number of hours she put in at work (thus giving her more time with her family).

THE BREAKTHROUGH

Jessica got more out of our values conversation than just a new financial plan. She told me later that she also came away with a sense of clarity about her life's purpose that she hadn't really had before. "It made me realize that much of what I was doing with my time had little or nothing to do with my own values about who I am and who I want to be," she said. As a result, she added, "Now when I am doing something, I am much clearer with myself. I always ask myself, 'Is this in line with my values?' If it's not, I try to not do it." Of course, as Jessica acknowledged, there are some things that can't be avoided, but at least she now knows where her focus is supposed to be.

Equally important, the conversation also made Jessica realize that she didn't need nearly as much money as she had thought in order to get what she really wanted out of life. As she told me, "It showed me that while I've been spending so much time trying to increase my income, I've actually been squandering money on things that have nothing to do with the values that are important to me. I realized that a new dress, a fancy car, and the latest iPhone were not worth all the weekends I was spending at the office."

Once that became clear, she said, she found it much easier to cut back on unnecessary expenses. "I immediately felt calmer about who I was and where I was going," she reported. "I hadn't had such a sense of inner peace in a long time. It's hard to believe that a question as simple as 'What's important about money to you?' can lead to such an important breakthrough, but it definitely can."

IF IT'S NOT ABOUT RETURNS, WHAT *IS* IT ABOUT?

Values exercises are not just for younger women. Taking a good look inside yourself can be a worthwhile undertaking no matter what your age—especially in this era of economic boom and record stock prices, when so many of us have become so obsessed with growth figures and rates of return that the point of saving and investing sometimes gets forgotten.

Take Helen, an older client of mine who came to my office one day, very upset. Even though it's been more than 20 years since that meeting, I can still vividly remember how concerned Helen was about her finances, despite the fact that she seemed to be in a great place financially. At 72 years old, Helen was a "child of the Great Depression" and had always watched her spending and savings very carefully. Ever since her husband had passed away six years prior to our meeting, she had been living on Social Security and a widow's pension. In addition, she had some $500,000 in bank certificates of deposit that had been paying her 8 percent annual interest (or

$40,000 a year)—a rate that seems almost mythical to modern savers. In short, she had more than enough money to live on.

So what was bothering her? Well, it seemed that her bank had informed her that her CDs were about to mature, and if she wished to roll over her savings into new CDs, the best interest rate she could get now was only 5 percent.

"What am I going to do?" Helen asked me. "These rates are so low, yet I can't afford to take any risk with my money."

When I asked Helen how she spent the $40,000 a year she earned from her CDs, she gave me a look and said she put the money into a savings account at the bank. In other words, she didn't need it to live on.

With that in mind, I asked her what was so important about this $40,000 a year in interest that she was earning but not spending. She said it gave her a sense of security. As we continued what quickly became a full-fledged values conversation, she explained that she wanted to know that she would always be independent; for her, being independent meant never having to be a burden on her family. Her grandchildren, she said, meant the world to her. "I just love them so much," Helen added fervently. "I want to be able to give to them and not need to take."

"And what would you like to give them?" I asked.

Helen's eyes lit up. "You know," she said, "I've always thought it would be so special to take the whole family on a cruise to Alaska." As she told me about this dream trip, she glowed. Her smile disappeared, however, when I asked her why she didn't just do it.

"Oh, David," she said, "it would cost at least ten thousand dollars."

"So?" I replied. "You've been earning more than four times that on your CDs every year." I shook my head. "Helen," I said, "you have your health, you have all these assets, and you have this wonderful dream of taking your family on a trip—and what are you doing? You're sitting in my office worrying about whether your CDs

HELEN'S VALUES LADDER

WIA = What's important about   **TY** = to you

(ALWAYS START WITH)
"What's important about money to you?"

are going to pay you eight percent or five percent. What does it matter what the interest rate is if you're not going to use your money to make your life the way you want it to be?" I then asked Helen the final question on the values ladder: Was there anything more important to her than her family?

As it turned out, there wasn't.

Within a week of our meeting, Helen booked the cruise we had discussed. The trip cost her about $12,500. It was the most money she had ever spent on a luxury in her entire life. What was important, however, was not what she spent but what she got—which was the joy of sharing a wonderful experience with her children and grandchildren.

Take a look at Helen's values ladder, and note how quickly we were able to use that simple question about the importance of money to help her build a future that was exciting for both her and her family.

The point of this story is that values-based financial planning helped Helen use her money the way money is supposed to be used—to make life better. If your money is not helping you make your life better, then something is wrong. Chances are you're not making a connection between your values and the role money plays in your life. The importance of making that connection is the point of this story and the point of this chapter.

CREATE YOUR OWN VALUES LADDER

Pretend you are arriving at my office in New York. You're going to meet with me, one on one, to create your own personal values ladder to the new you—a woman totally in control of her own financial situation.

You enter my office. In the middle of a round table at which you and I will sit is a piece of paper containing a blank values ladder just like the one that follows. We're going to use it to help you figure out what's important about money to you.

1. Start by relaxing. Take a minute to collect your thoughts. Our objective is for you to give answers that reflect how you really feel—not how you think someone else thinks you should feel. Remember, whatever your values are, they are the right ones for you.
2. Ready? Let's start with the single most important question. Ask yourself: *What's important about money to me?*
3. Write your answer on the bottom rung of the ladder.

    Remember that we're looking for values (basic aspirations such as *freedom, happiness, security,* and so on) and not goals (which generally involve specific amounts of money or particular acquisitions). If you've just gone through the jolt of a divorce and find yourself on your own with two kids to take care of, for example, your value might be "security." Or maybe you're a single entrepreneur who dreams of traveling around the world, in which case your initial value may be "freedom."
4. Now we need a little more perspective on the values you're listing, because the value you choose means different things to different people. Ask yourself: *What's important about* _____ [your value] *to me?* Write your answer on the next rung up the ladder.
5. Let's assume for a moment that _____ [your second value] has become a reality for you. Ask yourself: *What's important about* _____ [your second value] *to me?* Write your answer on the third rung of the ladder.
6. Continue climbing the ladder, filling in your answers as you go up. Don't cheat yourself. The biggest mistake people make when they conduct a values conversation on their own (and even sometimes in my office) is not taking the process deep enough. It's important to keep digging, because only rarely

will the values you hold most important be among the first ones you list. Just keep asking yourself: *What's important about* _____ [the last value you gave] *to me?* You'll know you're done when you can't think of anything more important than the last value you mentioned.

TAPPING INTO YOUR VALUES

For those of you who may be having trouble figuring out what is a value versus what is a goal—and many people do—I've listed some examples in the boxes that follow. By studying the lists, you'll get a better idea of the difference between the two. Don't cheat, though, and borrow some values from my list just because they sound good and you're having trouble filling out your ladder. If the values you write down don't truly reflect what you feel in your heart, then they won't work to motivate you.

What follows are examples of goals that people come up with when they do the values ladder exercise. Remember, we are not looking for goals. We are looking for values. (We'll get to goals in Step Three.)

SOME EXAMPLES OF VALUES

Freedom	Connection with others
Security	Independence
Happiness	Fulfillment
Peace of mind	Confidence
Power	Being the best
Helping others	Making a difference
Helping family	Fun
Realizing my true potential (self-actualization)	Growing
Greater spirituality	Adventure

YOUR VALUES LADDER

WIA = What's important about   TY = to you

(ALWAYS START WITH)
"What's important about money to you?"

SOME EXAMPLES OF GOALS

Pay down debt

Have $1 million

Not run out of money

Pay for college

Buy a house

Travel *(Travel is a goal; what traveling does for you is the value. I bring this up because travel is mentioned quite often in values conversations.)*

Get a new car

Redecorate

Retire rich

Donate money

Tithing *(As with travel, the reason you give to charity is a value; what or how much you give is the goal.)*

Put money in my retirement account

Not work

Start my own business

Put my child through college

Get divorced

Get married

Stay married *(Money affects marriages—no question about it. But contrary to what many people believe, it's not how much money you have that matters. It's how you communicate and make decisions about your money that determines whether financial issues will bring you together as a family or drive you apart.)*

WHAT IF I CAN'T COME UP WITH ENOUGH VALUES?

This almost never happens. Everyone has lots of values—more than you might think at first. Give yourself some time for them to occur to you. But don't turn it into a marathon. The whole exercise should not take more than 15 minutes! In my office, the average values conversation lasts less than 10 minutes.

Also, there are no right or wrong answers here. The only mistake you can make is to be less than honest. In my classes, I always jokingly tell the audience, "Don't look at your neighbor's paper. Those are her values, not yours."

GO ALL THE WAY!

The reason our values ladder is designed to elicit at least six personal values is that we are trying to get you to look deep within yourself—so deep that you will come away with a really intense awareness of what is most important to you. Understanding this, you should be able to stop wasting your time, energy, and money on things that don't really matter to you—and begin focusing your resources on the things that do!

As should be clear by now, although we are focusing on the question of money, what we really are getting at in our values conversation is the essence of what matters to you about life in general. That's what makes the technique so powerful. It enables you not only to lay out your values but to define who you are and what direction you want to take your life.

DON'T THINK YOU CAN SKIP THIS STEP

Don't be like some students who take my classes and try to skip this step in the mistaken belief that the values-based approach is nothing more than "New Age feel-good stuff." There's nothing New Age about getting in touch with your values. The Greek philosopher Socrates was talking about that sort of thing back in 400 B.C. The key to human advancement, he taught, could be expressed in two simple words: "Know thyself." So don't get sidetracked.

As you will see as we continue our journey, the eight-step approach builds on itself. If you don't complete this step, you'll find the next one much harder than it needs to be. That's because doing

Step Two gives you a certain momentum that makes Step Three really easy.

CONGRATULATIONS! YOU HAVE COMPLETED STEP TWO!

The thing to remember about this step is that we had you look closely at your values for a very practical reason: Knowing "what's important about money to you" not only makes it possible to plan your future intelligently, it also makes it easier to stick to your plan. Once they know what their values are, people will do more to protect them than just about anything else in the world. Values are not tasks or resolutions, like "eat less," "save more," or "keep the house clean." Values are not things we get bored with. Values are what we believe in; they are what motivate and shape us.

Now that you have constructed your own values ladder, keep it handy. We're going to use it in Step Three when we start defining your specific financial goals. But there's one more thing you've got to do before you're ready to design that road map to your financial future. *You need to figure out where you stand today financially.*

FIGURE OUT WHERE YOU STAND FINANCIALLY . . . AND WHERE YOU WANT TO GO

Imagine that you are trying to book tickets for a dream trip to Paris. You log on to your favorite flight deal site, but every time you click the "compare prices" button, you get an error message. You get more and more agitated, wondering what could possibly be wrong with the site. You've provided it the necessary information about when you'd like to travel and which Paris airport you'd like to land in. As you're just about to call the customer service line to ask why the stupid website isn't helping you book this trip, it suddenly dawns on you what you've done wrong.

You have told the travel website where you want to go, but you neglected to tell it where you are now. How can the site find you a flight if it doesn't know where you're leaving from?

When it comes to planning a trip, chances are you'd never make a mistake that elementary. But you'd be surprised how many people slip up in precisely the same way when it comes to planning their finances. They plunge into all sorts of detail about what they want to accomplish, what investment they should buy, and where they want to be, without first making sure they know where they stand now.

DO YOU KNOW WHERE YOUR MONEY IS?

If I asked you about your current financial status, could you, right now, list on a blank piece of paper all your assets and liabilities, including your investments, bank accounts, mortgages, and credit-card debts? Do you have an organized filing system in which all your financial documents can be found easily? Or have you left all that stuff to your spouse or your accountant? If you're working, do you know how the money in your company pension plan is invested?

You might want to turn back to Step One at this point and take a look at how you did on that quiz about your family's money. If you're like most people, you probably scored lower than you'd like. That's okay. This is where we start to fix the problems you found back there.

KNOWING WHERE YOUR MONEY IS SOUNDS OBVIOUS, BUT TRUST ME— MOST PEOPLE DON'T HAVE A CLUE

Having been a financial coach for hundreds of clients, I can tell you from firsthand experience that most people really don't know where they spend their money and where their money is invested. I've had clients come into my office with shopping bags filled with mutual-fund statements, bank statements, 401(k) printouts, you name it. Take Karen and Tom, a successful couple in their fifties.

They came into my office one day, dumped the contents of a bulging department-store shopping bag onto my desk, and announced ruefully, "David, we're the people you talk about in your seminars!"

We started going through their statements together, and you know what? Even though Karen and Tom had been organized enough to save the statements they'd been sent, most of the envelopes had never been opened! They hadn't looked at their accounts for months.

Now, I'm sure that you're not like this, but I'll bet many of your friends are.

SIX IRAS, FIVE BANK ACCOUNTS, FOUR INSURANCE PLANS ...

After two hours of going through Karen and Tom's stuff, we managed to figure out where all their money was: It was stashed in twelve separate mutual funds, six different IRA accounts, five bank accounts, two old and two new 401(k) plans, and four separate insurance policies.

Unbelievable, right? Wrong. Karen and Tom are typical of many successful people. As Karen explained it, somewhat defensively, "Tom puts all the responsibility of managing the money in my hands, but with a career and three kids I don't have time to keep track of it all. I really don't know how others find the time."

"You're right, Karen," I said, "No one has the time to monitor what they have, unless they are professional money managers. And I know a lot of professionals who don't take care of their own money because they're so busy taking care of other people's!"

MAKE GETTING YOUR FINANCIAL HOUSE IN ORDER NOW A PRIORITY!

Old or young, rich or poor, married or single, it doesn't matter— one of the first things we do at AE Wealth Management after discussing our clients' values is to figure out their current financial condition.

To accomplish this, I have my clients fill out what we call a **FinishRich Inventory Planner**™. You'll find a copy in Appendix 2.

NOTE: *Don't complete the worksheet until after you've finished reading this book! Why? Sad but true, most people never get past the first few chapters of books like this one if they have to stop reading and fill out a form. So wait until you've gotten through the whole book before you start on the worksheet.*

If you are like most people, you probably already have all your financial information totally organized. In fact, I'm sure that right now all of your financial documents are sitting in an easy-to-use filing system with brightly colored folders and neatly typed labels. And because all your financial documents are so well organized and easy for you to review, completing the worksheet in the back of the book shouldn't take you more than 30 minutes, right?

Obviously, I'm being a bit facetious here. Usually when I discuss filling out the FinishRich Inventory Planner™ in my investment classes, I call this project a "homework assignment." And when I get to the part about most people having all their financial information in color-coded files, the women in the room either laugh or groan. At that point, I say, "For those of you who use the shopping-bag approach to filing, it may take a little longer."

To be honest, I have had some clients who've told me that this "homework" took them only about 15 minutes (usually because they had everything on a financial software program like Quicken or on a Web-based personal finance tracker like **Mint.com** or **ClarityMoney .com**). But for most people, it generally takes at least an hour or two.

And don't worry if it takes you even longer than that. Some people find the assignment requires an entire weekend. If you're one of them, don't be daunted. It simply means that you really need to do it!

GETTING ORGANIZED IS ONE OF THE KEYS
TO FINANCIAL SECURITY

Admittedly, getting organized can sometimes be a painful experience. I've had some clients who thought they were financially secure, only to discover, after listing all their assets and liabilities, that they weren't doing as well as they had imagined. Then again, I've had plenty of others who completed the worksheet and found they were much closer to financial independence than they realized. Either way, they were much better off knowing the truth about their financial situation.

Take Betsy and Victor, two clients of mine who got a lot out of the process. Their story is quite typical, and I hope it will inspire you to emulate their example.

BETSY'S STORY: LEARNING WHERE YOU STAND

"When I first took David's investment class, I got really excited about the opportunity to become involved in my family's finances. I have to admit, however, that the homework assignment of 'getting my financial house in order' did seem a bit intimidating.

"The thing I liked best about the FinishRich Inventory Planner™ was that it was something that produced immediate results. I knew my family's financial documents were totally disorganized. I also knew that my husband, Victor, probably didn't know what our net worth was.

"The other thing I really liked about this step was that it gave me an easy way to approach my husband about getting involved with our finances. I basically came home from the class and said, 'Victor, I've got a huge homework assignment and I know I'm going to need your help. Do you think we could work together on it this weekend, because I'm not sure I can do it without you?'

"That approach really worked with Victor, since it wasn't like I was accusing him of anything or trying to take control of the finances. And when I showed him what the assignment was, he readily admitted it was something that we should have done years ago. As Victor put it, he had always wanted to get our financial documents organized, but it was a lot like cleaning out the garage—easy to put off.

"In the end, it wound up taking us almost the entire day to do—a lot longer than the 30 minutes David had promised. But as David said, the fact that it took so much longer meant we really needed to do it.

"When we were through, I could really see for the first time just where our family stood financially. I realized for the first time that we were actually doing a pretty good job of saving money. We had very little debt and our retirement accounts were really starting to add up. Seeing this all on paper got me excited about looking at what else I could do to improve our financial situation."

VICTOR'S STORY: A WEIGHT OFF HIS SHOULDERS

"When Betsy came home with this homework assignment to get our financial house in order, quite frankly I was embarrassed. I knew I had taken on the responsibility of managing the family's money, and I felt I had been doing an okay job—but I also knew there was a lot of stuff all over the place, not well organized.

"I have to admit it really felt good when we finished filling out the FinishRich Inventory Planner™ that weekend. For the first time in years, Betsy and I really discussed where our financial life was. By getting all of our assets and liabilities down on paper, we were finally able to see in black and white where we actually stood and how much our family was worth. While I always sort of had a running total in my head, filling out the inventory worksheet made it clearer and easier to deal with. I have to say—it's quite a weight off my shoulders to have Betsy involved with our money now. It takes some of the pressure off of me."

FROM MY POINT OF VIEW ...

When I met with Betsy and Victor in my office after their week-end "housecleaning" session, we had a great time. They really had enjoyed getting their finances organized and were excited to talk about where they stood.

Because they had done such a thorough job filling out the work-sheet, my job actually was quite easy. One of the first things I noticed was that they had both been opening individual retirement accounts (IRAs) at different banks each year for nearly eight years. They had done this because they thought that's how you get the best return on your money—and also because they had heard that "diversifying" was important, and they believed that going to a lot of different banks was how you diversified.

Actually, what they really were doing was letting their retirement dollars lay dormant at a measly 2 percent annual rate, which didn't even keep up with inflation. I was able to help them consolidate all their accounts into one custodial IRA and then reposition the money they had invested into more appropriate growth invest-ments. I will explain how we did this—and how you can too—in Step Five, when we discuss your "retirement basket." For now, what matters is that by getting organized, Betsy and Victor were able to see where they stood and what they needed to do to achieve their goals.

DO YOUR HOMEWORK

The way we work at my office is simple. We send prospective cli-ents the FinishRich Inventory Planner™ and ask them to fill it out completely before they come in. Nonetheless, some clients show up without having filled out their sheets. Often I'll kid them and ask if they were the kind of students who never did their home-work on time. Joking aside, however, there's no getting around the fundamental reality: Until you get your finances organized, you can't get started creating financial security—and ultimately your financial dreams.

So no excuses. When you finish this book, you must fill out the **FinishRich Inventory Planner**™ in Appendix 2 (you can also find a link to a PDF version on page 383). It's the best way to start getting organized and involved in your finances and, most important, determine your net worth. (This is key, since if you don't know what you are worth, you won't know where you are starting from.) By the time you are done, you will have a better grasp of your financial situation than the vast majority of Americans. You will know not only your personal net worth but also where you spend your money and how your newfound wealth is going to be built. You—not someone else—will be in charge of your financial destiny.

YOUR FIRST JOB: FIND YOUR STUFF

Completing the FinishRich Inventory Planner™ is probably the most crucial homework assignment you'll get in the course of this book. But don't start working on it yet. At this point, all I want you to do is begin finding your "stuff." To make this easier, I'm going to share with you an incredibly simple yet powerful way to organize your stuff at home. If you do this now, you'll find it much easier to fill out your worksheet later. So let's get going.

THE FINISHRICH FILE FOLDER SYSTEM™

So here's what I want you to do. First, get yourself a dozen or so hanging folders and a box of at least 50 file folders to put inside them. (Alternatively, if you keep all of your information digitally, then you can create these folders on your computer or on the cloud.) Then label the hanging folders as follows:

❏ 1. Label the first one "**Tax Returns**." In it, put eight file folders, one for each of the past seven years plus one for this year. Mark the year on each folder's tab and put into it all of that year's important tax documents, such as W-2 forms, 1099s, and (most important) a copy of all the tax returns you filed for that year. Hopefully, you've at least saved your old tax returns. If you haven't but used a professional tax preparer in the past, call him or her and ask for back copies. As a rule, you should keep old tax records for at least seven years because that's how far back the law allows the IRS to go when it wants to audit you. I recommend hanging on to them even longer, but that's up to you.

❏ 2. Label the second hanging folder "**Retirement Accounts**." This is where you're going to keep all of your retirement-account statements. You should create a file for each retirement account you have. If you have three IRAs and a 401(k) plan, then you should have a separate file for each. The most important things to keep in these folders are the quarterly statements. You *don't* need to keep the prospectuses that the mutual-fund companies mail you each quarter. However, if you have a company retirement account, you should definitely keep the sign-up package because it tells you what investment options you have—something you should review annually.

❏ 3. Label the third hanging folder "**Social Security**." You should put your most recent Social Security Benefits Statement in this folder. If you haven't already signed up for a "*my* Social Security" account, you can go online to **www.ssa.gov/myaccount/** to do so. Once you're there, you can print out a copy of your most recent Social

Security Benefits Statement. You can also request a copy by mail.

❏ 4. Label the fourth hanging folder "**Investment Accounts**." In this folder, you put files for each investment account you have that is not a retirement account. If you own mutual funds, maintain a brokerage account, or own individual stocks, each and every statement you receive that is related to these investments should go in a particular folder.

❏ 5. Label the fifth hanging folder "**Savings and Checking Accounts**." If you have separate checking and savings accounts, create separate file folders for them. Keep your monthly bank statements here.

❏ 6. Label the sixth hanging folder "**Household Accounts**." If you own your own home, this one should contain the following file folders: "House Title," into which you'll put all your title information (if you can't find this stuff, call your real estate agent or title company); "Home Improvements," where you'll keep all your receipts for any home-improvement work you do (since home-improvement expenses can be added to the cost basis of your house when you sell it, you should keep these receipts for as long as you own your house); and "Home Mortgage," for all your mortgage statements (which you should check regularly, since mortgage companies often DON'T CREDIT YOU PROPERLY). If you're a renter, this folder should contain your lease, the receipt for your security deposit, and the receipts for your rental payments.

❏ 7. Label the seventh hanging folder "**Credit-Card DEBT**." Make sure you capitalize the word "DEBT" so it stands out and bothers you every time you see it. I'm

not kidding. I'll explain later how to deal with credit-
card debt. For the time being, my hope is that this
won't be one of your larger hanging folders. You should
create a separate file for each credit-card account you
have. For many women, this folder may contain more
than a dozen files. I've actually met some women with
as many as 30. However many files you have, keep all
your monthly statements in them. And hang on to
them. As with tax returns, I keep all my credit-card
records for at least seven years in case the IRS ever
decides to audit me. If you no longer receive credit-
card statements in the mail, print out the most current
statement for each credit card to place in these folders.
It's a good idea to have a tangible reminder of your
liabilities.

❏ 8. Label the eighth hanging folder "**Other Liabilities**."
In here go all of your records dealing with debts other
than your mortgage and your credit-card accounts.
These would include college loans, car loans, personal
loans, etc. Each debt should have its own file, which
should contain the loan note and your payment
records.

❏ 9. Label the ninth hanging folder "**Insurance**." It will
contain separate folders for each of your insurance
policies, including health, life, car, homeowners or
renters, disability, long-term care, etc. In each of these
folders put the appropriate policy and all the related
payment records.

❏ 10. Label the tenth hanging folder "**Family Will or Trust**."
This should have a copy of your most recent will or
living trust, along with the business card of the attorney
who set it up.

❏ 11. If you have children, put together a folder labeled "**Children's Accounts**." It should hold all statements and other records pertaining to college savings accounts or other investments that you have made for your kids.

❏ 12. Finally, create a folder called **FinishRich Inventory Planner**™. Here's where you're going to put the worksheet found on page 375 (Appendix 2) after you've filled it out. This folder will also contain a file in which you keep a running semiannual total of your net worth—a vital record that will help you keep track of your financial progress.

That's it. You're done. A dozen folders—eleven if you don't have children. Not so bad, is it? I really do still recommend you do the old-school things of creating files—in a file drawer. All too often if people do this on their computer and only in the "cloud," when one person dies, the other person or the beneficiaries can't find the stuff (unless they have the passwords).

As you dig into this assignment, you may realize that you don't have all of these documents. In some cases, you may have lost them or thrown them away. In others, you may never have had them in the first place. For example, chances are you've never bothered to sign up for a "*my* Social Security" account with the Social Security Administration. Or maybe you don't have disability insurance. Whatever the case, it does not matter at this point. All I want you to do now is create the aforementioned files, whether you have anything to put in them or not. It shouldn't take very long. After all, there are only 12 of them.

Once you're done, put the folders in a file cabinet and feel good about yourself. You are already more organized than you were when you first picked up this book and are better prepared to complete the FinishRich Inventory Planner™.

IF YOU'RE PART OF A COUPLE ...

If you are married (or are in some similarly committed relationship), you definitely should try to get your significant other involved in this project. But be diplomatic. After all, while you've been getting excited about getting organized, your mate has been innocently going about the day with no idea that you are planning to "clean house" financially. A word of advice: Don't suddenly start jumping all over your partner for being disorganized. Remember—your partner hasn't read this book. (At least not yet.)

As I tell the women who take my seminars, it's probably not a good idea to run home and tell your spouse, "Honey, there's this financial advisor named David Bach and he says that as a man you are more than likely doing a really terrible job managing our finances, so from now on I'm going to be in charge of our money. Now, show me where it is!" Nor should you announce, "I just learned that you will probably die before me. And if you don't drop dead soon, I'll still need to protect myself in case you meet some bimbo and decide to divorce me. So show me where all the money is!"

Now, obviously, I'm exaggerating a little bit. I doubt you would ever be so blatant. But I also know that it is very easy to get excited by a set of new ideas.

And I do want you to get excited. That's the whole point of this book—to get you excited enough to make drastic changes in your life. Still, I don't want a bunch of angry men out there looking for my head. More important, I don't want you to be met with an immediate wall of defensiveness and negative feedback if your spouse isn't immediately on board with such drastic changes.

My grandmother taught me that you can accomplish anything in life if your approach is right. In this case, the right approach involves recognizing that if you are part of a couple (and this goes for same-sex relationships as well), money issues should be handled jointly. Chances are, at this point yours are not.

That's one of the great things about this financial housecleaning process. Not only does it show you where you stand financially, it's also, as Betsy pointed out, a very proactive way for couples to start working on their finances together. In filling out the worksheet, nobody is judging or criticizing anyone. All you are doing is getting your stuff organized. If your husband or significant other says, "It's taken care of, honey—don't worry about it," you simply reply, "Great. Show me how it's taken care of and let's discuss it together." If your spouse continues to balk, explain how important it is to you to get involved with the family's finances and that knowing where to find everything is simply a fundamental part of the process.

WHAT IF YOUR SPOUSE WON'T COOPERATE?

For most of you, this process of discussing your finances with your significant other is not going to be a big deal. My experience is that most spouses really do want their mates to be involved with the family's finances. I can't tell you how many men have said to me over the years, "I'm so glad my wife is taking an interest in this stuff. She never seemed to care before, and I always worried about how she would cope if something were to happen to me. Having her involved is a real relief."

The key is how you present it. Some men have fragile egos. What can I say? We like to think we are in charge and that we know what we are doing. Of course, for the most part you know that we are not in charge and that you are. That's fine—just don't let us know that you know it.

> **Five-Star Tip:** If you're concerned that your husband, boyfriend, or partner won't read a book entitled *Smart Women Finish Rich,* consider getting *Smart Couples Finish Rich* and using it as a guide to plan your financial future as a team. You can visit our website at

www.smartcouplesfinishrich.com and read a few chapters of the book for free.

In the event your family already has someone who helps to manage your money (a financial advisor or an attorney or an accountant), then I strongly suggest that you make an appointment to meet with that person. Most likely, he or she does not know exactly where you stand, and completing the Finish Rich Inventory Planner™ really will help the person to better help you. The initial phone call can be as simple as this: "I'm making an effort to get involved in handling the family's financial decisions. My spouse and I would like to meet with you to discuss where we stand financially so we are all on the same page."

When you make the appointment, you and your significant other should go to this meeting—and all future meetings—together. I can't stress this enough: Financial planning should involve both of you equally. The biggest mistake I see couples make is not handling it together. In our office, if a man calls to make an appointment and tells us that his wife does not need to come with him because he's "in charge of the money," we won't take the meeting. That's how strongly we feel about the importance of doing financial planning as a couple.

HEADING IN THE RIGHT DIRECTION

Microsoft, which in my opinion is still one of the smartest companies in the world today, used to run what I thought was one of the world's smartest advertising campaigns. The campaign wasn't about software but rather about our lives and where they might be headed. Their television commercials asked the question straight out: "Where do you want to go today?" (with the idea obviously being that Microsoft could get you there).

As a Smart Woman, the challenge you face now is to answer that question for yourself—to take the foundational work we have just done (including looking at your values and getting your family finances organized) and use it to create a compelling future that inspires and excites you.

So where do you start? Well, here's a hint . . .

Success leaves clues.

Have you ever noticed that some people seem to have it all? Their lives always seem to be going in the direction that they want. They always seem to be moving forward, never pushed off course by life's daily demands and challenges. No matter what happens to them, they come out on top.

Don't you just hate those people?

I threw that in just to see if you were paying attention. Of course, you don't really hate them. But doesn't it make you wonder? Why is it that some people can be so successful, have so much fun, and make it seem so easy?

The answer, I believe, lies in the fact that for the most part successful people have specific goals. In the book *The Eleven Commandments of Wildly Successful Women*, author Pamela Gilberd interviewed 125 women who achieved extraordinary success in both their work and their personal lives. What she found was that most of these women had one thing in common: They all knew where they wanted to go. They had goals. They created their own plans and they focused on making them happen.

The master motivator Napoleon Hill, who wrote the renowned book *Think and Grow Rich*, phrased it differently, but it amounted to the same thing. According to Hill, to achieve your dreams you have to focus on what you want your life to be about. He called this developing "Definiteness of Purpose." After studying the most successful people of his time, Hill concluded that individuals who had this "definiteness of purpose" found it easier to prioritize their time, effort, and money—and, ultimately, to reach their dreams.

Now, "developing definiteness of purpose" is nothing more than a fancy way of saying "setting yourself specific goals." And what Hill teaches us is that successful people do just that. When you ask them, they can tell you where it is they want their life to end up and what they are doing to make sure they get there.

GETTING BEYOND "SHOULDA, COULDA, WOULDA"

It's been said many times that if you want to be successful, you should do what successful people do. I wholeheartedly subscribe to this belief. (This is what I was getting at before when I said that success leaves clues.) In other words, if successful people set specific goals for themselves, maybe that's something you should be doing too.

With that in mind, let's spend a moment talking about what a goal is . . . and what it is not. The dictionary defines a goal as the purpose toward which an endeavor is directed. That's clear enough, but it's only part of the story. The fact is, not just any purpose will do. In order to empower us, a goal must be specific. Otherwise, we will treat it as nothing more than a wish—what I call the "shoulda, coulda, woulda" phenomenon.

You know what I'm talking about. It's possible that at times you have succumbed to this phenomenon yourself. I certainly have. As you will learn in Step Four, I used to be a raging shopper. I'd get home from a shopping spree and think, *I really should have left those credit cards home* or *I should have bought less stuff.* My point here is that back when I was shopping too much, spending less was for me a wish, not a goal. Spending less didn't become a real goal for me until I took a piece of paper and a pen and wrote down the words: "I will not buy anything with my credit cards anymore. I will use only cash."

ACHIEVING YOUR GOALS ISN'T SOMETHING THAT JUST HAPPENS

If goals were easy to achieve, then the entire world would be successful. But that's okay. You didn't buy this book because you expect life to be easy. Rather, you are a woman who knows that to make things happen in life, you have to get involved. But let me ask you something: Do you have written goals right now? Is there a piece of paper somewhere in your home or office on which you have written down what it is you are striving for?

More than likely the answer is no. In fact, studies show that less than 1 percent of Americans write down specific goals for themselves each year. That's a shame, because writing down your goals is powerful. And over the years I have definitely seen it work.

WRITING A $10 MILLION CHECK ... TO YOURSELF!

One of my favorite stories about the power of writing down your goals involves the actor Jim Carrey, the star of such hit movies as *Dumb and Dumber*, *How the Grinch Stole Christmas*, and *Bruce Almighty*.

In the late 1980s, Carrey's career was starting to stall. He had managed to get a few small TV jobs but seemed nowhere near to realizing his dreams of major stardom. It was at this point in his life, when he was struggling to the top, that he went for a drive in the Hollywood Hills and visualized what it would be like to be rich and famous. Carrey did more than just dream, however. He parked his car, pulled out his checkbook, and wrote himself a check for $10 million. He dated it: "Thanksgiving Day, 1995," and wrote "for acting services rendered" in the memo line.

For the next several years, Carrey kept that check in his wallet. When times got tough, he would take it out and stare at it, thinking about what his life would someday be like when his talents and efforts finally were rewarded.

The rest, of course, is history. Carrey got noticed on the TV series *In Living Color*, and his first two movies, *Ace Ventura* and *The Mask*, were huge hits. Late in November 1995, he was offered $15 million to star in *Ace Ventura: When Nature Calls*. The following year, with *The Cable Guy*, his price went up to $20 million a picture!

Now, you can be a skeptic like many people and say, "Oh, that was just dumb luck." Or you can focus on the fact that Jim Carrey had Napoleon Hill's "Definiteness of Purpose." He didn't "shoulda, coulda, woulda" his goals into wishes that fade away. He put them in writing, and by making them specific, he was able to make them happen.

SEE, HEAR, FEEL, AND SMELL YOUR WAY TO YOUR DREAMS

In my seminars, when we get to talking about creating goals, I often tell a story about two women. One is named Jill and the other is named Jane. Jill and Jane both want to have successful financial futures, and both believe in keeping a written list of their financial goals. As it happens, they have at least one goal in common: They both want to own a vacation home. But while Jill writes down her goal as "Buy vacation home," Jane is a lot more specific. "I will own a vacation home by the time I celebrate my 45th birthday," she writes. "It will be a three-bedroom house with two baths located on the west side of Lake Tahoe. The mortgage will range between

$400,000 and $450,000. I will take out a 30-year mortgage but make extra payments to pay it off in 18 years. I will save $80,000 over the next 36 months to make my down payment."

Now let me ask you the question I ask the students who attend my seminars: Which of these two women do you think is more likely to reach her goal of owning a second home?

The answer, obviously, is Jane. The reason: Jane has been incredibly specific about what she wants and how she intends to get it. Indeed, she has been so specific that she practically can see, hear, feel, and smell that lakeside home. And that's the key. Specificity transforms a vague dream into a concrete, achievable goal. If you can practically see, hear, feel, and smell a goal, the chances are excellent that you'll not only know what's required to make it real, you'll actually do what's required to make it real.

The challenge facing you is to create goals that are equally specific and empowering.

THE "SMART WOMEN FINISH RICH" QUANTUM LEAP SYSTEM

Let's say for a moment that you buy what I'm saying. Let's say you accept that you should have goals and that you believe they should be in writing and you want to make them as specific as possible. Now I want to show you a way to formulate a series of goals that will allow you to take a quantum leap toward your dreams in the years ahead. I promise you—if you follow the rules I'm going to lay out, your life just 12 months from now will both surprise and delight you.

> ### RULE NO. I
> **Until it's written down, it's not a goal—
> it's just a slogan.**

If you don't put what you want in writing, then you might as well not even waste your time thinking about it. You are kidding yourself. Your goals must be written down. Think about it. How many times have you had a "great idea" that you thought could make you a fortune, only to forget what it was a week later? Why? Because you didn't write it down. If your goals are worth focusing your effort and time on, then they must be worth recording—and if you don't record them, who will?

In a nutshell, writing down your goals makes them real and easy to focus on. So from now on, you must commit yourself to recording all your goals on paper. No excuses.

> ### RULE NO. 2
> **Goals must be specific, measurable, and provable.**

Even if it's in writing, if you are not specific about what it is you want to attain—or if you've written down something that really can't be measured or proven—then, once again, what you've got isn't a goal, it's a wish.

For instance, there is no point in writing down "I want to be wealthy in the year 2022." That is useless. What you should be writing down is something much more specific—something like "I will put aside 10 percent of my gross income every month for the next 36 months, at which time I will have a minimum of $48,000 in a pretax retirement account." (I'll explain what a pretax retirement account is in Step Five.) Similarly, you shouldn't write down "I will be debt free." Rather, you should write something like "I will pay off my VISA bill over the next 12 months. I will pay cash for all purchases until my credit-card debt is completely gone, and I will never spend over $100 on an item without leaving the store and giving myself 48 hours to consider whether I really need that item."

The point is that a goal is very difficult to attain if it's vague.

You have to be able to show someone (the most important someone being yourself) exactly where the finish line is. After all, if you don't know precisely what your goal is, how will you be able to tell whether you've attained it or not?

> **RULE NO. 3**
> **Take some immediate action within the next 48 hours to start moving toward your goal.**

Let's say that, like Jill and Jane, your goal is to be able to purchase a vacation home on Lake Tahoe. Now, that's a long-term goal; realistically, you don't expect to accomplish it for at least five years. But that doesn't mean there isn't anything you can do right now, in the next 48 hours, to move toward that goal. You could, for example, go online to take a look at houses that are currently for sale within your price range and interest. You could set up online alerts to let you know when houses that meet your specific requirements go on sale, so that you can have a sense of what the local real estate market is like. You could subscribe to the local Tahoe newspaper online in order to keep abreast of what is happening in the community.

There are many things you could do. The key is to do something. Take an action—any action—that will make the goal you have written down feel more real and specific!

> **RULE NO. 4**
> **Once you have written down your goals, put them someplace where you can see them every day.**

I keep my list of goals in my phone, on my computer, and on a piece of paper posted above my computer in the office where I see it every day. Some people I know tape theirs on the mirror in their bathroom. The point is that you should read your goals every day.

By seeing your goals each day (preferably in the morning when you first wake up), you reaffirm to yourself what you are focusing your life on. As a result, you will find yourself subconsciously seeking out information and contacts that can help you attain your goals. In addition, reviewing your goals every day helps to make them clear and, ultimately, very personal and real to you.

> **RULE NO. 5**
> **Share your goals with someone you love and trust.**

I have heard it said time and time again that you should keep your goals and dreams to yourself, because "other people will try to talk you out of them or squash them." Well, that's total nonsense!

I can't tell you how mad it makes me to think of all the years I wasted keeping my goals and dreams to myself because of bad advice like that. The fact is, the best way to reach your goals is to get help. But if you don't share them with anyone, how are your friends or coworkers going to be able to offer you support and assistance?

I first learned the power of this rule at one of Tony Robbins's "Date with Destiny" seminars. Tony was doing a session on goal setting, and he told the group, "If you keep your goals inside you, you are missing out on the world that wants to help you." Well, I didn't really believe that the world wanted to help me. Then again, this was Tony Robbins, one of the greatest motivational experts in the world, so I figured, "What the heck, it can't hurt to try."

At that point, Tony broke us up into groups and told us to share our biggest dream or goal for the year. Once my group formed, I hesitatingly announced, "I want to write a book for women on investing called *Smart Women Finish Rich*." Everyone nodded and said that sounded great. Ten minutes later, after the group had dispersed, an incredible woman named Vicki St. George tapped me on the shoulder. "I heard you want to write an investment book for women," she said. "I've worked with Tony for ten years and now I run my own writing company called Just Write. I'd love to work with you to help you make your book a reality."

I ended up hiring Vicki about three months later, and the book proposal she helped me create was instrumental in getting me one of the top literary agents in the country.

ONLY YOU KNOW WHAT YOU CAN DO

If you share your goal with someone you love and he or she says, "Oh, you can't do that" or "No, that won't work," remember—that person really doesn't know what you can or cannot do. He or she knows only what he or she can or cannot do. Many well-intentioned people will tell you that you can't do something simply because it's beyond their own capabilities. Ignore these people; their negative beliefs are their problems, not yours. Keep sharing your goals until you find someone who will support you.

And here is something else to think about: If your friends really don't support you and your goals, maybe you need a new set of friends. I consider myself very fortunate because I am surrounded by incredible friends. When I originally told them I wanted to write a book, each and every one of them said, "That's great, go for it, I can't wait to read it." And periodically after that, they would ask me how my book was coming along. This inspired me even more. It also put a little pressure on me to keep focusing on my goal. Both the support and the pressure really helped me get the job done.

The key point here is that few things affect how successful you will be as much as the people with whom you surround yourself. If becoming financially independent is really important to you right now but you don't have any close friends to whom you feel you can turn for support, then go out and make some new friends. Join a women's investment club in your area. Take some evening classes on retirement planning. Do something that forces you to get out of your immediate comfort zone and meet some new people. There are many organizations you can join to get help and learn new skills. Take advantage of them.

RULE NO. 6
Develop goals that fit in with your values.

In Step Two, we went through a process specifically designed to help you get in touch with your values about money. Use what you discovered about yourself and what you are looking for in life to create goals that will make your dreams a reality.

For instance, if the phrase at the top of your values ladder is "spend more time with my family," then write that down on your goal list. But remember, you must make the goal measurable and specific. So be sure to indicate how you want to spend time with your family—what you want to do and when you will do it. And involve your family; enlist their ideas and opinions. Tell them, "I've determined that one of my most important values is to spend more quality time with you, and I'd like to plan some special family time together." Get them to suggest specifics, and then, together, write them all down on paper.

If you do this, not only will your goals be written and specific, but your family will be your support team because you've gotten them involved in your newfound spirit.

RULE NO. 7
Review your goals at least once every 12 months.

At an absolute minimum, you should review your goals and redo this process once each year. Ideally, I recommend you carry out this review process the last week in December so you can start the new year with total passion and renewed enthusiasm. I go through this process each December myself. In addition, every three months I spend an entire day reviewing both how I am doing and where I want to go. In this way, I am forced to recommit emotionally to my written goals, which in turn helps me refocus my efforts to make them become a reality. If I find I can't recommit to all my goals, that's a major sign it's time to rethink—and probably rewrite— what's on my list.

Remember, this is your list and your life. You should be in charge of what is and what is not important to you. And don't consider a change of heart to be a failure on your part. Your goal list is not a to-do list. It is much more important. It is your life-planning process!

LET'S GET STARTED!

Both in my office and in my class, I always ask my clients and students the same question to elicit their goals.

> *"In a perfect world, if you and I were sitting together three years from today, what would have to happen for you to feel you have made not just good, but GREAT financial progress with your life?"*

The point of this question is quite simple. Before you get into investment strategies, what you need to do to become financially secure is be clear about exactly what it is that you want and feel you need.

Think back to Step Two, in which you worked out what was important to you about money. The point of writing down your values then was to make it easier for you now to articulate a series of goals that can help you put your values into practice.

So based on what you said in Step Two, and how you feel now, what is it that you would like to see happen in your life over the next three years that will require money? Do you want to see yourself get out of credit-card debt? Do you want to own a home? Is your goal to be able to afford to retire in three years? Maybe you would like to move to Paris and study art. Or start your own business. Or expand a business that you already own. Whatever the case may be, use the values you came up with in Step Two and write down, on the chart that follows, what would have to happen for you to feel three years from now that you have made successful progress.

Do it now.

FIGURING OUT WHERE YOU WANT TO BE

Many people call what we have just done together goal setting. I call it *Designing a Proactive Life!* However you label it, one thing is inarguable: If you can't figure out where you want to be in three years, how are you ever going to be able to plan out your life 10 to 20 years from now? Equally important, how will you know how much money you are going to need to reach your goals? The answers are, you won't and you can't.

Why three years? Three years is a very useful amount of time to work with. You can accomplish a tremendous amount in three years. In fact, you can change your life.

Consider the story of Lucy, a woman who used these questions to make massive changes in her life. Lucy took my Smart Women Finish Rich! seminar a few years ago, but unlike many of my students, she didn't come to my office to review her finances when the class was over. In fact, I didn't hear from her for almost an entire year.

When we finally sat down together, my first question to Lucy was why she had waited so long to come see me.

"Well, David," she began, "when you asked us in class where we wanted our lives to be in three years, I realized that I had some serious decisions to make."

Indeed, it turned out that my question had led Lucy to transform her life totally.

GOALS

Designing a Proactive Life!

THERE ARE TWO PARTS TO THIS EXERCISE:
- Ten blanks for writing down your goals between now and three years from now
- A form in which you specify your five most important goals over the next three years

STEPS:
- On this page, below, fill in the ten blanks with as many goals as possible that you want to accomplish during the next three years.
- On the next page, specify:
  1. Five Most Important Goals
  2. Make Specific, Measurable, and Provable (i.e.: How much will it cost?)
  3. Immediate Action in the Next 48 Hours
  4. Whom Will You Share Your Goals With?
  5. What Values Does It Help You Accomplish?
  6. What Challenges Will You Face?
  7. Strategies to Overcome Anticipated Challenges

1.   6.

2.   7.

3.   8.

4.   9.

5.   10.

FIVE MOST IMPORTANT GOALS	MAKE SPECIFIC, MEASURABLE, AND PROVABLE	IMMEDIATE ACTION IN THE NEXT 48 HOURS	WHOM WILL YOU SHARE YOUR GOALS WITH?	WHAT VALUES DOES IT HELP YOU ACCOMPLISH?	WHAT CHALLENGES WILL YOU FACE?	STRATEGIES TO OVERCOME ANTICIPATED CHALLENGES
1						
2						
3						
4						
5						

LUCY'S STORY: TURNING OFF THE AUTOMATIC PILOT

"What I realized after thinking about that question of David's was that after 32 years of marriage, I was not happy. I was living a loveless life. I also realized that more money was not going to make my marriage any better—not then or in three years. So for me the question was: Do I have enough money to get divorced? If I don't want to be married, can I afford to be single?

"The more I thought about this, the more I realized it wasn't simply an issue of money. I truly did not want to go on with my life the way it was. My kids were grown, I was just starting the 'fun' phase of my life, as David had put it in the class, and I realized that the time was now to make a decision. So I made one.

"On the worksheet I had received in class, I wrote down, 'Get separated and independent of Sam within three years.'

"Once I had written that down, I got to thinking. *Why should this take three years?* I realized it shouldn't. I also realized that I had probably wasted the last ten years of my life with Sam, because I had never really stopped to ask myself where it was I wanted my life to head. Looking back, I see now that I had let my life get on 'automatic pilot.' Unfortunately, as a result of being on automatic pilot, I had ended up at a destination that did not work for me.

"Now, however, thanks to the three-year question and the technique of writing down your goals, my life has been dramatically changed for the better."

FROM MY POINT OF VIEW . . .

I find Lucy's story incredibly empowering. Less than three years after she took stock of her values and goals, she is a new person. First and foremost, she is divorced. And while I am not an advocate of divorce, in Lucy's case it happened to be necessary. Was it hard for her? You bet it was. But, in fact, both of her children supported her decision. (Indeed, they wanted to know why she had waited so long.)

Second, as a result of the divorce settlement, Lucy has been able to pay off her home mortgage completely, and we have positioned her additional assets to grow for her retirement. With a well-defined plan in place, Lucy can look forward to retiring in ten years without having to worry about money.

Third, she has upgraded her career from a position in retail sales to office management at a law firm, and she is increasing her job skills on a daily basis.

Finally, and most important of all, Lucy is happier than she has been in years.

IS YOUR LIFE ON AUTOMATIC PILOT?

Letting your life go on automatic pilot has a tendency to lead to disaster. Yet we do it all the time, usually without noticing it.

The best and quickest way I know to protect yourself from this syndrome is to stop, think, and put in writing what it is you specifically want out of life. In addition to formulating these wants in terms of three-year goals, I suggest you also write out intermediate and long-term goals. If you haven't already done so, remember to use the "Designing a Proactive Life!" worksheet on pages 94–95.

Remember to use the seven rules of goal setting I listed earlier. Most important, remember that this is your opportunity to create the future you want. Have fun with this. If you create a really compelling future for yourself, you will find yourself jumping out of bed every morning, knowing you are facing not just another day, but a day full of promise that will bring you closer to the future that you want!

DON'T LET CHALLENGES GET YOU DOWN!

Guess what? It's possible that you could do this entire exercise and still not stay on track and reach your desired goals. Why? Because life is filled with "challenges," both financial and personal, and unless you prepare for them, you could get stopped dead in your tracks.

So here is what I want you to do. After you write down your goals, I want you to list in detail all the potential challenges that could derail you from attaining them. Notice I don't call them "problems." I want you to wipe that word out of your vocabulary. Short of death (which is the only permanent problem I know of), there are no problems. There are only challenges.

Now, with that in mind, I want you to put down on paper everything you can think of that possibly could prevent you from achieving your goals. You may be thinking that I'm being pessimistic, but trust me on this—I'm not being pessimistic, I'm being realistic. By highlighting all the potential challenges on paper, you are acknowledging two very important realities: that there are challenges, and that you can come up with ways to overcome them.

In fact, that is the next step. Once you've listed all the challenges you can come up with (and I'll bet that right now without realizing it you are thinking subconsciously of all the reasons why you might not be able to make your goal a reality), I want you to write down a specific "solution" for each of them. And don't despair—all challenges have solutions.

I call this process drafting your "Personal Plan for Success." An example of a Personal Plan for Success that I used with a client when discussing retirement planning follows. Take a look at it and then create one for yourself and your number one goal.

CHALLENGES ARE YOUR BUILDING BLOCKS TO THE FUTURE YOU WANT!

As you finish Step Three, I want you to think about the following question: When was the last time you did something perfectly the first time you tried it?

The answer is probably never.

Imagine if when you were a toddler, crawling around on all fours, your parents had berated you for not being born a "walker." Imagine if instead of encouraging you, they criticized and yelled, saying things like "I can't believe you can't walk—you'll never be able to walk." It would have been not only cruel but dumb. The fact is, sensible adults do the exact opposite with their kids. We not only encourage them when they start trying to walk, we whip out our phones and tablets to record it all. We take endless videos to make sure we capture the moment when the child finally takes his or her first step.

So why is it that we start criticizing ourselves for not "walking" the first time we try to take a step? If this is the first time you have ever put down in writing what you want your life to be about, what your goals for the future are, you should be congratulating yourself—not feeling bad if your initial attempt doesn't turn out perfectly!

Remember, your first attempt to record your goals is not supposed to be perfect. Each time you do this exercise, it will become easier, and you will become better at designing your life. The exciting thing you should realize is that by making the effort to write down your goals, you are saying to yourself, "I am responsible for my future." Nothing could make you more powerful.

By itself, the single act of writing down your goals makes you special. Don't believe me. Test it. Do this entire step, put everything down in writing that I have suggested, then ask your friends and family if they have written goals. Not "ideas" about where they want their life to go, but actual written goals. Most likely, you will find that you are now unique. In fact, my guess is that when they learn you have put your goals in writing, your friends and family will begin to hold you in higher esteem. You also may find them deciding that they too should have written goals. So share this chapter with them. You may become the inspiration that your friends and family need to make their lives even better.

A Personal Plan for Success
Designing a Specific Plan to Overcome Your Challenges

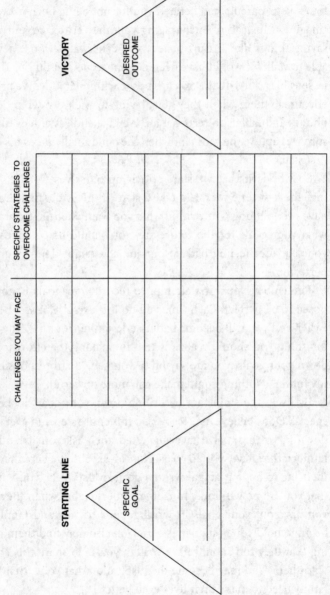

VICTORY

DESIRED OUTCOME

SPECIFIC STRATEGIES TO OVERCOME CHALLENGES

CHALLENGES YOU MAY FACE

STARTING LINE

SPECIFIC GOAL

A Personal Plan for Success
Designing a Specific Plan to Overcome Your Challenges

STARTING LINE

SPECIFIC GOAL

Date: 2018

Barbara's number-one goal is to retire at age 58 with $1 million.

Current retirement assets are $250,000.

CHALLENGES YOU MAY FACE	SPECIFIC STRATEGIES TO OVERCOME CHALLENGES
Not saving enough money	Maximize contributions starting tomorrow in company-sponsored 401(k) plan
Spending too much money	Spend cash only
Too much credit-card debt	Cut up credit cards; stop using them
Too much credit-card debt	Make goal to pay off credit cards, starting with smallest debt first
Not making enough money	Look for specific ways at work to "add more value"; meet with boss, discuss strategy to get a raise
Family spends too much money	Discuss specific financial goals and get their input on ways we can work as a team
College costs	Explain financial goals and challenges of retirement to son, Tom, and explain the importance of Tom's getting a job now to help with college costs
Not enough time to get everything done	Wake up an hour early each day and focus on goals and plans.

VICTORY

DESIRED OUTCOME

Desired Date: 2038

Barbara wants to live a worry-free retirement that includes travel and lots of fun.

Based on her expenses, $1 million will provide her with an income she cannot outlive.

CONGRATULATIONS! YOU HAVE FINISHED STEP THREE

Now let's take the goals and dreams you have written down and learn about a powerful system that will enable you to achieve them without having suddenly to start earning a lot of money. This system employs something I call "the Latte Factor®," and it is the most powerful and easy way I know of to transform a woman's financial goals and dreams into reality.

USE THE POWER OF THE LATTE FACTOR® ... HOW TO CREATE MASSIVE WEALTH ON JUST A FEW DOLLARS A WEEK!

Have you ever heard someone say, "If only I could make more money, then I could really start to become a saver, or maybe even an investor"? Perhaps you've even said something like that yourself.

If so, you may have been mistaken. Making more money won't necessarily make you a better saver or investor. Look at the newspapers—virtually every day someone famous, someone you or

I might reasonably regard as a huge money earner, declares bankruptcy. Take M. C. Hammer, the hip-hop star. In the early 1990s, Hammer was one of the world's highest-paid performers, earning a reported $35 million in one year. Almost overnight, he had gone from being a bat boy for the Oakland Athletics to a millionaire many times over. I remember thinking how incredible it must have felt to become so wealthy so quickly. Then one day I saw Hammer on television taking a reporter through the extravagant house he was building in Fremont, California. The place was huge. Though it was only half-finished, it was rumored to have cost him more than $10 million already.

When I saw how out of control his spending was, I told friends that M. C. Hammer would be bankrupt in five years. I was wrong. It was only about three years later that he declared bankruptcy. Unfortunately for M. C. Hammer, being rich and famous did not lead to financial security. But M. C. Hammer is not alone . . .

DO YOU RECOGNIZE ANY OF THESE PEOPLE?

Larry King, 50 Cent, Francis Ford Coppola, Debbie Reynolds, Kim Basinger, Mike Tyson, Dorothy Hamill, Wayne Newton, Drake Bell, Burt Reynolds, Toni Braxton. Do you know what they all have in common? Aside from being famous, they have all filed for bankruptcy. So did more than 790,000 other Americans in 2017. What accounts for this epidemic of insolvency? Well, among other things, Americans have become addicted to spending money by using "plastic cash." According to the website Nerd Wallet, as of September 2017, consumer debt hit a record $905 billion! Which leads me to suggest . . .

It's time to keep more . . . and spend less.

As I noted back in Step One, the reason most people fail financially is not because their incomes are too small, but because their spending habits are too big. In other words, they spend more money than they make. This may sound awfully basic, but it's true. If you spend more than you make, you will always be in debt, always stressed, rarely happy, and eventually poor or bankrupt.

Controlling your spending, though, isn't all there is to being a Smart Woman and finishing rich. You also must make a point of saving a portion of every dollar you earn. No matter how large your paycheck is, if you don't save, you will never live a life of financial abundance. (Just ask M. C. Hammer.)

Whether you are a highly compensated doctor or lawyer supporting mortgages on two homes, a more modestly paid teacher or office worker, or a sales trainee who barely makes the rent each month, the key to financial independence can be summed up in three little words . . .

Pay yourself first.

Why in the world would you work 40 (or 50, or 60, or more!) hours a week, and then pay someone else first? Search me, but most Americans pay *everyone* else before they pay themselves. Most of us pay the IRS first (through our withholding tax), then our mortgage or our rent, then our utilities, then our car loans, then our VISA or American Express bills, and on and on. If by some miracle there is something left over after all those payments—meaning there have been no "Murphy's law" disasters, like the car breaking down or the washing machine dying—then maybe (and I mean just maybe) we might manage to put away a few dollars for our future.

I call this the "Pay Everyone Else First, You Last" system, and it stinks. It's like having "investor dyslexia"; it's all backward. Among other things, it's why the average American has so little in the bank and so much in credit-card debt.

WHATEVER YOU DO, DON'T PAY
UNCLE SAM FIRST!

Of all the crazy things people do with their money, the one I really can't fathom is paying their taxes before they pay themselves. Not even the government expects you to do that. If the government did expect to get paid first, it wouldn't have enacted laws that allow us to put part of our earnings into retirement accounts such as IRAs and 401(k) plans *before* the tax man takes his cut. This is called "pretax" investing, and it is the single smartest thing you can do to build wealth.

Unfortunately, millions of Americans don't take advantage of pretax investing. Instead, they let state and federal tax authorities funnel off as much as 40 percent of each paycheck—that's 40 cents out of every dollar they earn—before they even get to see it. This is a huge mistake. In Step Five, you'll learn all about pretax retirement accounts. Until then, just remember that the government really does want you to have financial security—so much so that it's willing to give you a break on your taxes if you use part of your earnings to fund a retirement account. Whatever you do, don't pass up this break. You've earned it!

THE 12 PERCENT SOLUTION

So what does "pay yourself first" mean? It means that whenever you make any money, no matter how much or how little, before you spend any of it on anything else, you should put some of it aside for your future.

Now, when I say, "before you spend any of it on anything else," I mean *anything* else. That includes your rent or mortgage, your credit-card bills, even your payroll withholding tax. Ideally, you should pay 12 percent of the gross—meaning your total earnings *before taxes*—into some sort of retirement account that you will never touch until you actually retire. Of course, it's possible that because of how much you make or the kind of retirement account you have, you may not be eligible to put that much into a pretax retirement account. In that case, you should make up the difference by putting money into an after-tax account.

Why do I suggest putting away 12 percent of your gross income? Well, for years the financial experts have been suggesting that to prepare properly for retirement, everyone should be saving at least 10 percent of what he or she makes. Of course, when they say "everyone," the experts are generally treating men as the default—and in this case, at least, what's good enough for men isn't necessarily good enough for women. After all, women live longer than men—and as a result, they need to put away more money for their retirement. How much more? Well, if women's retirements tend to last 20 percent longer than men's—and that's what the statistics tell us—then women's retirement nest eggs need to be 20 percent larger. In other words, if the experts say that men should be putting away 10 percent of their pretax income, then as a woman, you should be putting away 12 percent of yours.

Now, I realize that saving 12 percent of your income may sound like a lot. But believe me, it's not as hard as you might think. The trick is not to let the figure overwhelm you. Rome wasn't built in a day, and neither is a new financial future. If you can't imagine saving 12 percent of your income right now, then start with 6 percent and make it a goal to bump up your savings rate by 1 percent a month for the next six months.

If even 6 percent seems like too much, do what I often suggest to clients of mine who really have a problem with the idea of saving. Start off putting away just 1 percent of your income. (I have never met anyone who could look me in the eye and tell me they couldn't save 1 percent of their income.) Then increase the amount by 1 percent a month for a year. At the end of a year, you will be saving 12 percent of your income and you will barely have noticed the difference.

It's a lot like getting in shape to run a marathon. People who train for a marathon don't say to themselves, "Today I think I'll run a marathon" and then go out and run 26 miles. They start off running a block, then 2 blocks, then a mile, then 2 miles . . . until one day they are running 26 miles (and are actually enjoying it). Think about your goal of saving 12 percent of your income the same way. Day by day you are striving to become financially stronger. Before you know it, you will be in great financial shape!

One more key thing to consider: *Twelve percent of your gross income is equal to right around one hour a day of your income.* My question to you is why would you work nine hours a day and not keep the first hour a day of your income for YOU? Trust me—keep the first hour a day of your income and you will build financial security for life.

WHAT ABOUT THE REAL WORLD?

Paying yourself first is one of those concepts that strike a lot of people as sounding great in principle but having very little application in the real world. And I wouldn't be at all surprised if right now you are thinking, *Sure, I'd love to pay myself first. Just tell me where I'm going to get the money.*

Well, I'll let you in on a secret: You already have it.

That's right. No matter how much or how little you earn, you already make enough money to pay yourself first. Your problem—and it's not just *your* problem, it's almost everyone's problem—is not that you don't make enough, but that you spend too much.

Learn to control your spending, and everything else will fall into place.

SPEND A DOLLAR TODAY AND
YOU LOSE IT FOREVER

When I was a student at the University of Southern California, my favorite pastime was shopping. Some people get black belts in karate; I had a black belt in shopping. I could go to the mall with my friends and easily spend thousands of dollars in just a few hours. Every week I would come home with bags and bags of clothes. As I often tell my students today, you know you're shopping too much when you can go into your closet and find clothes you don't remember buying. Well, I could. My wardrobe was to die for. Unfortunately, the bills were to die for too—literally! Every month I would close my eyes as I opened my VISA bill.

The truth was that my spending was out of control. It never mattered how much money I made, I always spent more. As soon as my credit-card bills were paid, I'd go off on another spending spree.

My life changed when I packed up everything I owned one summer and put it in a storage unit. (At USC, you couldn't leave your possessions in your campus apartment over the summer.) As I was filling up this $50-a-month storage facility under a freeway in L.A., I started thinking, *What if there's an earthquake and this freeway collapses and destroys the warehouse? My clothes would get ruined!*

All of a sudden it hit me: I'm looking at a storage unit with "stuff" in it and worrying. Of all the potential consequences of a devastating earthquake, here I am more concerned about *stuff* than about people. Even worse, I'm paying *money* to store stuff that I haven't even paid for yet because it's still on my credit card!

I started laughing so hard I had to sit down. It dawned on me there was an entire industry of storage units around the country filled with people's "stuff." Think about it! How absurd is it to buy so much stuff that you have to pay someone else to store it because you don't have anywhere to put it yourself! The moral seemed clear.

Buy less stuff and you'll be rich!

That insight changed my life. Suddenly I realized that instead of spending money I didn't really have on things I didn't really need, I should be putting my resources into something that mattered. And what could possibly matter more to me than my future? Forget about things; what I really should be concerning myself with was doing whatever I could to ensure myself the kind of life I felt I wanted and deserved. And that's just what I did. From that day on, I stopped wasting my money on ridiculous shopping sprees and started investing in myself.

Trust me—if a world-class, black-belt shopper like me can cut back, you can too. It's not easy, but it can be done, and it will change your life just like it changed mine.

Now, just because you're not buying new clothes every week like I used to doesn't mean you're not spending money you should be saving. You'd be surprised how easy it is to be wastefully extravagant without realizing it. The fact is, often the "little" purchases in life—what I call the Latte Factor®—make the difference between being a millionaire and being broke.

WORK FOR YOU

In my investment classes, I tell my students that any woman can become an investor—and in the process put herself on the road to financial security—simply by putting aside as little as $50 a month. Invariably, someone in the audience will raise her hand at this point and say, "David, I'm living paycheck to paycheck. I'm in debt, and I'm barely making it. I don't have this $50 a month you keep talking about."

One day I challenged just such a young woman on her assertion that she didn't have enough money to invest. Deborah was 22 years old and worked at an advertising agency. She wasn't being paid a whole lot, and she insisted there was no way she possibly could put $50 a month into her retirement plan at work. As she put it, she was "dead broke and destitute." So I asked her to take me through her average day.

"Well," she began, "I go to work and then I research—"

"Do you start your day with coffee?" I interrupted her.

A friend of Deborah's who was sitting next to her started to laugh. "Deborah without coffee in the morning is not a good thing," she said.

Picking up on that, I asked Deborah if she drank the office coffee.

"No way," Deborah replied. "The office coffee is the worst. I go downstairs and buy a latte every morning."

I asked, "Do you buy a single or a double latte?"

"I always buy a double nonfat latte."

"Great," I said. "Now, what does this double nonfat latte cost you every morning?

"Oh, about $4.00."

"Do you just get a latte, or do you also get a muffin or a bagel with that?"

"I usually get a biscotti."

"Do you get the biscotti with chocolate on top?"

"Oh, yes," Deborah enthused. "I love the ones with chocolate."

"Great, Deborah. Now, what does the chocolate biscotti cost?"

"I guess about $1.50."

"So you're spending over $5 a day for latte and biscotti. Interesting."

I let Deborah continue taking me through her day. In the process, we found another $10 in miscellaneous costs—a candy bar here, a Power Bar there, a protein shake in the afternoon, and so on.

When she was done, I pointed out that just by cutting out her latte, a couple of Diet Cokes, and a candy bar, Deborah could save at least $8 a day—and that $8 a day equaled roughly $240 a month, or almost $3,000 a year. This $3,000 could be put into her retirement plan at work, where it could grow tax-free until she retired. If she put in $3,000 every year, and she invested it all in stocks (which have enjoyed an average growth rate of nearly 10 percent a year over the last 50 years), chances are that by the time she reached 65, she would have more than $1.6 million sitting in her account. In other words, she would be able to retire a millionaire!

By the time I had finished, Deborah's eyes were as big as saucers. "That is so amazing," she said. "I never realized my double nonfat lattes were costing me more than a million dollars!"

So I ask you now . . .

Are you latte-ing away your financial future?

I'm not trying to pick on you if you are a coffee lover. I happen to enjoy a great cup of coffee in the morning myself. I just want to point out a simple fact:

Everyone makes enough money to become rich.

What keeps us living paycheck to paycheck is that we spend more than we make on stuff we don't need. Take the $5 you were going to waste over the next few days on bottled water (water is still free), the $9 you would spend on junk food (you'll be healthier without it), and the $11 you were going to throw away on two cups of fancy coffee during the workweek (break-room coffee is just as caffeinated), and you'll have $25 this very week that you can devote to savings. Keep this up and you'll soon be putting away 12 percent of what you earn. Before you know it, your life will begin changing dramatically for the better. Once you see the 12 percent solution at work, you automatically will start looking for ways to save even more. The process creates a new habit—one that will make you feel great!

GETTING YOUR SPENDING UNDER CONTROL

The hardest part of any undertaking—whether you're preparing for a marathon or trying to contain your spending—is getting started. With that in mind, here are six exercises that should help you get your spending under control ... and ultimately make it easy for you to pay yourself first.

EXERCISE NO. 1
Know what you earn.

This may seem obvious, but in these days of direct-deposit payroll programs and automatic checking, many of us don't know exactly how much we actually earn, both before and after taxes. Go get your last paycheck. What does it say your monthly gross income is? What's your net? Write down those numbers below.

> *I currently earn $_____ a month before taxes,*
> *and $_____ after taxes.*

EXERCISE NO. 2
Estimate what you spend each month.

In Step Three, I asked you to figure out where your money is. Now I want you to figure out where your money goes.

Most people do not have a clue about how much they really spend each month and on what. To be financially healthy, however, you need to have a solid grasp of your spending patterns. Only after you've seen the numbers in black and white can you figure out where you can cut back.

In Appendix 1, you'll find a form with the heading "Where Does Your Money *Really* Go?" Use it to estimate how much you spend each month on everything from food and shelter to cosmetics and movie tickets. Then add 10 percent for what I call "Murphy's law" expenses—those unexpected bills for car repairs and plumbing problems that always seem to crop up when you least expect (or can afford) them. To make sure your estimate is in the right ballpark, review your last three months' worth of bank statements, receipts, and credit-card bills. Once you're satisfied you have a reasonably accurate figure, write it down.

I currently spend $____ a month.

Now subtract your monthly spending total from your monthly after-tax income. Is your cash flow positive or negative? Your goal, obviously, is to have a positive cash flow. The next four rules should help you do just that.

I earn a month after taxes		_____
I spend a month approximately	–	_____
Cash flow monthly	=	_____

EXERCISE NO. 3
Track what you really spend.

For the next seven days, I want you to record every single penny you spend. I call this the "Seven-Day Financial Challenge." Eventually you should do this for a full month, but right now, to get yourself started, I want you to try it for just seven days. Get yourself an inexpensive notepad, and throughout the coming week, write down every purchase you make, no matter how big or small. (This means *everything*: highway tolls, candy bars, the cost of download- ing a new song from iTunes—everything.)

This seven-day challenge actually can be fun. The trick is to be yourself. That is, don't change your behavior. Spend money just as you always have. The only thing you should be doing differently is writing everything down. Once you have captured your spending habits on paper, you will quickly see where you are wasting money and you can decide where it makes sense to cut back. (One woman I know found that the simple act of writing down expenditures made her so self-conscious about being extravagant that her ex- cess spending stopped cold. "I just hated the idea of having to write down that I was spending $80 on a sweater I didn't need," she said. "So rather than having to write it down, I didn't buy the sweater.")

If you know you're more likely to follow through with tracking your spending on an app, here are three great apps that can help you keep track of your money automatically:

- **ClarityMoney.com.** I am an advisor for this new app, and I am excited about how it can help users take control of their finances. When you sign up, the app gives you a daily summary of your spending, including automatic categorization of your purchases. You can also set up automatic savings and figure out where you can cut expenses through this program.
- **Mint.com** was the first free Web-based financial tracker, and it continues to offer great automatic tracking and user-friendly graphs and charts of your habits. Mint is available both online and as an app.
- **YNAB (YouNeedABudget.com).** I've always said I don't believe in budgeting, but many readers have let me know how much they enjoy the You Need a Budget program,

which is based on the envelope method of setting money aside for specific spending categories. This app is one of the few programs that easily allows users to track cash spending as well as providing automatic tracking.

EXERCISE NO. 4
Start paying cash.

After you have tracked a typical week's expenses and are ready to start changing your ways, the easiest thing you can do to reduce your spending automatically is to start paying for everything with cash. That's right, cash! Remember that green stuff with the pictures of the dead presidents on it? It's time to start using it again.

When you buy things with credit cards or a payment app, you don't feel the significance of your spending. I dare you to stick $500 in cash in your wallet and try to spend it frivolously on some impulse purchase like a new sweater or a pair of shoes or the latest electronic gadget. You won't be able to do it. That's because cash makes you think more about exactly how much you are spending and for what. (As one client of mine told me, a pair of shoes marked down to $160 doesn't seem like that much of a bargain when buying it means taking eight twenties out of your wallet.)

You'd be surprised what a dramatic change this single action can make. I can't tell you how many of my students have told me that when they went to a cash-only system, their spending dropped by 20 percent in a single month!

EXERCISE NO. 5
Give yourself a credit-card haircut.

Here's an idea that I am sure occurs to you every time you get a large credit-card bill: Take a pair of scissors and cut up one of your credit cards. Just one. (I don't expect you to cut them all up—not, at least, on your first attempt.) When you finish reading this chapter, go through all your credit-card bills, pull out the biggest one, and then cut that card into about ten pieces.

The feeling of power you will get from this small token gesture can be tremendous. Just try it. If you think you can handle it, cut up more than one card. Remember, if worse comes to worst, you can always call the credit-card company and order a new one. And if your credit card is set up to automatically populate on your computer, delete your card (especially on websites like Amazon). If you use Apple Pay or a phone payment app, delete it. This will slow down impulse purchases.

> ### EXERCISE NO. 6
> **Never spend more than $100 on anything without taking 48 hours to think about it.**

The idea here is simple. Most Americans spend far too much money on impulse purchases they really don't need to make. It can be a pair of shoes, a new phone, an expensive dinner. The point is, stores are designed to make sure you get caught up in the excitement of shopping, and before you know what's happened, you've bought something.

So set yourself a ceiling. I suggest $100, but it can be any amount that makes sense to you. Once you've set it, do not permit yourself to buy anything for that amount or more without first leaving the store and giving yourself 48 hours to think about it. By forcing yourself into this "cooling-off" period, you give yourself a chance to decide rationally whether the purchase really is necessary. If you still feel like buying it two days later, great! Chances are the item in question will still be there—maybe even on sale!

I know how effective this exercise can be from personal experience. As I mentioned earlier, I used to be a world-class shopper.

But once I imposed the $100 ceiling on myself, I found that just "casually shopping" wasn't so much fun anymore. Items I had thought I "just had to have" no longer seemed so important once I got home and thought about them. Because I was buying less and less, shopping began to feel more and more like a waste of time. Before long I found myself going shopping less often. These days I go shopping only once or twice a year, and only with the specific purpose of getting something I need. I'm telling you, these exercises work!

The basic point of getting your spending under control is, of course, to allow you to save more. Ultimately, your goal should be to get your savings rate as high as 20 percent. For now, however, try to start saving at least 6 percent of your gross income and commit to raising that to 12 percent within 12 months.

THE MAGIC OF COMPOUND INTEREST

You may wonder what good it will do to put aside less than an eighth of your income if your income isn't very big to begin with. But remember, even if you earn what seems to you like a modest salary, the amount of money that will pass through your hands during your lifetime is truly phenomenal. For a quick reminder of just how phenomenal, go back and review the chart on page 26 in Step One.

Pretty awesome, isn't it? And here's some more good news . . .

> *The sooner you start saving, the less you*
> *will need to put away!*

Take a look at the following chart. It shows how quickly the magic of compound interest can help you accumulate a significant amount of assets. To me, "significant" means at least $1 million worth. Now, some skeptics may argue that $1 million doesn't go very far anymore, but regardless of how much it does or doesn't buy these days, wouldn't you rather have $1 million than not? In any case, given that GoBankingRates has found that over three-quarters of middle-aged Americans have less than $10,000 saved and the Federal Reserve says 47 percent of Americans can't get their hands on $400 in case of emergency, let's run with the idea that earning your "first" million is probably a worthy goal to shoot for.

The chart illustrates that simply by putting aside a couple of dollars a day and giving your money a chance to work for you, you can become a millionaire! While it is easy to think "a dollar here, a dollar there" is no big deal, it *is* a big deal. Depending on how quickly you decide to make your financial future a priority, it can be a *million-dollar deal*!

Stop reading for a second and think about the day you just had. What is your personal Latte Factor®? What did you buy today that you could do without tomorrow and thus save a few dollars? Take a few moments right now and think of three things you could cut out of your daily spending tomorrow. What are they? How much money would you save a day? How much would it save you a month? While $100 a month in savings may not sound like a lot, look at the chart on page 120. Saving $100 a month can quickly add up to a lot of money.

Now, how do you make sure that this money you are now not going to spend on things you don't really need doesn't disappear down some other drain? It's simple, really. The trick to making sure your money goes where it's supposed to go—that is, that your spending matches up with your values—is to arrange things so you don't have any choice in the matter. There's no getting around it. We may like to think of ourselves as being self-disciplined and conscientious, and many of us actually are. But there is only one way to

BUILDING A MILLION-DOLLAR NEST EGG			

How to Accumulate $1,000,000
Regular Deposits Required to Accumulate $1,000,000
by Age 65 at Stated Rate of Return

$1,000,000
10% Annual Interest Rate

Starting Age	Daily Savings	Monthly Savings	Yearly Savings
20	$ 3.47	$ 106	$ 1,267
25	$ 5.63	$ 172	$ 2,055
30	$ 9.20	$ 281	$ 3,358
35	$ 15.15	$ 462	$ 5,530
36	$ 16.77	$ 512	$ 6,122
37	$ 18.57	$ 566	$ 6,778
38	$ 20.57	$ 627	$ 7,508
39	$ 22.82	$ 696	$ 8,329
40	$ 25.33	$ 773	$ 9,245
41	$ 28.15	$ 859	$ 10,275
42	$ 31.32	$ 955	$ 11,432
43	$ 34.89	$ 1,064	$ 12,735
44	$ 38.92	$ 1,187	$ 14,208
45	$ 43.50	$ 1,327	$ 15,878
46	$ 48.70	$ 1,485	$ 17,776
47	$ 54.63	$ 1,666	$ 19,940
48	$ 61.47	$ 1,875	$ 22,437
49	$ 69.30	$ 2,114	$ 25,295
50	$ 78.40	$ 2,391	$ 28,616
51	$ 89.05	$ 2,716	$ 32,503
52	$ 101.58	$ 3,098	$ 37,077
53	$ 116.48	$ 3,553	$ 42,515
54	$ 134.41	$ 4,100	$ 49,060
55	$ 156.28	$ 4,767	$ 57,042

The figures shown above represent the amount of money you would have to save (i.e., daily, monthly, yearly), at the stated interest rate, in order to accumulate $1,000,000 by the time you reach age 65. These figures DO NOT take into account any federal or state taxes that may be incurred. Monthly and yearly figures are rounded to the nearest dollar.

make sure you will consistently pay yourself first, and that is to put yourself on an automatic system. To put it another way ...

Smart women pay themselves first . . . automatically!

What this means is that if you work for a company that offers some sort of contributory retirement program—such as a 401(k) plan—you should definitely sign up. (We'll discuss this in detail in Step Five.) Under most such plans, after you've signed up, you don't have to do a thing. Every pay period, your employer will take a portion of your gross pay (i.e., *before* taxes are withheld) and put it in a retirement account for you. No muss, no fuss, no chance to succumb to temptation.

If you don't have access to this sort of company-sponsored program, then you must set up the appropriate retirement account on your own. (Again, we'll provide details in Step Five.) You also must arrange your own automatic payroll-deduction system. You may be able to do this through your company payroll department. If not, you can do it on your own by telling your bank to automatically transfer a given amount from your checking account to your retirement account on the same day you deposit your paycheck.

The key is to make sure the transfer is done automatically. Otherwise, you probably won't do it consistently. Just as most people can't stick to budgets, most people who promise to "pay themselves first" don't . . . unless the money is taken out of their paycheck and put into a retirement account before they have a chance to do anything else with it. If you are married and your husband works, make sure he does this too!

IT'S NEVER TOO LATE

There's no question that the sooner you get started paying yourself first, the better off you will be. The following chart shows it plainly.

		TO BUILD WEALTH . . . PAY YOURSELF FIRST AND DO IT MONTHLY				
YOUR MONTHLY INVESTMENT	YOUR AGE	TOTAL AMOUNT OF MONTHLY INVESTMENTS THROUGH AGE 65	AT A 4% RATE OF RETURN	AT A 7% RATE OF RETURN	AT A 9% RATE OF RETURN	AT A 12% RATE OF RETURN
$100	25	48,000	118,590	264,012	471,643	1,188,242
	30	42,000	91,678	181,156	296,385	649,527
	40	30,000	51,584	81,480	112,953	189,764
	50	18,000	24,691	31,881	38,124	50,458
$150	25	72,000	177,294	393,722	702,198	1,764,716
	30	63,000	137,060	270,158	441,268	964,644
	40	45,000	77,119	121,511	168,168	281,827
	50	27,000	36,914	47,544	56,761	74,937
$200	25	96,000	237,180	528,025	943,286	2,376,484
	30	84,000	183,355	362,312	592,770	1,299,054
	40	60,000	103,169	162,959	225,906	379,527
	50	36,000	49,382	63,762	76,249	100,915

Incredible, isn't it? But wait. If you study this chart closely, you might come to the conclusion that the key to success is to start young. What if you are older? What if you weren't fortunate enough to start saving when you were in your twenties or thirties? Don't worry. The miracle of compound interest does not depend on how old you are. The only thing that matters is how long your money has been invested and at what rate it is growing.

When students of mine who are in their forties and fifties insist to me that it's too late for them to get started saving, I point out that simply by investing a mere $10 a day in a mutual fund that returns 15 percent a year (and plenty have exceeded this rate), over a period of 25 years they will accumulate well in excess of $1 million!

Remember—the combined power of the Latte Factor® and the miracle of compound interest is truly amazing. The only thing that can short-circuit it is the all-too-human tendency to procrastinate. Too many people put off doing what they know they should, and as a result these two powerful tools never get the chance to work for them. Don't make this mistake.

DON'T LABEL YOURSELF A PROCRASTINATOR

Even if everything I've just said makes sense to you intellectually, I know it is still very possible that you simply won't be able to pay yourself first. What many people say is, "I know I should do this, but I'm just a procrastinator."

Well, I have never met a real procrastinator. Whenever someone tells me she is a procrastinator, I respond by asking her, "Did you eat this week?" Of course, she will always answer yes. The fact is, no one procrastinates *all* the time. What you may be is a selective procrastinator—which means that if something is important enough (like eating), you are perfectly capable of taking care of it right away.

So what makes us procrastinate about saving? Most of us do it for one reason: *fear of change.* Why do we fear change? Because we associate change with pain. Saving means reducing your spending. Reducing your spending means changing (however slightly) the way you live. And changing (however slightly) the way you live means . . . who knows what? *Probably something terrible!*

I often run into this when I address employee groups. Many people tell me they know my "idea" of contributing a portion of their gross pay to a retirement plan makes sense, but they just can't see how they could possibly get by if their take-home pay were suddenly reduced by 10 percent.

I recall one incident in particular: I was at a Fortune 500 company, speaking at a sign-up seminar for the firm's retirement plan, when a gentleman named Dan stood up and challenged my assertion that it was possible "to give yourself a pay cut."

"David," he said, very agitated, "I don't think you are in touch with reality. Many of us here today are in our mid-forties and fifties. We have expenses, like homes, car payments, and college costs. We are basically living from paycheck to paycheck, and when you are doing that, you can't take a 10 percent pay cut. It's simply not possible."

A murmur of agreement rippled across the room. Clearly many of Dan's coworkers shared his fears. Justified or not, those fears deserved to be addressed.

"What would you do," I asked Dan, "if your boss came into your office tomorrow and told you that because of a corporate restructuring, you had to choose between losing your job or taking a 10 percent pay cut?"

Dan looked startled, then stared at his feet and mumbled, "I'd take the 10 percent pay cut."

"And how would that affect you?" I continued. "Would it make you so depressed that you couldn't get out of bed in the morning?"

Dan looked at me a little strangely. "Of course not," he said. "I'd be bummed, but I'd still be able to get up in the morning."

"Good," I responded. "So we know that being forced to take a 10 percent pay cut wouldn't incapacitate you. Now, what about your house? Would you lose your home if you got a 10 percent pay cut?"

"No," Dan replied. "We'd figure out a way to cut back."

I told him that was good too. "Now we know that a pay cut will neither incapacitate you nor leave you homeless. What about your wife? Would she leave you if your pay got cut?"

"No, of course not," he answered.

"I didn't think so," I said. I went on to explain to Dan that the point of my questions wasn't to make fun of his concerns. What I was trying to do was show him and everyone else in the room that there are really two options in life: You can be either reactive or proactive to circumstances. And it's a lot more fun and a lot less painful to be proactive—to make decisions about your life before events take control of *you*.

IT'S TIME TO GIVE YOURSELF THAT PAY CUT!

If for any reason (a company restructuring, a war, a death, a divorce, whatever), you suddenly found yourself forced to take a pay cut, you'd manage to cope somehow, wouldn't you? So why wait for something to happen and then react to it? Why not take control over your own destiny and create your own future now?

Finally, remember that the key to the Latte Factor® is recognizing that small things (like a $4 cup of coffee) can make a big difference. A dollar here, a dollar there, if invested regularly through an automatic pay-yourself-first system, can make you financially secure for life. And, quite frankly, you deserve to be!

CONGRATULATIONS, YOU'VE COMPLETED STEP FOUR

You've taken advantage of the Latte Factor® to reduce your spending, you've made a commitment to pay yourself first, and you've arranged to put aside a portion of your gross income (ideally, 12 percent—one hour a day of your income) automatically each month. You are now ready to move on to Step Five, in which we'll figure out exactly what to do with all this money you are now paying yourself.

PRACTICE GRANDMA'S THREE-BASKET APPROACH TO FINANCIAL SECURITY

As I mentioned in the introduction, it was my grandma Bach who encouraged me to make my first investment—in three shares of McDonald's. I was seven at the time, and the idea of being a stockholder was so exciting to me that as soon as I managed to save up some more money, I bought another share. And then another. And another.

Finally, my grandmother took me aside. "David," she said, "McDonald's is a fine company, but it's not the only one on the Stock Exchange."

"But I like McDonald's," I protested.

"I know," she replied, "but the sensible thing to do is to spread your money around. Haven't you ever heard the expression 'Don't put all your eggs in one basket'?"

I hadn't—not until then, at any rate. But once my grandmother explained it to me, it made complete sense, and to this day it remains one of the fundamental principles of my approach to financial planning.

Most people assume that financial planning is difficult, complicated, and exhausting. It's not. The fact is, if you do it correctly, actually it's pretty easy. One of the keys is to remember my grandmother's advice: Don't put all your eggs in one basket.

As it happens, there are *three* baskets into which you should put your eggs. I call them **the security basket**, **the retirement basket**, and **the dream basket**. The security basket protects you and your family against the unexpected (such as a medical emergency, the death of a loved one, or the loss of a job), the retirement basket safeguards your future, and the dream basket enables you to fulfill those deeply held desires that make life worthwhile. This three-basket approach may sound simple, but don't let that fool you. If you fill the baskets properly, you can create for yourself a financial life filled with abundance and, most important, security.

The "eggs" we're talking about are, of course, the extra dollars you learned to put aside in Step Four. You are going to use them to fill these three baskets—in some cases by investing the cash directly in money-market accounts or retirement plans, in other cases by buying things such as insurance policies.

We are going to discuss the security basket first—mainly because it involves a bunch of things that you need to take care of immediately. In practice, however, you will be filling up both your security basket and your retirement basket at the same time. Once you've taken care of your security and retirement baskets, you can start filling your dream basket.

We'll get to the details of exactly how retirement saving works in a little while. Right now, let's talk about security.

BASKET ONE:
YOUR SECURITY BASKET

Your security basket is meant to protect you and your family in the event of some unexpected financial hardship, such as the loss of a job or some other major income source. It also can help you cope with life's little unplanned surprises, like the car breaking down, the refrigerator needing repair, or the dog eating your child's retainer, which just cost you $496! The security basket does this by providing you with a financial cushion—an air bag, if you will—that softens the blow in case of accident. Not only will having this sort of cushion contribute to your peace of mind, but when trouble strikes, it can (quite literally) buy you the time you will need to get back on your feet.

SIX THINGS TO DO RIGHT AWAY
FOR PROTECTION

In order to be properly protected, you must make sure that your security basket contains most—if not all—of the following seven elements.

> **SAFEGUARD NO. 1**
> **You must have at least 3 to 24 months' worth of living expenses saved in case of emergency.**

The goal here is to put away "rainy-day money" to cover expenses in case you lose your income. Exactly how much money you need to put away depends on what you spend each month. (You can figure this out with the help of the Where Does Your Money *Really* Go?

form in Appendix 1.) I generally recommend to my students and clients that they put away somewhere between 3 and 24 months' worth of expense money. By this measure, a Smart Woman whose basic spending runs about $2,000 a month should aim to have at least $6,000 in cash in her security basket.

That 3- to 24-month range covers a lot of ground. What's right for you depends in large part on your particular emotional makeup. Some of my clients simply do not feel safe if they have anything less than two years' worth of cash sitting in a money-market account. I happen to think that's a bit excessive, but if that's what it takes to make you feel comfortable, then by all means make it your goal.

In general, the size of your cushion should depend on how easy it would be to replace your current income. Say you currently earn $75,000 a year. If you suddenly lost your job, how long would it take for you to find a new one paying that much or more? If you are easily re-employable and are confident that you could land a new $75,000-a-year job relatively quickly, then you probably don't need to have much more than three months' worth of expenses in your security basket. If, on the other hand, you think it would take you six months to a year to find another job paying that much, then you should probably have a lot more money—at least six months' to a year's worth of expenses—in your security basket.

DON'T LET THE BANKS RIP YOU OFF!

How much you save in your security basket is critical. But where you save it is equally important! As far as I'm concerned, there is only one sensible place to keep your security savings. They must be placed in a money-market account that pays a fair rate of return.

Many women today keep their rainy-day money in a bank savings account. In some cases, it's barely earning any interest at all. Please, please don't make this mistake. The fact that banks can rip you off like this absolutely infuriates me. Quite frankly, I think Congress should make it illegal for financial institutions to pay you a less than competitive rate of return on your savings. But since it hasn't, you as a consumer need to protect yourself by shopping around for the best rate of return available either in your area or online. I can't stress enough how important it is that you do this. Indeed, if the only action you take as a result of reading this book is moving your savings from a low-interest account to one that earns a competitive money-market rate, that alone will earn you back what you paid for this book in just the first 30 days.

In addition to brokerage and mutual-fund firms, most online banks today offer money-market accounts that are not only safe and pay competitive interest rates but also come with ATM cards and check-writing privileges—although you are generally limited to about three to six checks per month.

As of this writing, these sorts of accounts are paying depositors between 1 and 2 percent a year. That's much higher than the average bank savings account rate, which tends to be about one-hundredth of a percent unless you carry a huge balance. Other great options are online savings accounts at Internet-only banks. These banks typically have no physical branches, which means they have lower overhead than brick-and-mortar banks, so they can afford to offer annual yields as high as 1.55 percent. Online banks also provide some nice perks, including ATM access (which is often free) and no required minimum balance. (To find out more about where to get the best rates, you can visit **www.bankrate.com**.)

If you have $10,000 sitting in a savings or checking account earning only 0.01 percent annually when it could be earning 1.6 percent, you are cheating yourself out of $160 a year in interest. The way I see it, that's a fancy night out on the town or more money in your retirement account! In other words, that so-called free savings account at the bank really isn't. Quite the contrary, it's costing you a fortune.

WHY DIDN'T WE KNOW THERE WERE ACCOUNTS THAT PAID ALMOST 2 PERCENT?

If all this about money-market and high interest savings accounts comes as news to you, don't worry—you're not alone.

I can't tell you how many times I've talked about them during lectures and seminars and TV shows, and had people come up to me afterward asking me how they can get one. That's not surprising, since the banks don't want you to know about them. As rates head up, remember that means "cash is back." There will be higher rates available, so pay attention as rates move up and better deals compete for your cash.

The fact is, these accounts have been around for years. The key difference today is that you no longer have to be rich to open one. You used to need an initial deposit of $10,000 or more to be able to open a money-market account. These days, you can open one with as little as $100—and in some cases, with no minimum amount at all.

To save myself the trouble of having to answer all the e-mails I'm bound to get on this question, here is a sample list of several reputable institutions that offer these kinds of accounts. This list is not intended to be exhaustive, nor am I endorsing any of these brokerage firms. It's just meant to give you somewhere to start. In any case, there's no reason to go crazy researching where to open a money-market account. I haven't listed the rates—they change regularly and you can find the most current rates at the websites listed. Not all of these accounts offer checking.

Ally Bank (no minimum to invest)
(877) 247-2559
www.ally.com

Barclays (no minimum to invest)
(888) 710-8756
www.banking.barclaysus.com

Capital One (no minimum to invest)
(800) 289-1992
www.capitalone.com

Charles Schwab ($2,500 minimum)
(866) 855-9102
www.schwab.com

Edward Jones ($1,000 minimum)
www.edwardjones.com

EverBank ($5,000 minimum)
(888) 882-3837
www.everbank.com

Fidelity Investments ($2,500 minimum)
(800) FIDELITY
www.fidelity.com

Marcus (Goldman Sachs; no minimum to invest)
MARCUS1 (844) 627-2871
www.marcus.com

Merrill Lynch ($2,000 minimum)
(877) 653-4732
www.ml.com

Morgan Stanley ($2,000 minimum)
(800) 688-6896
www.morganstanley.com

Synchrony (no minimum to invest)
(866) 226-5638
www.synchronybank.com

TDAmeritrade (no minimum to invest)
(800) 669-3900
www.tdameritrade.com

UFB ($5,000 minimum)
(877) 472-9200
www.ufbdirect.com

Vanguard ($3,000 minimum)
(877) 662-7447
www.vanguard.com

> **Five-Star Tip:** Interest rates change daily! To find the current rates on money market accounts and compare them, visit **www.bankrate .com** and its proprietary site **www.ratepro.co** (no "m" on the end). RatePro reviews nearly 5,000 funds and highlights the highest rates.

> **SAFEGUARD NO. 2**
> **You absolutely, positively, no matter what, must have an up-to-date will or living trust.**

Two out of three Americans die intestate. That's legal jargon for dying without having written a will or set up a living trust that explains how your assets should be distributed after your death. Not taking steps to plan for what happens after you're gone is incredibly irresponsible. In effect, what you are saying to your loved ones is the following:

To those I love—
While I understand that I have the right to determine who will inherit my property when I die, I have decided to let the courts make that decision for me, even though that might mean that people I never knew or never liked could wind up as my heirs.

I also understand that there are perfectly legitimate ways of minimizing the estate taxes my loved ones will have to pay. However, because of the government's generosity to me through-out my lifetime, I have decided to let Uncle Sam take the biggest bite he can.

In addition, rather than deciding who should take care of my children, I've decided that I'd rather have my family fight about it and then let the courts just go ahead and appoint anyone they feel like.

Finally, I know that as a result of not leaving a will, a signifi-cant portion of my assets could be eaten up by lawyers' bills and that all the private details of my financial affairs will be made public.

Now, clearly, that's not what most people want to have happen when they die. Yet millions and millions of Americans have no will or living trust in place.

Please don't make this terrible mistake. Yes, making out a will or setting up a living trust can be difficult; it forces you to consider all sorts of contingencies you'd probably rather not think about. But remember—if you die without a will or living trust in place, it falls to the government to figure out what should be done with the fruits of your life's work. Do you really want the government to decide how your estate should be divided up? Even worse, by dying intestate, you make it possible for swindlers to lay claim to your estate, and you virtually guarantee that your entire private life will be made public.

The most common excuse for not having a will or living trust is laziness. Well, Smart Women aren't lazy! After you finish reading this chapter, call your family attorney and set up an appointment to draft a will or a living trust. Your lawyer can advise you on which would make the most sense for your situation. For what it's worth,

I generally advise my clients in almost every case to go for the living trust.

WHAT IS A LIVING TRUST?

Before we go any further, I probably should explain a little about living trusts. A living trust is basically a legal document that does two things. First, it allows you to transfer the ownership of any of your assets (your house, your car, your investment accounts, whatever you like) to a trust while you are still alive. Second, it designates who should be given those assets after you die. By naming yourself the trustee of your trust, you can continue to control your assets—which means that as long as you live, the transfer of ownership will have no practical impact on your ability to enjoy and manage your property.

The main advantage a living trust has over a simple will is that if you create a living trust properly and fund it correctly, your assets won't have to go through probate—that is, the courts won't review your instructions regarding the distribution of your assets. This is very, very important. By avoiding probate, you can save thousands of dollars in attorney fees.

In addition, you will be able to maintain your estate's privacy. (Once an estate goes through probate, all the details become a matter of public record.) In a perfect world, this might not matter, but the world isn't perfect. Sadly, there are people out there who make their living reading probate records and trying to figure out how they can get their hands on your money. The fact is, anyone can say that they were promised a piece of your estate. They can show up in court and insist they were your best friend and that you promised to leave them $50,000 when you died. Even if it's a total fabrication, your family will still have to pay some attorney good money to fight the claim.

Another big advantage of a trust is that it can save your heirs money in estate taxes. The 2017 Tax Cuts and Jobs Act significantly increased the estate exemptions to $11.2 million for individuals and $22.4 million for couples—which means that any estate worth less will not have to pay estate taxes. This is a huge win for really wealthy families. With that said, it is important to still note that these new tax rules expire January 1, 2026. Time will tell what happens. Regardless of these new tax rules, I still recommend that most people consider a trust and work with an attorney. Trusts are not "do it yourself" projects. I recommend you get professional assistance and work with an attorney who specializes in trusts and estates.

The cost of setting up a living trust typically ranges from $1,000 to $2,500, depending on the complexity of your estate. But setting it up isn't enough. The trick to making a living trust work for you is to fund it correctly. Many well-intentioned people set up a trust, but then they never get around to putting their house or their brokerage accounts in the trust. Say I set up the David Bach Family Trust. If I neglect to switch my brokerage account from my own name to the trust's name, that account will end up in probate when I die—all because I forgot to change the name on it. Changing the name on an account is called "replating." It's an easy process, and your financial advisor or attorney will be happy to help you with it.

There are too many different kinds of trusts for me to be able to list them all. The key thing to know about trusts is that there are primarily two types: one that is **revocable** and the other type that is **irrevocable.** You can change or cancel revocable trusts at any time. With an irrevocable trust, you've made a decision for life (that's a big deal, as circumstances do change). Irrevocable trusts are typically used to hold insurance policies and can be very helpful to reduce estate taxes. Just be very careful before you sign an irrevocable trust, because it's a permanent decision.

The next thing to know is that trusts are either "living trusts" or "testamentary trusts." In other words, a living trust benefits you while you are alive and is transferred to your beneficiaries when you die—an example being a "revocable living trust." A testamentary trust is a trust that goes into place after death. This is very common for parents to set up for their kids or grandchildren, to take effect upon the death of the parents.

Here is a list of some common types of trusts. It is not exhaustive, but should give you a helpful overview.

Revocable Living Trust. This kind of trust is designed to protect your home and your brokerage accounts, and to help your estate avoid probate. It is extremely flexible and easy to set up, and can be changed whenever you like throughout your lifetime. It's the most commonly used trust, and you don't need to be rich to want to have one of these—you simply want to avoid probate.

Marital and Bypass Trust. This is also a revocable living trust, and is often referred to as an "AB" trust. In the past, these trusts were often used to reduce estate taxes, and they were hugely popular when this book was originally written. However, now that the estate tax exemption has been increased to $11.2 million ($22.4 million per couple), there is far less need for estate tax reduction. In addition, due to changes in tax laws, AB trusts may now leave beneficiaries vulnerable to capital gains taxes. This means there are many fewer people who would benefit from an AB trust these days.

Qualified Terminable Interest Property Trust. The QTIP trust is often used by people who've been married more than once. Say you've got a new spouse and want him or her to be provided for, but intend that your family fortune eventually go to your children by a previous marriage. A QTIP trust will provide income to your surviving spouse for the rest of his or her life, then pass to your children (or whomever you happen to name as the ultimate beneficiary).

Special Needs Trust. This kind of trust allows parents of special needs children to leave money for their children's benefit, even if the children are not able to handle the money on their own. This kind of trust is particularly important for special needs children because of the requirements for Supplemental Security Income, which is only available for individuals who have less than $2,000 in personal assets. Leaving your child money in such a trust will keep his or her assets below the disqualifying $2,000 threshold while still ensuring that your money is available for your child.

Charitable Remainder Trust. This trust allows you to continue to live off the proceeds of your estate even after you've donated it all to a charity (and presumably reaped some hefty tax advantages in the process). Typically set up by very wealthy families, it can provide you and your designated heirs with income for the rest of your lives, but once you are all gone, the estate will go to the charity.

Irrevocable Life Insurance Trust. This is a great way to protect the real value of your life insurance from the brutal impact of estate taxes. Unfortunately, once you've set it up, it can't be changed, nor can you easily access your policy's cash value.

Because estate planning is so important and so complicated, I strongly recommend that you hire a qualified professional who specializes in this sort of thing. Hire an estate-planning expert who specializes in drafting trusts.

WHAT TO DO IF YOU ALREADY HAVE A WILL OR LIVING TRUST

If you already have a will or a living trust, that's great. If it was written more than five years ago, however, don't assume it's still good. In all likelihood, some things in your life have changed, and your will or trust probably needs updating. I have sat with clients reviewing wills that still talked about who would take care of the kids—even though the "kids" were now in their fifties. (People always laugh when I tell that story, but the situation is more common than you would believe.)

Once you've written or updated your will or living trust, make sure your loved ones know where you've stored it. And *don't* keep it in a safety deposit box. If your heirs don't have the keys to your box, they may need to obtain a court order to get it opened—and that could take weeks (sometimes even months). If you store important documents in a safe or strongbox in your home or office, make sure someone (such as your attorney or your children) knows where it is and how to find the combination. You might think this is obvious, but even professionals sometimes forget. Not too long ago, my own father, who's been a financial advisor for more than 30 years, casually happened to mention that he and my mother kept their wills and other important papers in a "hidden safe" in their house. It was the first I'd ever heard of it.

The point is, if you are hiding any valuables, make sure your heirs know where they're hidden. Because if you don't, they may well stay hidden after you pass away.

And don't be penny wise and pound foolish and try to draft a will or trust by yourself. Just one mistake on a self-created will can make the entire document invalid—in which case your estate will end up in the courts, at a cost to your family of thousands of dollars and endless heartache. Spend the money (and time) to have your will drafted properly by a professional. As I mentioned, the bill may run from $1,000 to $2,500, but I promise you, it will be worth it.

Finally, if you have older parents and you don't know if they have a will or living trust in place, you really should have a talk with them about getting things organized. The conversation may be uncomfortable, but it will almost certainly spare you and your family much heartache later on.

Five-Star Tip: Since the first edition of this book was published, I've had a number of people tell me that they prepared their own wills with the assistance of a self-help legal information service called Nolo Press. I've visited the Nolo website (**www.nolopress .com**) and I was impressed by what I found, particularly their will-making software. I still think that an attorney is a better way to go, but if you can't afford to spend $1,000 on a will, writing your own with Nolo's help is probably better than not doing anything at all.

Bonus Five-Star Tip: Check out **Everplans.com**. This new website allows you to store and share everything important to you and your family regarding your will and family wishes. It's an online vault for your digital archive of your will, trust, insurance policies, health-care directives, passwords, and more. They have a free and really robust resource area on wills, estate planning, etc.

SAFEGUARD NO. 3
Get the best health insurance you can afford.

When I originally wrote this book, I said, "The U.S. healthcare industry is a mess, and it's probably going to get worse before it gets better." To say that was an understatement is putting it mildly. It's almost impossible to update this section of this book right now as our politicians fight about the direction of our healthcare system and the healthcare system is in such flux. The truly sad part about healthcare is that it's simply not affordable for too many people. And yet we all need medical insurance!

Government data on Heathcare.gov shows that the average three-day stay in a hospital can cost about $30,000. On average around the country, the minimum hospital stay is around $1,500 to $2,000 a day, not including the actual treatment you may be receiving or your doctors' fees. I had a client who was never sick a day in his life suddenly discover he had cancer. He wound up spending $50,000 on chemotherapy in just a few months. Another otherwise healthy client of mine was involved in a car accident. In less than two weeks, he ran up medical bills totaling more than $100,000. In fact, a similar thing happened to me. When I was 15, I got hit by a car while I was riding my moped. It took six surgeries and three months in the hospital, followed by a year of physical therapy, before I was able to walk again. The bills totaled well into six figures. Fortunately, both my clients and my parents had medical insurance that covered virtually all the costs. Unfortunately, not everyone is so lucky. According to a recent study by the Kaiser Family Foundation, about 29 million people still lack health insurance. This is frightening.

So no debating here. You must have health insurance. The only question in your mind should be how you get it and what your options are.

Most people fall into one of two categories. Either you or your spouse works for a company that provides you with some healthcare options, or you don't—meaning your company doesn't offer health insurance or you are self-employed. If you are one of the latter, you will need to do some research and find a plan on your own. This process today is done through an insurance broker or through the ACA healthcare portal at **www.healthcare.gov**. I would start by going to www.healthcare.gov and checking the open enrollment dates. From that website, you will ultimately link to the website for your state. Depending on your state, you should also have links to the type of financial assistance you may qualify for. In most cases, you can complete the application online, or you can do it by phone or even in person. The health plans now come in four tiers: *Bronze, Silver, Gold,* and *Platinum*. According to 2014 *USA Today* article, nearly two-thirds of participants chose the Silver tier health plan.

My advice about health insurance hasn't changed with this update. When it comes to choosing a plan, I still recommend you purchase the best insurance you can afford. My caveat today, however, is that you make sure the plan you buy is NOT a plan that you can *barely afford*, because when rates go up you may simply not be able to afford it at all.

If individual coverage turns out to be too expensive for you, you may be able to get a group rate through a professional organization or association. You might even check with your church or syna-gogue.

In the end, however, everyone—even those whose companies do offer coverage—has to make some basic decisions on their own.

WHAT A SMART WOMAN NEEDS TO KNOW ABOUT HEALTH INSURANCE

There are basically two types of health insurance programs to choose from these days: fee-for-service plans and managed care. Fee-for-service (also known as an indemnity plan) allows patients the kind of healthcare most of us grew up with. Unfortunately, because of the cost, fewer and fewer companies are offering it to their employees. Managed care is less expensive and, as a result, far more popular.

FEE-FOR-SERVICE PLANS

Once upon a time, most Americans had a family doctor whom they really knew and who really knew them. They went to this doctor whenever something was wrong with them, and if that something turned out to be especially complicated or obscure, the family doctor would refer them to a specialist.

Under a fee-for-service or indemnity plan, you can still be treated this way. You can continue to see your old family doctor, whether or not he or she is part of any program. You can switch physicians any-time you'd like, without needing anyone's permission. If you want to see a particular specialist, you go to that particular specialist. Once you've paid the deductible, the plan typically pays 80 percent of your bill up to an annual cap.

There is, of course, a catch. The premiums for these sorts of poli-cies are huge—so huge in fact that few companies are still willing to offer fee-for-service or indemnity coverage to their employees.

Despite the cost, if your employer happens to be one of the few who still offer the option of electing an indemnity or fee-for-service plan, I would urge you to consider it seriously. Yes, it will probably be the most expensive plan you can choose, but it's also bound to be the most flexible one, providing you with the most freedom and the most choices. Personally, when it comes to my healthcare, I like having the freedom to choose. It's highly unlikely this will be the type of plan you consider today because it is simply not an option for the majority of Americans.

MANAGED CARE

Because of its lower cost, most employers—not to mention most self-employed people—prefer managed-care plans these days. Managed care comes in three basic forms: health maintenance organizations (HMOs), preferred-provider organizations (PPOs), and point-of-service (POS) plans.

HMO COVERAGE

A health maintenance organization is, in effect, a group of healthcare providers who have joined together to provide comprehensive healthcare coverage for subscribers. HMOs are generally the oldest managed-care systems around. They are also among the most restrictive.

When you sign up with an HMO, you are given a list of doctors from which you must select a primary-care physician. Otherwise known as a "gatekeeper," this doctor is the one you must see whenever you have a medical problem, regardless of what the problem might be. In other words, if you wake up one morning and notice a spot on your leg, you can't go directly to your dermatologist. You have to make an appointment with your gatekeeper first. If it turns out you need to see a specialist, the gatekeeper will refer you to one within the HMO. If for some reason you want to see a specialist who's not part of your HMO, too bad. The visit will not be covered.

The good news about HMOs is that they are relatively inexpensive. Chances are they'll be the cheapest healthcare option your employer offers. In most cases, you'll only have to make a $10 to $50 copayment when you visit your primary-care physician. The same is generally true for prescription drugs; indeed, some HMOs don't make you pay anything for drugs.

HMOs vary widely in cost and quality of service. Some people love their HMOs and will tell you they are the only way to go because they are so affordable and easy to use. Others will complain bitterly about not being able to see the doctors they want or get the treatment they feel they need. All things being equal, I'd spend more money and consider either a PPO or POS plan.

PPO COVERAGE

A preferred-provider organization usually consists of a group of individual physicians, medical practices, and hospitals that have joined together in a loose coalition to create a "group network." In some ways, PPOs look and feel a lot like HMOs, but there are some distinct differences that I think make the PPO approach much better. For one thing, PPOs don't require you to have a gatekeeper. You still have a primary-care physician, but if you want to see a specialist, you can go on your own without a referral. Also, you can use a specialist who's not a member of your PPO's group network and the PPO will still cover at least part of the bill.

Not surprisingly, all this flexibility comes at a price—literally. PPOs are more expensive than HMOs. Their premiums are slightly higher, the copayment will be higher, and some PPOs require you to pay an annual out-of-pocket deductible of anywhere from $250 to $500, or even $1,000 before their coverage kicks in. But, again, the costs depend on the deductible and tier you select—they could be much higher.

EPO COVERAGE

Exclusive provider organizations are a lot like HMOs; they generally DO NOT provide out-of-network coverage. There has been a lot of controversy over these plans; class action lawsuits have claimed the EPOs did not clearly disclose that people were signing up for an EPO and instead thought they were getting a PPO. Be very careful about these before you go forward—get the clear facts. The fees cover a wide range based on the plan level and deductible.

POS COVERAGE

Point-of-service plans are becoming increasingly popular, probably because they offer subscribers the widest array of choices of any managed-care plan. Combining features from both HMOs and PPOs, the POS plan allows you either to stay within the plan's network of doctors (thus saving money) or elect to go outside, in which case you have to pay a deductible (as with a PPO). This is often referred to as a "hybrid" plan because it's a combination of an HMO and a PPO.

CONCIERGE MEDICINE

Concierge medicine is a new and fast-growing medical service that hearkens back to the old way of healthcare. This kind of practice offers patients higher-touch service at a higher cost. You can generally expect to pay between $2,000 and $5,000 annually, depending on the practice, service, and location, but the big draw is that you can get appointments quickly and some doctors will even make house calls. Some of the doctors or medical practices accept insurance and some do not.

More affordable versions of concierge services are also becoming more common. I recently joined a new practice in New York City called One Medical (**www.onemedical.com**); membership costs $199 a year (on top of my insurance, which allows me to use them). This service lets me do everything online with an app, and I was blown away by my ability to get a next-day appointment with my doctor, especially considering that the average time it takes to book a doctor is 29 days, according to *The New York Times*. One Medical is currently available in eight cities, and many other medical practices are becoming available in the twenty-first century that are on the cutting edge of service and technology. If you don't have one now, it may be time to take a look.

HOW DO I CHOOSE WHICH PLAN IS BEST FOR ME?

I used to recommend that you select the most expensive choice. I said this because in almost every case the most expensive choice will provide you with the most options, and when it comes to your healthcare you want to try to cover all the bases.

But today, with health insurance costing literally two to three times more than it did 20 years ago, I can't make a recommendation as simple as advising that you select the most expensive choice with the most options. I realize you may barely be able to afford what you have *now*. You are going to need to really look into your plan options. If you change providers, can you continue to see your current doctors? If not, are you comfortable with the new plan's doctor and hospital options? Does it cover your drug needs? What *does* the plan cover? How big is the deductible? Can you afford the deductible? And, most important, can you ultimately afford the plan you just selected?

If you're married and both you and your spouse happen to have corporate coverage, I'd suggest that you compare plans. One of them may be noticeably better than the other, in which case you may want to cancel the lesser plan and use the superior one to cover both of you. Over the long run, doubling up on one good plan may be cheaper than being on two separate ones. One caveat to this, however, is the fact that some corporate healthcare coverage discourages married couples from doubling up on one plan. If both spouses have access to healthcare coverage through work, either or both insurers might require each spouse to use his or her own insurance or face a penalty for signing up for the other's insurance. Make sure you understand the requirements, rules, and fees of each of your policies to make sure you're making the best decision for you both.

And don't forget: *In many cases, it makes sense to have two separate healthcare plans to protect you in case one of you loses your job.*

If you're planning to have children . . .

Needless to say, women who are thinking about having children should make sure they choose a medical plan that offers first-rate maternity coverage. If you are planning to have a baby in the next year or two, call your company's benefits department and ask them which plan they recommend for prospective mothers. If they won't give you any guidance, ask any coworkers you know who have had children.

It's also always a good idea to contact the healthcare providers directly. A really smart strategy is to select your medical plan *after* you select your doctor and your hospital. First, find the doctor and hospital you want. Then ask them which plans cover their services. Hopefully, you'll be able to sign up for one of these plans.

WHAT IF I'M SELF-EMPLOYED?

Just because you're self-employed is no excuse not to have healthcare coverage. Many entrepreneurs belong to professional organizations, and many of these offer group plans at reasonable rates. If you don't belong to such a group, why not consider joining one? Beyond that, you can always ask an independent insurance professional about getting coverage. Or you can go online and do your own research. The following websites are a good place to start.

eHealthInsurance.com
(844) 839-4346
www.ehealthinsurance.com

e-INSURE Services, Inc.
(855) 372-7400
www.einsurance.com

Freelancers Union
www.freelancersunion.org

Health Insurance
(844) 337-4826
www.healthinsurance.org

Insure.com
www.insure.com

Of course, if you're married and your spouse works for a company that offers healthcare coverage, your problem may be solved—simply go on your spouse's plan. If you're in a relationship but the two of you aren't married, see if your partner's employer covers domestic partnerships. Happily, an increasing number of companies are starting to do this.

> ### SAFEGUARD NO. 4
> **If you have dependents, you should have life insurance.**

If you have dependents—children or other relatives who depend on you financially—you must protect them by buying life insurance. Most people hate to talk about life insurance, but if someone is depending on you and your income, then you need to have some sort of protection plan in place in case something happens to you. And that's all life insurance is—a protection plan.

LIKE IT OR NOT, MEN DIE

One of the sadder aspects of my career over the years has been how often I hear horror stories about women who thought their husbands had life-insurance coverage—only to find out after it was too late that they didn't. Remember, no one really knows when he or she is going to go. That's why you have to have insurance . . . to protect against the unexpected.

As I noted in Step One, men are the worst when it comes to dealing with this reality. So if you are married, put this book down right now and go find out if you and your husband have life insurance. Then find the insurance policy and read it. (By the way, when you pull out the policy, if the pages are yellowed and stick to the plastic folder they came in, chances are you have a really old policy that definitely needs to be reviewed.)

If you are a single mom raising kids on your own, it's even more essential that you have life insurance to protect your children's future. Indeed, as a single mother, getting adequate life insurance could be the most important thing you ever do for your children.

When you start reading your policy, the first two things you really want to know are who is covered and how much money will be paid out if the insured individual dies.

IF YOU ARE MARRIED WITH CHILDREN, DON'T INSURE JUST YOUR HUSBAND

Many family men naively assume that if their wife is a stay-at-home mom, she doesn't need to be covered. This is a huge mistake. After all, if you are a stay-at-home mom and something happens to you, who is going to take care of the kids? Your husband will have to hire a nanny or stay at home himself (and thus have to stop or cut back working). Either way, that will require more money.

IF YOU ARE A SINGLE MOM, YOU'D BETTER OVERINSURE!

Life insurance is not the place to cut corners. Stop for a moment and think about it. If you were to pass away, who would take care of your kids? Would it be your parents? A relative such as a sister or brother? Or would your kids end up with your ex-husband? Whatever the case, you want them to be safe and secure, and this means, among other things, protecting them financially—that is, leaving them with enough money to live comfortably and ultimately with sufficient savings to pay for college.

So make sure you have enough life insurance not simply to provide for your children's needs over the next years if something were to happen to you, but to cover their expenses straight through four years of college.

That's bound to be a lot of money, of course, but if you don't provide it, who will? Don't make the terrible mistake I personally have seen too many single moms make and assume that your parents will be able to handle the financial burden of taking care of your children. Over the past few years I have had to sit in too many meetings with clients who are now struggling because of the obligations they inherited when a grown child of theirs died, leaving them to take care of their orphaned grandchildren.

SO HOW MUCH IS ENOUGH?

In order to come up with a ballpark number, you should ask yourself the following questions.

1. Who will be hurt financially if I should die? In other words, who relies on my income? (By the way, if you could be hurt financially by a death in the family—your spouse's, for example—then you definitely want to make sure you are protected yourself.)
2. What does it cost those who depend on me to live for a year? (This figure should include everything—mortgage, taxes, college costs, etc.)

3. Are there any major debts, such as a home or business loan, that would need to be paid immediately if I or my significant other were to pass away? (You'd be surprised how often smart people overlook these sorts of financial obligations. If you own a business, what costs would your family or children incur if you died? Do you own a second home? If you do, make sure the mortgage payments are covered. What about funeral expenses, estate taxes, and probate costs? These can amount to tens of thousands of dollars.)

MOST PEOPLE ARE UNDERINSURED

As a starting point to determine the minimum amount of life insurance you need, take your gross annual income (that is, your total earnings before taxes) and multiply it by 6. I say "minimum" because depending on the level of your debts and expenses, you might want a death benefit as high as 20 times your annual income.

Whether you insure yourself on the low or high end of that range depends on your situation. Some people like to have just enough insurance to cover their dependents' major expenses for a few years. Others want to make sure that if something happened to them, their family's independence would be ensured indefinitely. As with the amount of your security savings, this is a decision you must make for yourself personally. I recommend that you cover your family's living expenses for at least ten years—more if your dependents happen to be very young.

NOT EVERYONE NEEDS LIFE INSURANCE

Life insurance is meant to protect dependents who can't otherwise take care of themselves and would be at risk if you weren't around. It's not meant to leave your significant other in the lap of luxury.

Therefore, if you don't have kids (or some other relative who depends on you), there is no reason for you to make financial sacrifices to buy life insurance. I'd rather see you put the money away for retirement.

Indeed, if you are single and childless (and have no other dependents), then the only possible reason you should buy life insurance is because you want to leave an estate for a charity or you are using it as a retirement vehicle. As far as your security basket is concerned, the point of life insurance is to protect your dependents; if you don't have any, you don't need any.

SO WHAT KIND OF LIFE INSURANCE SHOULD I BUY?

If you are confused about life insurance, don't worry—you are not alone. Today there are more than 500 differently named types of policies. It's no wonder the public is confused. For the sake of your security basket, I am going to try to keep the insurance game simple.

First and foremost, there are really only two types of life insurance: term insurance and permanent insurance.

TERM INSURANCE

Term insurance is really very simple. You pay an insurance company a premium, and in return the insurance company promises to pay your beneficiary a death benefit if you die. Specifically, term insurance provides you with a set amount of protection for a set period of time.

The chief advantages of this type of insurance are that it is very cheap and generally it is very easy to get. The disadvantage of term insurance is that it does not allow you to build any "cash value." What this means is that you never accumulate any equity in the policy no matter how long you pay premiums to the insurance company. All term insurance provides is a death benefit. You can literally pay premiums into a term policy for 30 years, but if you then decide you don't want it anymore, you walk away with nothing.

Term insurance comes in two basic "flavors"—annual renewable term and level term.

Annual Renewable Term. With annual renewable term insurance, your death benefit remains the same while your premiums get larger each year. More than likely, this is the type of policy you have if you work for a company and signed up for life insurance through the benefits department. The biggest advantage of an annual renewable term policy is that it is really inexpensive when you are young. Indeed, it is by far the cheapest way to buy insurance when you are just starting out. The problem is that as you get older (and the likelihood of death increases), the premiums can become prohibitively expensive.

Level Term. Under a level term policy, both the death benefit and the premium remain the same for a period of time that you select when you first sign up. The period can range anywhere from 5 to 30 years. While this type of term insurance is initially more expensive than annual renewable term, it actually can turn out to be cheaper over the long run. If you choose this type of term insurance, I personally recommend you take it for a minimum of 15 to 20 years. If you are in your thirties or younger, a 20-year policy would at least protect your family in the years in which they are likely to have the greatest need for your income.

WHO SHOULD BUY TERM INSURANCE?

Unless you are looking for an investment vehicle, I would recommend that everyone with dependents to protect should buy term life insurance—ideally, a level term policy. Depending on your particular situation, you probably would do well to look into getting as long-term a policy as possible, at least 20 years. If better rates become available, you can always go shopping for a new policy. (If you do this, make sure you don't cancel your old policy before you've been approved for your new one.)

The great news about term insurance these days is that it has never been more affordable. In fact, if you have a life insurance policy that is more than five years old, you probably should get it updated. Typically, you should be able to buy a new policy that provides two to three times the death benefit for the same price you're paying now, or the same size death benefit at just half or a third of your current premium cost.

Why hasn't your insurance company told you about this? Come on. Do you really think your insurance company is going to phone you up and say, "Hey, guess what? We've cut our prices 50 percent, and we'd like to send you some of your money back"? Of course it won't—which is why you should be constantly reviewing your financial situation.

> **Five-Star Tip:** As attractive as it may seem, don't get term life insurance through your employer unless the policy the company is offering is guaranteed renewable and portable. This means that if you leave your job, you can take the policy with you. If your policy isn't portable, you could find yourself without a job and without insurance—a bad combination.

PERMANENT INSURANCE

Permanent insurance is known in the industry as "cash-value" insurance. Basically, it combines term insurance with a forced savings plan that can help you build a nice nest egg. Eventually, you can either dip into these forced savings for income or use them to pay the annual premiums on your policy. If used correctly, you can also borrow the money tax-free and use it during your lifetime, or leave a large cash cushion (potentially tax-free) to your beneficiaries. The catch here is that permanent insurance is a commitment and it's not cheap. Indeed, it can cost as much as 5 to 10 times more than term insurance.

There are four main types of permanent insurance: whole life, universal life, variable universal life, and indexed universal life. Let's go over the basics.

Whole Life. Imagine paying for term insurance, but adding a 50 percent surcharge to the cost of the annual premium and having some of that extra money put in a money-market account, where it can grow tax-deferred into a little nest egg for your old age. That's what whole life is. It's a term policy with a little cash-value basket added onto it. The problem is that the money is invested so conservatively that it seldom earns more than 4 or 5 percent a year—which is to say that the policy's cash value grows too slowly to really amount to anything. At the time of this update, the rates are even lower.

Universal Life. After decades of being sold on whole life insurance, people began to wake up and realize that it was not the great retirement vehicle they had been told it was. So the insurance industry came up with a new and improved angle. "Instead of just putting your extra premium money in a money-market account," the industry told potential customers, "we will invest it more aggressively and pay you a great rate." Some insurance agents sold these policies on the promise that policyholders could earn as much as 11 percent a year. They would flash fancy illustrations showing that if you earned 11 percent a year, your cash value would be just enormous in 20 years. These illustrations always looked really impressive. The problem was they were just illustrations, not guarantees. Universal life works great when rates are high and the insurance company invests well, but it can be a disaster when the company doesn't invest well or rates simply go down as they have in the past decade. Many people who bought universal life policies back when rates were in the high teens have been shocked in recent years by annual returns of just 6 percent—and they still have to make premium payments.

I intentionally left these numbers from the original book update to show how much things can change in a decade. Today people would be pretty happy with 6 percent. The point here, as I said before, is to focus on the guaranteed return, not the projected return.

Variable Universal Life (VUL) Insurance. If you feel strongly about purchasing permanent insurance—which is to say, if you want life insurance that can also double as a retirement vehicle—you might consider a VUL policy or an indexed universal life (IUL) policy (covered next). With VUL, you get a cash-value policy that allows you to control how the savings portion of your premium is invested. A good VUL policy may offer more than a dozen different high-quality mutual funds from which you can select. If you want to be conservative, you can choose a bond fund. If you want to be aggressive, you can choose growth funds. The point is, you are in charge. What makes this especially nice is that, as with a 401(k) plan or an IRA, the cash value of your policy can grow tax-deferred. That is, you can change investments, buying and selling funds as market conditions dictate, without having to pay taxes on any gains. Of course, as with any speculative investment, you can also lose money. There is no guarantee that your cash value will only go up.

Indexed Universal Life (IUL) Insurance. This is the biggest change in permanent insurance since this book was originally written. Often referred to as IUL or equity indexed universal life, this type of permanent life insurance takes a "hybrid" approach. Basically, you are able to get a guaranteed rate on your policy (a minimum fixed rate) and then an indexed account option. The best way to explain this in plain language is that you get the security of a universal policy with the potential growth of a variable policy linked to an index (for example, the S&P 500). The catch is that you don't get the full benefit of the market index (say, the S&P 500 returns), you get a predetermined percentage. Make sure you're really clear about the index the policy is tied to and the predetermined percentage you will receive before you sign on the dotted line. Also, ask a lot of questions about how the minimum rate is calculated, because it's complicated and you want to understand this clearly before you invest.

WHO SHOULD CONSIDER INDEXED UNIVERSAL LIFE AND VARIABLE UNIVERSAL LIFE INSURANCE?

While I think that term life insurance makes the most sense for most people, there are certain circumstances under which you might want to consider buying an indexed universal or variable universal life policy. If the following five characteristics apply to you, IUL or VUL may actually be a good idea.

1. You want to build cash value for retirement.
2. You have at least 10 to 15 years to invest in the policy.
3. You earn a high income (at least $100,000 a year).
4. You are already maxing out contributions to a qualified retirement plan.
5. You understand the risks associated with mutual funds and the market.

Keep in mind that IUL and VUL are complicated insurance products that are often sold to the wrong people. At the very least, you shouldn't even consider them if you're not already fully utilizing a 401(k) plan, deductible IRA, or other tax-deferred retirement account.

The reason some insurance agents and financial advisors are so motivated to sell you a permanent policy (whether in the form of whole life, universal life, or variable life) is that they make a lot of money from this kind of insurance. Which is fine, provided they explain this to you in detail, you understand it, and it's right for you. In some cases, the sales commission on a permanent insurance policy can be as much as 100 percent of the first year's premium. With all this said, I personally own a variable universal life policy (I bought it in my twenties); today, if I were doing this again and had to choose a policy, I would definitely select the indexed universal life over the variable universal life. (I think it is worth the trade-off of not getting all the upside of the index in exchange for the fixed guarantee.)

I do fundamentally believe in permanent insurance (IUL and VUL) for the right investor. The key words are *right investor*.

> **Five-Star Tip:** If you buy a variable policy, you must be prepared to accept a certain amount of risk and volatility. Because you are investing in securities that may go down as well as up, there is a chance you may lose a portion of your cash value and be forced to make additional premium payments. If you are extremely conservative and like "guarantees," don't consider a variable policy, because you won't be happy with the volatility. Remember, permanent insurance works only if you are committed to it—and if you can afford to make premium payments over a long period of time. On average, it takes about 10 to 15 years for a permanent policy to really work as an investment vehicle. If you are not sure you can commit to fund a policy for this long, don't buy variable coverage. Start with a level term policy instead. It will cost less and protect your family just as adequately. You always can get permanent insurance later.

WHERE SHOULD I START?

If you are going to buy life insurance, you should meet with a life-insurance professional—*not* a salesperson. Make a point of asking friends and getting recommendations. A good insurance professional can really add value, provided he or she is ethical and experienced.

Some people prefer not to buy through an agent or broker. Certainly, that can be more expensive than purchasing coverage directly from the company. If you're one of these people, do your research on the Internet. It's never been easier to buy life insurance on the Internet (specifically, *term* insurance), and it's never been cheaper. Here are some great sources you can use:

Ameritas
(800) 552-3553
www.ameritas.com

e-INSURE Services, Inc.
(855) 372-7400
www.einsurance.com

Geico
(800) 207-7847
www.geico.com

LadderLife
(855) 543-3944
www.ladderlife.com
LadderLife is a major new player in term insurance (it's all they do) and they say they can save you up to 40 percent on the price of term insurance. You can also get price quotes online from them in minutes.

Nerd Wallet
www.nerdwallet.com
Great website for financial content in general. Their insurance screening tool helps you compare insurance from 30 companies. (To find it from the homepage, click on "Insurance," then choose the "Life" tab.)

Select Quote

www.selectquote.com

Select Quote specializes in term insurance and helps you get quotes from more than 70 carriers.

USAA Life Insurance Company

(800) 531-8000

www.usaa.com

SAFEGUARD NO. 5

You need to protect your income with disability insurance.

I used to think disability insurance was a waste of money. I was wrong. Although far more people have life insurance than have disability insurance, the chances of your becoming sick or hurt are much greater than the chances of your dying prematurely. Without disability insurance, you are playing Russian roulette with your income.

Consider the following statistics. In one year . . .

- 1 out of every 106 people will die.
- 1 out of every 88 homes will catch fire.
- 1 out of every 70 cars will be involved in a serious accident. But . . .

One out of every 10 people will suffer a serious disability!

What this means to you and me is that the greatest threat to our ability to finish rich may be the risk we all face of serious injury or illness! And the younger you are, the greater your risk actually is. Indeed, the Council for Disability Awareness reports that one in every four of today's 20-year-olds will become disabled before they retire.

Other than your health, your income is probably your most important asset. Lose it and you could be losing your primary means of financial security. That's why we all need disability insurance.

WHAT IS DISABILITY INSURANCE?

Put simply, disability insurance provides income if you are unable to work due to an illness or injury. It will normally provide this income monthly, although there are new policies that can provide the income in one lump-sum amount.

HOW MUCH DISABILITY INSURANCE DO I NEED?

Disability insurance is not designed to make you rich. Rather, like life insurance, it is a protection plan for your current earning power. Ideally, therefore, an adequate disability policy is one that would pay you the equivalent of your current take-home pay.

Most disability plans offer a benefit equal to about 60 percent of your gross (or before-tax) income. That may not sound like much, but if you've paid for the disability policy yourself, any income you receive from it will be tax-free, so 60 percent of the gross probably will be enough to maintain your standard of living. (After all, 60 percent of the gross is about what most of us actually take home after taxes.)

If your employer pays for your disability insurance, any benefits you receive from it will be taxed. This means that if the policy pays only 60 percent of your gross income, you're going to come up short. Indeed, once you've paid the taxes on your disability benefit, you're likely to find yourself with only a fraction of your normal take-home pay. To guard against this, you should consider purchasing what is known as a "gap policy" to make up the difference.

DON'T ASSUME YOU HAVE
DISABILITY INSURANCE

Many people mistakenly assume they automatically get disability coverage from their employer. Don't assume anything of the kind. If you work for a company, first thing tomorrow check your benefits statement or phone your benefits department to find out whether you have disability insurance. If you don't, find out if you can get it through work and start the application process immediately. If you are a stay-at-home mom whose spouse works, check to see if he is covered. If you are self-employed and don't currently have disability insurance, make getting it a top priority.

You should apply for disability insurance now, while you are healthy. For some reason, people always seem to put this off, waiting until something is wrong with them before they start trying to get coverage. By then, of course, it is too late. And don't think you can fool the insurance company by fibbing on your policy application. Saying you're healthy when you know you're not, or that you don't smoke when in fact you do, is not only immoral, it's also pointless. Insurance companies will do just about anything they can to avoid having to pay out benefits—including hiring an investigator to thoroughly investigate your past medical history.

QUESTIONS TO ASK BEFORE YOU SIGN UP

1. Is the disability plan portable and guaranteed renewable?

If you purchase your policy through your employer, you must make sure that you can take the policy with you if you leave the company. You also want a policy that is guaranteed renewable; there is no bigger rip-off than an insurance company that makes you "qualify" each and every year. This is how a bad insurance company gets out of having to pay you when you file a claim!

2. Under what circumstances will the policy pay off?

Specifically, you want to know whether the policy will cover you in the event you're no longer able to do the work you currently do, or whether it pays off only if you are rendered unable to do work of any kind. In the insurance industry, this is known as "owner-occupation" and "any-occupation" coverage. Make sure you buy an owner-occupation policy. Why? Well, take me, for example. I happen to make my living talking on the phone to clients, doing speeches, television, radio, podcasts, etc. Now, if I lost my voice and couldn't talk, I would, for all intents and purposes, be out of a job. But unless I had owner-occupation coverage, the insurance company could say to me, "So what if you can't talk on the phone? There are plenty of other jobs you could do—like digging ditches. So we are not going to pay you any disability benefits." With owner-occupation coverage, they can't do that to me. This sort of coverage is more expensive, but it is much, much safer.

3. How long does it take for the coverage to kick in?

Most disability policies start paying benefits within three to six months after you've been declared disabled. The easiest way to reduce the cost of a disability policy is to lengthen that waiting period. The more cash you have in your security basket, the longer you can stretch it out.

4. How long will the policy cover me?

Ideally, your disability policy should pay you benefits at least until you turn 65.

5. Is my coverage limited to physical disability, or are mental and emotional disorders also covered?

A major cause of disability these days is stress. Not all disability policies cover it, however. If you are in a high-stress occupation, make sure yours does.

Five-Star Tip: As with all good and important things, there is a catch to disability insurance. It is expensive (plans often cost between 1 and 3 percent of your annual income), which is why most people don't have it. In fact, less than 35 percent of Americans carry long-term disability insurance. The reason it costs so much is that insurance companies know there is a good chance they will have to pay off on the policies they write. (This alone should convince you that you need disability insurance.) In any case, I recommend that you contact your company's benefits department first and see if you can get it through them. Group policies tend to be less expensive and easier to get. If your employer won't cover you—or if you are self-employed—check with the companies in the following list that specialize in disability insurance.

Once again, like life insurance, disability insurance is very complicated, and you may want to consider hiring a disability specialist to assist you.

The list that follows includes some of the larger firms that provide disability insurance. Again, talk to your insurance professional first if you work with one; he or she should be able to assist you.

Aflac
(866) 632-4648
www.aflac.com

Colonial Life
(800) 325-4348
www.coloniallife.com

Geico
(800) 207-7847
www.geico.com

LifeHappens.org

This nonprofit site (backed by insurance companies) provides additional educational materials on all forms of insurance including disability insurance. They have a nice section on disability insurance, and I like their simple-to-use calculators.

Mutual of Omaha Insurance Company
(800) 205-8193
www.mutualofomaha.com

Northwestern Mutual Life Insurance Company
(866) 950-4644
www.northwesternmutual.com

State Farm Insurance Companies
(855) 733-7333
www.statefarm.com

SAFEGUARD NO. 6
If you are in your sixties, it's time to consider long-term care coverage.

Once upon a time, individual families provided their own support systems to take care of sick or aged parents. Today, families are often spread out all over the country and as a result there is often no support system. With average life expectancies climbing, more and more elderly people are thus finding themselves in need of either home care or a long-term care (LTC) facility. Indeed, studies indicate that no fewer than one out of every three Americans over the age of 65 will eventually need this sort of help.

The cost of such care can be staggering. According to Genworth

Financial, median nursing home costs can top $80,000 annually. Assisted living can cost more than $40,000, and home health aides will run about $45,000. You may think that Medicare will cover your nursing-care needs. Unfortunately, the reality is that in most cases it won't.

BUSTING THE MEDICARE MYTH

According to AARP, many of us wrongly assume that Medicare will pay for our basic nursing-care needs when we get old. As I noted, we are in for an unpleasant surprise. The fact is, of the billions of dollars in nursing-home costs we incur every year, less than 10 percent are covered by Medicare.

The reason is simple. Most of the care that nursing homes provide to people with chronic, long-term illnesses or disabilities is custodial care, and Medicare does not pay for custodial care. Rather, Medicare is meant to take care of what are known as acute-care needs. For Medicare to cover a nursing-home stay, you must first spend three full days in an acute-care hospital and require skilled care or rehabilitation therapy at least five days a week. And even then, Medicare will cover you completely only for the first 20 days of your nursing-home stay. (After that, it may pay a portion of your care for the next 80 days, provided your health is actually improving as a result.)

And even if you turn out to be one of the lucky ones who meets the current qualification requirements, there's no guarantee that Medicare will be able to pay all of the promised benefits by the time you reach the age of eligibility. As of 2017, the Medicare trustees have predicted that the Medicare trust fund will be insolvent as of the year 2029.

What about Medicaid? Well, Medicaid is welfare, and to qualify for it you must be virtually destitute. That's *not* how a Smart Woman wants to end up.

DON'T JUMP THE GUN

As valuable as it can be, LTC coverage isn't necessarily something you need to buy right away (especially if you are under the age of 50). Most people start thinking about LTC coverage in their fifties and purchase it in their sixties. If you wait until you're in your seventies or eighties, it can become prohibitively expensive. Unless you're in terrible shape, you can still get a pretty good deal in your early sixties.

When you're looking for LTC coverage, the first thing you need to understand is what it will not do. Long-term care insurance will not pay for acute care that you get in a hospital (say, in the immediate aftermath of a heart attack or a broken hip). This is typically the province of health insurance and Medicare. What LTC insurance will cover is the kind of care you get in a nursing home, a residential-care facility, a convalescent facility, an extended-care facility, a community hospice or adult-care center, or in some cases your own home.

The type of LTC coverage you can buy varies from state to state. All things being equal, when you check out what's available in your state, I recommend that you consider a comprehensive policy. The reason is that right now you are probably healthy and as a result can't really predict what type of coverage you (or you and your spouse) will need in the future. A comprehensive policy will typically give you the most options. It will cost more, but should you eventually need the care, I'm confident it will more than justify the extra expense.

HOW TO KEEP YOUR LTC PREMIUMS DOWN

The cost of LTC coverage depends on a number of variables. These include your age, the level of care you want, the amount of coverage ($100 a day, $200 a day, and so on), the length of waiting time before your policy kicks in, your state of health, and how long you want your policy to last should you need to use it.

Not counting short stays of less than three months, statistics show that most people spend an average of about three years in a nursing-care facility. For most people, lifetime benefits for long-term care insurance are now becoming cost prohibitive and most companies are no longer offering them. I recommend looking for a five-year benefit with a six-month waiting period up front, since that will likely cover the average nursing-care stay. The six-month waiting period means that your policy will take longer to go into effect. Most LTC policies start paying off within 90 days after you enter a nursing facility or put in a claim for home care. By stretching that out a bit, you can bring down your premium costs quite nicely.

Delaying the start of coverage may sound scary, but it's actually quite sensible, since you will probably be able to afford the first few months on your own. It's later on that you will need the most help. By taking a higher deductible and getting a five-year benefit you are covering the worst-case possibility, which is why you are buying this type of coverage in the first place. (By the way, the cost of this type of insurance can be tax-deductible, so check with your accountant if you decide to purchase it.)

QUESTIONS TO ASK BEFORE YOU SIGN UP

1. What exactly does the policy cover?
Remember, there are several different types of coverage available and they vary from state to state. Make sure you know exactly what type of coverage you are being shown before you sign up.

2. How much will the policy pay out in daily benefits? Will it be adjusted for inflation? At what point do my benefits kick in and how long will they last?
As I noted, you can keep your premiums down by requesting a higher deductible.

3. **Does the policy contain a premium waiver or will I still have to pay the premiums after I start receiving benefits?**

With this waiver, you won't have to worry about continuing to pay premiums while you are in the nursing-care facility.

4. **Is there a grace period for late payments?**

Make sure there is. You would hate to find yourself in a situation where you accidentally missed a payment and then discovered that you'd lost your coverage.

5. **Are there any diseases or injuries that are not covered?**

The answer should be no.

BE CAREFUL WHOM YOU BUY FROM

Because LTC insurance is still a relatively new insurance product, I recommend that you avoid purchasing an LTC policy from any company that hasn't been in the business for at least ten years. Many companies that have entered this space since this book was originally written have gotten out of it, or they have been downgraded by the ratings agencies. There are five major services that rate insurance companies (A. M. Best, Standard & Poor's, Moody's, Duff & Phelps, and Weiss), and you shouldn't buy a policy from any company that hasn't earned a top grade from at least three of them. You can find out what sort of ratings a company has received by asking; if the company says it doesn't know or doesn't want to tell you, that's a good sign you should take your business elsewhere.

Before you buy any LTC policy, use Google to search and review the insurance rating. Also use Google to check for "complaints" about the company. I recommend purchasing LTC insurance through a professional independent insurance agent—let them do the work of explaining these policies and shopping for the best one for you. If you don't have an agent, here are some websites to use as starting points: **www.LTCtree.com**, **www.Prepsmart.com**, and **www.AALTCI.org**.

Here's how to directly contact some of the biggest providers of LTC insurance that currently have top insurance ratings. This list is not exhaustive.

Mass Mutual
(800) 966-4093
www.massmutual.com

Mutual of Omaha Insurance Company
(800) 205-8193
www.mutualofomaha.com

New York Life
(800) CALL-NYL
www.newyorklife.com

Northwestern Mutual Life
(800) 950-4644
www.northwesternmutual.com

In addition, make sure you find out what happens to your policy in the event the company is sold or goes out of business. Ideally, you want a guarantee that if your policy were to be transferred without your permission, the original terms on which you bought it would remain in effect.

You have now completed your security basket. In the process, you have done an amazing amount—far more than 95 percent of the population ever does—to protect both your future and that of your family.

BASKET TWO:
YOUR RETIREMENT BASKET

In Step Four we talked about the importance of paying yourself first—of putting aside a portion of your income (ideally, one hour a day of your income, roughly 12 percent of your income before taxes), and how you should have it transferred out of your paycheck automatically, before you even see it. Well, where this money actually goes is into your retirement basket.

Remember: Even though we discussed the security basket first, that doesn't mean you should put off funding your retirement basket until after you've funded your security basket. *You should be doing both at the same time!*

The point of paying yourself first is to put money away now so you can have a great retirement later. As you will see, accomplishing this is not only easy, it also can be a lot of fun. Why? Because nearly every dollar you put into this basket goes in tax-free! If that's not fun, I don't know what is. What's more, because your retirement money is not taxed as long as it stays in the basket, you are in essence getting "free money" from the government to invest. When was the last time that happened to you?

You may be wondering how this works. It's simple. When you put money into your retirement basket, you actually are putting it into what is known as a pretax retirement account.

WHAT EXACTLY IS A PRETAX
RETIREMENT ACCOUNT?

A pretax retirement account is a retirement account into which you are allowed to deposit a portion of your earnings before the government takes its usual bite out of them. What's great about this is that normally that bite amounts to at least 28 cents out of every dollar you earn. If you live in a state that has its own income tax, the damage is even worse. For example, California imposes a state income tax of up to 13.3 percent; as a result, my average client is lucky to keep barely 60 cents of every dollar she makes.

Funneling your hard-earned dollars into a pretax retirement account spares the money from this kind of shrinkage. When you put your earnings into a pretax retirement account, all 100 cents of each dollar go to work for you, and as long as the money stays in the account, it can continue to work for you without any interference from the tax man.

THE WONDERFUL WORLD OF RETIREMENT PLANS

There are basically two kinds of pretax retirement accounts: the kind your company provides for you (known as employer-sponsored retirement accounts) and the kind you provide for yourself (known as individual plans).

Over the next few pages, I'm going to describe how these work and how you go about setting them up and contributing to them. Regardless of your status—that is, whether you are self-employed or on a company payroll—I suggest you read about both types of accounts. After all, self-employed people do wind up working for companies sometimes. And in this era of corporate restructuring, company people all too often can find themselves suddenly self-employed. What's more, even if you are lucky enough to have a secure job with a company that offers a good retirement plan, opening an individual retirement account of your own still might make sense for you. So please don't skip over a section just because you don't think it applies to your situation right now.

HOW EMPLOYER-SPONSORED
RETIREMENT PLANS WORK

The most popular retirement program employers make available to workers these days is what is known as a 401(k) plan. Nonprofit organizations have 403(b) plans; some smaller companies may offer what is called a SIMPLE plan, a SEP-IRA, or a defined-contribution plan (which used to be known as a Keogh plan).

Whichever type your employer offers, you should be able to join it at no cost. If you've just started a new job, you may have to wait several months before you are eligible to join the retirement program. And even then, some plans allow new participants to enroll only at certain times of the year.

Whatever the case, once the "start" date has rolled around, the benefits person probably will give you what is called a sign-up package. Your job is to fill it out ASAP.

Many people mistakenly assume that signing up for a 401(k) plan is automatic. IT'S OFTEN NOT! The good news is that since I originally wrote this book, many companies have made "automatic enrollment" a part of their 401(k) plans. The best plans offer not just automatic enrollment features but also "automatic increase features" that increase the savings rate automatically on a set time frame (usually annually). This single change in the retirement planning industry has done more good than probably anything ever done in regard to savings. Companies that have automatic enrollment have seen up to 85 percent of employees participate in their 401(k) plans, according to Aon Hewitt, from an average participation rate of 62 percent. That's the good news. The bad news is that many of these plans are automatically opting employees in at 3 percent, and then the employees are leaving it at this low rate, thinking they are "good to go." If you have automatic enrollment, you MUST look at what the automatic enrollment level is and then increase it! Among companies *without* automatic enrollment, many unfortunately find that fewer than half of their eligible employees participate in their 401(k) plans. It's not hard to understand why. As a new employee, you are handed this huge package of material and you're so busy getting used to your new job that you simply don't have time to read it all. Or, worse, today everything is sent via e-mail and it just gets lost in your in-box. The next thing you know, six months have gone by and you are still not signed up for the plan.

So here's my recommendation. If you work for a company that offers a 401(k) plan, first thing tomorrow check with the benefits manager in your company's human resources department to make sure you are properly signed up. If it turns out that you are not enrolled, ask for a sign-up package. If your company does all of this online, then get online **right now, look at what your enrollment level is, and then increase it!** Some companies won't let you join their 401(k) plan until you've worked there for some minimum amount of time, usually 6 to 12 months. This is not a legal requirement but a matter of corporate policy. If you ask "loudly" enough, sometimes they will waive the rules and let you join early. If not, find out when you will be eligible and mark the date on your calendar. As soon as it arrives, run (don't walk) to the benefits department or go online and get signed up. Believe me, no one from the benefits department is going to remind you to sign up for the plan. Not to be negative, but they aren't watching this stuff. That's why you have to.

The most important piece of information you want to find out from your benefits person is the maximum amount of money that you can put into the plan each year. **By law, the maximum dollar amount you can contribute to a 401(k) plan in 2018 is $18,500 if you are under the age of 50 and up to $24,500 if you are over age 50.** The allowable contribution is raised each year by a specific amount, so keep checking with your benefits department to make sure your contribution level is up to date. You can also go to **www.irs.gov** each year to see if the amount you can save has increased. (Simply search "401(k) retirement maximum contributions" and you should find the latest rules.) Keep in mind that just because the government has raised the amount you can contribute to a 401(k) plan doesn't mean your employer will raise your contribution accordingly. Most likely, you will have to go back to your benefits department and give them specific instructions to increase the amount. This may sound like a bother, but believe me, it's worth it. Keeping an eye on these sorts of details is what makes the difference between having to struggle in retirement and finishing rich.

THE IMPORTANCE OF "MAXING OUT" YOUR RETIREMENT PLAN

Whatever your maximum allowable contribution happens to be, that's the amount you should be putting in. This is called "maxing out" your retirement plan, and it is by far the single most important thing you can do to create a secure financial future. There is nothing I know of that is better at transforming otherwise ordinary Americans into millionaires than the simple act of each month putting as much of their paycheck as they are allowed into a pretax retirement plan at work.

It's reported that less than half of Americans who are eligible for a retirement plan at work actually bother to sign up. And most of the people who do don't max out their contributions. Why? In a word, ignorance. I am convinced that if people knew what they were missing out on—how they were cheating themselves out of a secure and comfortable future—hardly anyone would fail to take full advantage of their retirement plans at work.

Here's a simple example that made a tremendous impact on me.

TWO WOMEN, SAME PLAN,
BUT A $600,000 DIFFERENCE!

Early in my career, I held what is known in the investment industry as an IRA rollover seminar for a local company. This is a seminar where you teach workers who are about to change employers or retire how to "roll over" the money they've saved in their company's 401(k) plan into an individual retirement account.

After this particular class, two women came into my office. One was named Betty; the other, Lynn. Both had worked for a utility company for more than 35 years. Indeed, they were best friends who had started work at this company the very same week.

I met with Lynn first, and after I reviewed her plan, I was able to tell her that she was in great shape to retire. Her account balance totaled $930,000—enough to produce plenty of income for her to live comfortably for the rest of her life. Not surprisingly, Lynn left my office with a big smile on her face.

Betty, by contrast, wore a worried expression when she came in. "You know," she told me, "even though Lynn and I started at the same time and have made close to the same amount of money, I'm not in nearly as good a shape as she is financially."

"Oh, really," I said. "And why is that?"

Betty then took out her retirement plan and showed it to me. Her balance was a little less than $300,000. Not bad, but not nearly as good as her friend's $930,000. "David," she said with a sigh, "I can remember it like it was yesterday. Sitting down at lunch 35 years ago, Lynn and I discussed how much of our income we were going to put into the plan. Lynn told me she was going to max hers out and put away the full 15 percent. She figured it might hurt the first few months, but after that she wouldn't really notice it. I said, 'Fifteen percent? No way! That's just too much.' I figured I'd start with the minimum, which was 4 percent, and when I got a raise, I'd increase my contributions."

Betty shook her head ruefully. "You know what? So many raises came and went, but I never got around to increasing the size of my contribution. There always seemed to be some new expense that came first—a new car, a special vacation, college costs. Now Lynn gets to retire and I have to go find another job. I'll probably need to work for another 15 years. Pretty stupid, huh?"

My heart went out to Betty. But there wasn't much I could do. Don't make the same mistake she did. Maximize your retirement contribution now.

ARE YOU WHERE YOU SHOULD BE?

If you are currently enrolled in a retirement plan but don't know if you are maxing out, you need to educate yourself immediately. Do this **today!** Contact your employer's benefits person, and check out what percentage of your income you are saving and then increase it. If it turns out that you're contributing anything less than the maximum, make it a priority to get your contributions up to the ceiling as quickly as you can. If you are not working but have a spouse who is, make sure he's enrolled in his employer's retirement plan and that his contributions are maxing out.

Five-Star Tip: Check your company's 401(k) match. Since the recession ended, more companies are now offer a matching contribution to your 401(k) savings. According to the Society for Human Resource Management, 42 percent of companies are now matching some amount of employee contributions. Make sure you understand what that amount is—and how many years it takes for the "match to be vested"—meaning it is yours to keep. As I always say "don't count your match until it hatches" (i.e., vests).

HOW DOES MY MONEY GET
INTO THE PLAN?

Once you have completed your sign-up package and are enrolled in your firm's retirement program, your employer will begin taking your contribution out of your paycheck automatically. This automatic salary deduction has two tremendous advantages. First, because it is automatic, you don't have to worry about it (and run the risk of changing your mind). Second, the money you've decided to put aside goes directly into the plan, avoiding that 40 percent tax bite I mentioned earlier.

Oh, and don't worry: Your decision to contribute the maximum allowable amount is not chiseled in stone. If you find you need to reduce your contributions temporarily, at most companies you can do so on as little as 90 days' notice.

WHERE DOES MY RETIREMENT MONEY
REALLY GO?

The application form you fill out to enroll in the plan asks you more than just how much you want to contribute. It also asks you where you want your money to be invested. Most plans today offer participants at least three choices: (1) Your money can be invested in your company's own stock (assuming that you work for a company with publicly traded stock); (2) it can go into a target dated mutual fund or a selection of mutual funds; or (3) it can be put in some vehicle that offers a guaranteed fixed rate. It's up to you to decide what combination of the available options makes the most sense for you and how much of your contribution you want to put into each of them.

This decision is potentially one of the most important financial decisions you will ever make. Let me repeat that.

*How you decide to invest the money in your
retirement plan is one of the most important
financial decisions you will ever make!*

So take this decision seriously. Don't just turn to your neighbor at work and ask him or her, "What are you doing?" He or she may not have a clue.

Instead, study your options carefully and discuss them, both with your significant other (if you've got one) and with a knowledgeable financial advisor. At the end of this chapter, you will find a list of rules aimed at helping you make the smartest decision possible. Follow them, and I think you will be in great shape.

WHAT ABOUT ROTH 401(K) PLANS?

Since I originally wrote this book, the biggest change to the 401(k) space is the *Roth 401(k)* option. The Roth 401(k) allows you to invest after-tax dollars (that means no tax deduction up front) into the plan, and then the money grows tax-free and comes out later tax-free. Because you won't get a tax deduction up front, it basically costs you more out of pocket to fund it. I personally like the tax deduction up front, and I have used only tax-deductible retirement accounts myself. Many investors are now choosing to use both options (if their plan allows). This is how it works: Some money goes into a tax-deductible traditional 401(k) and some goes into a Roth 401(k). If you're not sure which way to go, using both is a solid option. Typically, people who do this split their contributions 50/50.

HOW DO I GET MY MONEY OUT
OF THE PLAN?

As long as you remain employed by the company where you opened your 401(k) account, your funds typically stay in the company plan. You can take money out anytime you want, but if you're younger than 59½, you will end up paying ordinary income tax on your withdrawal, plus a 10 percent penalty. (There are a few ways of avoiding this penalty; we'll cover them later in this chapter.) If you change jobs or leave the company for any other reason before you reach retirement age, you can "roll over" your 401(k) funds either to a new employer's 401(k) plan or to a new IRA of your own. If done properly, the IRS will not consider this transfer of funds a withdrawal, and you won't be subject to any taxes or penalties.

Once you've turned 59½, you can start taking money out of your retirement plan. (You are not required to—not at least until you're 70½—but you can if you want.) Whatever money you withdraw from then on will be treated by the government as ordinary income, which means you will have to pay income taxes on it.

IF YOUR COMPANY DOESN'T HAVE A RETIREMENT PLAN

In my view, companies that don't offer retirement plans are doing their employees a disservice. I happen to believe that employers have a moral obligation to provide programs that allow workers to secure their own financial futures by contributing to tax-advantaged savings and investment accounts.

Some employers—especially the owners of small businesses—complain that they simply can't afford to offer such programs. In recent years, however, the cost of setting up and administering retirement plans has dropped to the point where even small businesses should be able to manage it. Setting up and administering a 401(k) plan is both simple and inexpensive. For a company with fewer than 100 employees, it shouldn't cost more than a few thousand dollars a year. Indeed, when you figure everything in, it's probably less expensive for an employer to set up a retirement plan than to replace a fed-up worker who has quit to join a competitor that cares about its employees' futures!

As an employee, you should make sure your boss knows how unhappy you are about not having a retirement plan. You might add that if she expects you to make a long-term commitment to her company, she'd better do something about putting this sort of benefit in place.

One of the best ways to make sure your employer does the right thing is to do the basic research for your employer. Not only will you be showing your employer just how important a retirement plan is to you and your coworkers, but you'll also be making it easier for the company to get the process started.

There are many companies that offer "turnkey" 401(k) plans for small businesses. You can contact a few of them and request some information about how the process works, which you can then pass along to your boss. Among the companies that can help you with this are Insperity (reachable at 877-516-8977 or **www.insperity.com**), Fidelity Investments (800-343-3548 or **www.fidelity.com**), the Vanguard Group (877-662-7447 or **www.vanguard.com**), T. Rowe Price (800-422-2577 or **www.troweprice.com**), and America's Best 401k (great option for small companies; call 855-905-4015 or go to **www.americasbest401k.com**). Reaching out to such companies is only a starting point, but by doing some of the early legwork you stand a better chance of getting your company to set up a plan. In addition, your boss may even be impressed by your initiative.

That being said, it's still entirely possible to love your job even though your company does not now and never will provide you with a retirement plan. If that describes you, don't worry. You don't have to quit. But you do have to do something.

It's quite simple, really. If your employer won't provide a retirement plan for you, you must provide one for yourself. In other words . . .

You should open an individual retirement account.

Opening an IRA is a relatively simple procedure.

With a traditional account, your contributions may be tax-deductible (depending on your income and whether you contributed to a 401(k) plan), and they get to grow free of all federal taxes until you take them out. With a Roth IRA, you pay income taxes on your money before you put it in, but that's it—if you follow the rules, you never pay a penny more in federal taxes on your nest egg, no matter how large it grows over the years (provided you don't touch the money until after you turn 59½).

Let's go over the basics.

THE TRADITIONAL IRA

The rules governing this type of IRA, originally created in 1974, are relatively straightforward.

1. Who is eligible?

Anyone under the age of 70½ who earns income from a job (as opposed to interest or investment income) or is married to someone who earns income from a job.

2. What if my employer offers a retirement plan?

Even if you participate in a retirement plan at work, you still may be able to contribute to a traditional IRA, although how much of your contribution will be deductible depends on the size of your income. As with all tax issues, I strongly recommend you consult a tax advisor.

3. How much can I put in?

By law in 2018, an eligible individual is allowed to invest up to $5,500 a year in a traditional IRA if you are under age 50 and up to $6,500 if you are 50 or older.

4. What are the tax advantages?

Depending on your income (or, if you are married, on your joint income) and whether or not you participate in a company-sponsored retirement plan, part or all of your IRA contributions may be tax-deductible. As long as it stays in the account, your money will grow tax-deferred—meaning you do not have to pay any taxes on any interest earnings or capital gains.

5. When can I take my money out?

Once you reach the age of 59½ (or anytime after that), you can withdraw any or all of your savings. The government will regard every withdrawal you make as ordinary income and will expect you to pay income taxes on it. (There is an exception to this rule: If you've funded your IRA account with after-tax money—that is, you didn't take a tax deduction on the original deposit—then you'll be taxed only on the earnings and the growth your investment generated over the years, not on the investment itself.)

6. Do I *have* to start taking money out of my IRA when I turn 59½?

No, but you can't leave it there forever. IRS regulations require you to start making what is called a required minimum distribution from your IRA no later than six months after your seventieth birthday. To figure out exactly what your mandatory minimum amounts to, check with your accountant or call the IRS and ask for Publication 590, which explains how to calculate it. (By the way, if you have elderly parents, make sure they are aware of the minimum distribution requirement. Failing to take a minimum distribution can leave them liable to a penalty equal to 50 percent of the amount they should have taken out.)

7. **What if I need my money before I reach retirement age?**

If you withdraw any or all of your IRA savings before the age of 59½, in additional to paying ordinary income tax on the money you have taken out, you may have to pay a 10 percent penalty on whatever interest or investment earnings your initial deposit generated over the years. This penalty does not apply if your withdrawal is used for one of three major "life events": to pay college bills for yourself, your children, or your grandchildren; to help finance a first-time home purchase (up to a maximum of $10,000); or to cover health insurance premiums, extraordinary medical expenses, or long-term disability costs.

There is another way to avoid the penalty—an obscure section of the tax code known as Internal Revenue Service Rule 72(t)(2)(A)(iv), generally referred to as "72T." According to this little-known regulation, you don't have to pay the early withdrawal penalty if you take your money in what the IRS defines as "substantially equal and periodic payments that are based on life-expectancy tables." This is an extremely complicated undertaking that you shouldn't attempt without professional guidance. Done correctly, however, it can be hugely valuable—especially if you are planning to retire in your early fifties. So if early retirement is a possibility for you, make a point of finding a financial specialist who knows the ins and outs of rule "72T." It could save you a bundle in tax penalties.

MAXING OUT YOUR IRA

Though IRA contribution limits have not increased since 2013, the limits are set to increase with the inflation rate in $500 increments—which is why they have remained the same for the past five years, during which time inflation wasn't high enough to trigger the next increment. However, maxing out your IRA contribution every year is an excellent way to sock away money for your retirement. And with "catch-up" provisions allowing women over

50 to contribute more, these accounts offer an exciting option for retirement savings.

THE ROTH IRA

When the Roth IRA was introduced in 1997, many experts were skeptical that it would really be worthwhile for the average American. In the decades since then, however, skepticism has been replaced by enthusiasm. The Roth IRA—which is named for the late Senator William Roth, who sponsored the legislation that created it—is quite similar to the traditional IRA, except for two things. The first difference is that with a Roth IRA, your contributions are not tax-deductible. Once your money is in the account, however, it grows tax-deferred, just as it would in a traditional IRA. And when you take a distribution, you encounter the second big difference: Provided you're older than 59½ and the money has been in the account for at least five years, it's *totally tax-free*! That's right—you pay no income taxes, no capital gains taxes, nothing!

Sounds like a great deal, doesn't it? It is, but as always, there is a catch. Remember, there's no tax deduction for the money you put into a Roth IRA. That deduction, of course, is what made traditional IRAs so popular in the first place. So it's a trade-off. Which is worth more to you: the money you'll save in taxes now by being able to deduct your IRA contributions this year or the money you'll save later by not having to pay any taxes on your IRA withdrawals when you retire? The current rule of thumb on this is that if you are more than ten years away from retirement, you'll come out ahead with a Roth IRA.

Here is a rundown of the basic rules governing Roth IRAs.

1. Who is eligible?

As with a traditional IRA, you must have earned income to be able to open a Roth IRA. But you can't earn too much if you are also eligible for a 401(k) at work. The cutoff point starts at a modified adjusted gross income (known as "MAGI") of $120,000 for single filers and $189,000 for married filers. Depending on what year you read this book, these rules could change, so go to IRS.gov (always go here for tax information related to rules like this) and plug in "Roth IRA Contribution Limits" in the search bar. Bam! You will have the latest rules. Don't Google this stuff. Too often, there are mistakes online in outdated articles. For tax limit rules, assume the IRS website is the source to go to.

2. How much can I put in?

Just like the regular (deductible) IRAs, as of 2018 you can contribute up to $5,500 per year and up to $6,500 a year if you are age 50 or older.

3. If I participate in a 401(k) plan at work, can I still open a Roth IRA?

Yes! I love pointing this out at my seminars because so few people are aware of it. I suggest is that you first make sure that you are maxing out your contributions to your 401(k) plans. Women who maximize their 401(k) plans and then contribute to Roth IRAs are setting themselves up to Finish Rich! I strongly recommend this if you can pull off the extra savings and you qualify based on your income.

4. What are the tax advantages of a Roth IRA?

While contributions to a Roth IRA are not tax-deductible, your money will grow tax-deferred—and provided it's been in the account for at least five years, you can take it out totally tax-free anytime after you turn 59½. This ability to take out money without paying any additional taxes is a tremendous advantage over a traditional IRA.

5. When can I take my money out?

Once you reach the age of 59½ (or anytime after that), you can withdraw any or all of your savings without penalty. Unlike a traditional IRA, however, you can leave your money in a Roth account as long as you like; you do not have to start making minimum withdrawals when you turn 70½. This too is a significant advantage over a traditional IRA.

6. What if I need my money before I turn 59½?
The rules here are exactly the same as for traditional IRAs.

SO WHICH RETIREMENT PLAN IS BEST FOR ME?

Determining which plan makes the most sense for you depends on your income, your age, and your goals. That notwithstanding, company-sponsored plans are almost always the best way to go. If you want to put away more money for retirement, you always can supplement your company plan with an IRA. As to choosing between a traditional IRA and a Roth IRA, if you are more than ten years away from retirement, go with the Roth; the benefits of the tax-free distribution later probably will outweigh the benefits of the tax deduction now. Otherwise, if you are eligible for a deduction through a traditional IRA, then this is probably preferable. In either case, if you are at all unsure of what's right for you, talk to your accountant or other professional financial advisor.

WHAT ABOUT CONVERTING MY OLD TRADITIONAL IRA TO A NEW ROTH IRA?

While Roth IRAs do offer some terrific advantages, especially for younger investors, that doesn't mean everyone under the age of 55 should convert all his or her old traditional IRAs to Roth accounts. I mention this because ever since Roth IRAs were first introduced, many banks, brokers, and financial advisors have been enthusiastically urging their clients to do just that. I have two words of advice on this subject: **Be careful. An IRA conversion is a very serious decision, and there isn't any one-size-fits-all answer.**

Remember that on a conversion you in effect have to cash it out. While you won't be hit with any penalties, you will have to report as income all the money you have accumulated in the account, which means you will have to pay income taxes on your nest egg. Ouch. Say you decide to convert a traditional IRA in which you've got a current balance of $50,000. In order to do so, you've got to declare that $50,000 as ordinary income earned during the year in which you're making the conversion. Chances are, this will bump you into a higher tax bracket and make for a painful tax bill come April 15. In any case, suddenly you'd have to pay Uncle Sam a big chunk of the money you have been working so hard to grow.

Typically, what happens is that people pull money out of their IRAs in order to pay the extra tax they've incurred by converting to a Roth. And in most cases, that makes no sense. Take our $50,000 example. If you withdrew $15,000 from your retirement account to pay the tax bill resulting from the conversion, that would leave you with only $35,000 invested in your new Roth IRA. That's a 30 percent reduction in your wealth. Is the Roth's tax advantage worth that much? Probably not.

Now, some people will suggest that if you have "extra money" sitting around, you could use that to pay your tax bill. But seriously, who has "extra money?" In any case, if you use the tools this book provides, your money won't ever be "sitting around," it will be working hard for you. So be sure to get solid financial and tax advice before making any decisions about converting your old IRAs.

WHAT IF I OWN MY OWN BUSINESS?

First, let me say congratulations! I say this because I admire entrepreneurs and because, as a business owner, you are eligible for the best retirement accounts around. Second, let me urge you to avoid a mistake that too many business owners make: deciding that setting up a retirement plan is too much of a bother.

Remember, you are in business to build a financially secure future for yourself and your family—and how can you do that unless you pay yourself first? As a business owner, the best way to pay yourself first is by setting up one of the four types of retirement plans meant for self-employed people:

- Simplified Employee Pension Plan (also known as a SEP-IRA)
- Solo 401(k) plan
- Defined-benefit plan
- Savings Incentive Match Plan for Employees (known as a SIMPLE IRA)

Establishing one of these may take a little effort on your part, but, hey, you're an entrepreneur—you should be used to going the extra mile. In any case, it's more than worth it. While the regulations regarding distributions and early withdrawals are pretty much the same as the ones that govern IRAs and 401(k) plans, the rules on contributions to retirement plans for business owners are much, much better, allowing you to put away up to $55,000 a year, tax-deferred—and possibly even more; up to 100 percent of your compensation with a cap of $220,000!

SIMPLIFIED EMPLOYEE PENSION PLANS (SEPS)

SEP-IRAs are very attractive to small business owners because they are easy to set up and require the least paperwork. If you run a small business, are a sole proprietor, participate in a small partnership, or are a Subchapter S corporation, this is probably the type of retirement account you'll want to set up. These accounts are truly amazing.

You can now contribute as much as 25 percent of gross income to a SEP-IRA, up to a maximum of $55,000 for 2018 (the amount is adjusted for inflation every year; always double-check the rules at **www.irs.gov**). If you are self-employed and don't have any employees, run—don't walk—to the nearest bank or brokerage (or go online) and open a SEP-IRA today. Setting up a SEP-IRA can often be done in less than 15 minutes, and can be taken care of online by most brokerage firms.

If you have employees, however, certain obligations go along with establishing a SEP-IRA. If you have people working for you who are over 21 and have been on your payroll for at least three of the last five years, you also must include them in your SEP-IRA, contributing on their behalf the same percentage of their annual compensation that you do of your own. In other words, if you put in 10 percent of your compensation, you also must contribute an amount equal to 10 percent of theirs. (By the same token, if you decide not to put in any money for yourself one year, you don't have to put any money in for them.)

The one disadvantage of a SEP-IRA is that the contributions you make for your employees are immediately 100 percent vested (which means the money you put in for them is theirs to keep, even if they leave your employ the next day).

THE SOLO 401(K) PLAN

If you think the SEP-IRA is great, you're going to love this. Originally created in 2002, the **Solo 401(k) plan** is an amazing account for any business owner (and her spouse) with no nonfamily employees. What makes these accounts so great? You can put more money more quickly into the Solo 401(k) than you can into a SEP-IRA.

Here's how it works: To start, you may deposit 100 percent of the first $18,500 you earn in 2018 (or more later, depending on the rules). In addition, you can use the profit-sharing portion of the plan to contribute up to another 25 percent of your income. This means the maximum combined total you can contribute in 2018 is $55,000.

Let's check out that math. A self-employed businesswoman earned $100,000. Her Solo 401(k) plan will allow her to put the first $18,500 she earned into the salary-deferred solo plan, and then she could later put another $25,000 into the profit-sharing portion (that is, 25 percent of her $100,000 salary). That's a total of $43,500 tax-deductible into the plan—on $100,000 in income. With a SEP-IRA the most you could put away on $100,000 income is $25,000 (still a lot), but for a business owner looking to build wealth faster, this is a better plan that allows you to save more money faster. Most major full-service brokerage firms today offer these plans.

DEFINED-BENEFIT PLANS

A defined-benefit plan allows business owners to put away more money than any other type of plan around. This is why I recommend defined-benefit plans to business owners who are over the age of 50 with no employees and with a high level of dependable income. If this describes you, and you can afford to contribute more than $55,000 per year and feel confident you can continue to do so each year until you reach age 59½, then this is the plan you want.

So how much more than $55,000 annually are we talking about? A lot more! *In 2018 you can put up to 100 percent of your compensation, not to exceed $220,000.* Yes, you read that correctly! You can put up to $220,000 tax-deductible into a defined-benefit plan. That's huge! We're talking big money here! If you have a nice, large income and you are over age 50 you should really look into these plans while they are still available.

The caveat is that this is not an easy do-it-yourself sort of retirement account. Business owners who set up defined-benefit plans will need to hire a financial advisor who specializes in these sorts of plans and a third-party administrator to write the plan document for you. Working closely with an accountant is also vital, since you need to make sure your plan conforms to all IRS guidelines and that you're correctly filing all of your annual reporting forms. But this extra work to set up a defined-benefit plan shouldn't scare you away from these great accounts. Over just ten years, anyone with a sufficiently high income could put enough into a defined-benefits plan to be able to retire!

It is important to note, however, that if you have nonfamily employees, there are huge liabilities to defined-benefit plans. This is the ideal plan for a high-income family-run business or solo business.

> **Five-Star Tip:** If you find all this confusing, you are not alone. This is why self-employed people who don't have employees normally go for SEP-IRAs, which are much easier to set up and monitor. So if you don't have any employees and want to get moving, start with a SEP-IRA. You can always upgrade later to a defined-benefit plan.

THE SIMPLE IRA

Introduced in 1997, the SIMPLE IRA is meant for small companies (those with less than 100 employees) looking for an easy and affordable retirement program—in other words, something simpler and cheaper than a 401(k) plan.

As with a SEP-IRA, the employer must contribute to the plan on the employees' behalf, and these contributions vest immediately. Then again, they are relatively small—limited to 3 percent of each employee's total compensation. Employees are able to defer up to $12,500 in 2018. Unlike the SEP-IRA, the SIMPLE IRA has a required employer contribution, and these employer contributions are tax-deductible. All things being equal, if you have employees, I recommend you open up a regular 401(k) plan for your company and pass on the SIMPLE IRA. These vehicles are not as simple as they sound. There are plenty of companies today offering 401(k) plans to small businesses.

SUMMARY OF RETIREMENT ACCOUNT ANNUAL CONTRIBUTION LIMITS							
TRADITIONAL & ROTH IRA (UNDER 50)	**TRADITIONAL & ROTH IRA (OVER 50)**	**401(K) & 403(B) PLAN (UNDER 50)**	**401(K) & 403(B) PLAN (OVER 50)**	**SEP-IRA**	**SOLO 401(K)**	**DEFINED-BENEFIT PLAN**	**SIMPLE IRA**
$5,500	$6,500	$18,500	$24,500	Up to $55,000	Up to $55,000	Up to $220,000	$12,500

Five-Star Tip: Don't forget that if you're over age 50 you can take advantage of the "catch-up provisions." On 401(k) and 403(b) plans you can add up to an extra $6,000 each year! On IRAs you can add up to an extra $1,000 per year. On SIMPLE plans you can add an extra $3,000 per year. **These numbers are all based on 2018**, so if you read this in later years, please check **IRS.gov** for updates.

WHAT DO I DO WITH MY CONTRIBUTIONS?

Okay, so you've decided what type of retirement account makes the most sense for you, and you've figured out how much you are going to contribute to it this year. Now comes the really big decision.

As I noted earlier, deciding where and how to invest your retirement money probably is the most important financial decision you ever will make.

Some of you may find that baffling. I can hear you asking, "Haven't I just made that decision? I'm investing my money in a retirement account."

No, you are not. A retirement account—whether it's an IRA, a SEP-IRA, a defined-contribution plan, a SIMPLE plan, a 403(b), or a 401(k)—is not an investment. It is, rather, just a holding tank for your retirement money.

People are often confused about this. They will tell you that they've gone to the bank and "bought an IRA." Sorry, but you can't "buy" an IRA. That's like saying you bought a checking account.

What you do with an IRA—and the same goes for employer-sponsored accounts like 401(k) plans—is this: You open it, and then you put money into it, and then you inform the bank (or brokerage or plan administrator) *how you want the funds invested.*

I once explained this to a class of mine, only to have a woman named Brenda stand up and tell me that I didn't know what I was talking about. "I've been buying IRAs at my bank for years," Brenda insisted.

When I asked her how she had invested her IRA funds, she shook her head angrily. "You're not listening to me, young man," she snapped. "I said I *bought* an IRA, I don't take risks with my money with foolish investments."

"Brenda," I said, "I'll bet you ten bucks that your IRA money is invested in a certificate of deposit that's paying you less than 5 percent a year."

"You're on," she replied.

As it turned out, I was wrong. When she brought her IRA statements to my office, I discovered that she was *not* invested in a CD. Rather, she was invested in nothing! It's true. When we called Brenda's bank to find out what exactly her IRA funds had been doing for the last ten years, the officer who answered the phone told us the money was sitting in a savings account.

"Great," I said. "And what rate of return is the savings account paying her?"

The bank officer stammered a bit. "Well," he said finally, "it's not actually paying her anything. It's just a place where we hold money until the client tells us how they want it invested."

Can you believe it? Brenda had her IRA money sitting in a holding account earning nothing for ten years! In other words, when you figure in inflation, her nest egg had shrunk, not grown.

If you think that's dumb, you are right. The only thing dumber is that there are literally thousands of Americans walking around right now thinking they "own" IRAs, when in fact they have no idea how their retirement money is invested or what it is earning. Equally bad is the fact that millions of Americans really don't know what their 401(k) money or 403(b) money is invested in.

Please, please don't be one of these people. Pull out all your IRA and/or company retirement-account statements right now and review them.

> *Make sure your retirement money is working as hard for you as you worked for it!*

Don't let it sit in some miscellaneous bank account that pays you just 0.1 percent a year—or even worse, maybe nothing at all!

To help you make the most of your retirement money, here are some rules I've compiled over the years.

RULE NO. 1
With retirement funds, invest for growth!

This may strike you as painfully obvious, but it's so important that I think it's worth emphasizing. All too often, women come into my office and show me retirement accounts that are invested in certificates of deposit or other fixed-rate securities. Now, with their guaranteed returns, CDs are perfectly appropriate if your goal is what the professionals call "short-term capital preservation"—that is, you've got a bunch of money that you're going to need to use sometime soon, and you want to make sure nothing happens to it in the meantime.

Unless you are planning to retire in the next five years, however, your goal with your retirement account is not short-term capital preservation. It's long-term growth. So don't make this mistake. Review your retirement plan options carefully and make sure your choices include at least some growth-oriented investments. What you truly need is a well-diversified account.

If you are at all unsure about what the best available investment options may be for you, seek professional guidance. Speak with your company's benefits director or call your personal financial advisor and ask him or her to go over your retirement-plan options with you. At *AE Wealth Management* our advisors do this sort of thing for our clients all the time—at no cost. If your financial advisor isn't willing to review your 401(k) investment options, you probably should look for a new advisor.

WHY INVEST FOR GROWTH?

Many people make the crucial mistake of thinking that when it comes to their retirement money, the thing to do is play it safe. They couldn't be more wrong when you're saving and investing for retirement. When you're close to retirement and retired you can begin to play it safer. Remember that inflation chart back on page 37? It showed that over the past two decades, the cost of living has been climbing steadily at an average of slightly more than 2 percent a year. Playing it safe will not allow you to beat that rate, and if your retirement account doesn't grow faster than inflation, you are not going to have very much to live on 20 or 30 or 40 years from now.

To secure your future, in other words, what you've got to do with your retirement money is go for growth. Yes, seeking growth requires you to invest in stocks, and they are generally more volatile and riskier over the short term than some other types of investments. But over the long term—and that's what we're concerned with here, the long term—they can be significantly more rewarding. Consider the tables on page 197—it's incredible, isn't it?

THE VALUE OF A HYPOTHETICAL $100,000 INVESTMENT AFTER 25 YEARS

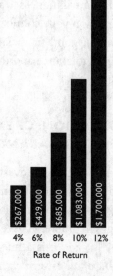

$267,000 $429,000 $685,000 $1,083,000 $1,700,000

4%   6%   8%   10%   12%

Rate of Return

AVERAGE ANNUAL TOTAL RETURNS: 1926–2017

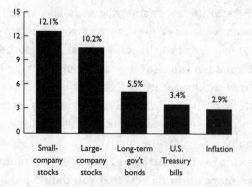

12.1% — Small-company stocks
10.2% — Large-company stocks
5.5% — Long-term gov't bonds
3.4% — U.S. Treasury bills
2.9% — Inflation

Source: Sterling Capital Inc. © Ibbotson Associates, Inc. All rights reserved. Returns based on Ibbotson® SBBI®—Stocks, Bonds, Bills and Inflation. **Past performance is no guarantee of future results.** This chart is for illustrative purposes only.

The obvious lesson here is that you should invest a portion of your retirement money in stocks or mutual funds that invest in stocks. How big a portion? Well, that really depends on your age, your personal goals, and your willingness to accept a certain amount of volatility. It also depends on your comfort with risk—everyone's risk tolerance is different. A good financial advisor can help you really understand your risk tolerance and then build a portfolio to match it and your goals.

ASSET ALLOCATION: CREATING THE PERFECT BALANCE

Figuring out the right mix of growth investments versus fixed investments is what is known in the investment industry as determining your asset allocation. Asset allocation is a fancy way of saying, "You need to put your eggs in different baskets." This may not sound like a big deal, but it is. In fact, it is a huge deal. *Studies indicate that more than 91 percent of all investment returns are attributable to proper asset allocation, as opposed to clever stock selection or good market timing.*

The first step in determining the asset allocation of your retirement plan is to decide how much of your money you want to put into growth vehicles (basically, stocks and stock-based mutual funds) and how much you want to put into safer but slower-growing fixed-income securities (basically, bonds or bond funds).

I use the following fundamental rule of thumb to help determine how much money a particular individual should invest in stocks versus bonds:

Take your age and subtract it from 110. The number you get is the percentage of your assets that you should put in stocks or stock-based mutual funds. The rest of your assets should go into something less volatile, such as bonds or fixed-rate securities.

For example, let's say you are 40 years old. Following the rule, you subtract 40 from 110, which leaves you with 70. That means you should consider putting about 70 percent of your retirement fund into stock-related investments, with the remaining 30 percent going into bonds.

Obviously, the older you are, the smaller your stock investment will be. (According to the rule, a 50-year-old should have 60 percent of her assets in stocks, while a 30-year-old should have 80 percent.) This makes sense, since the closer you are to retirement age, the less risk you want to incur.

This process may sound simplistic, but it is widely used and based on a theory created by an acclaimed scholar named Dr. Harry Markowitz, who was awarded a Nobel Prize in economics for his work on modern portfolio theory.

Once you have determined the ratio of stocks to bonds that is right for you, you will need to figure out more specifically what kinds of investments you should make in each category. Again, this is something you should consider discussing in detail with a trusted and knowledgeable financial advisor. (Later in this chapter, I'll give you some tips on how to find a terrific financial advisor.)

LOOK FOR "TARGET DATED MUTUAL FUNDS"—IN YOUR 401(K) PLAN

Investing, and specifically 401(k) investing, has radically changed since I first wrote this book because of one particular innovation: target dated mutual funds. These funds offer a one-step solution to investing in your 401(k) by providing investors with a single fund that is both totally diversified and professionally managed based upon your anticipated retirement date. If you have a company retirement plan, chances are high that you have a target dated mutual fund option.

The target dated mutual fund is professionally managed, and the asset allocation (the mixture of the investments from stocks to bonds) becomes more conservative as you approach retirement. You should select a target dated fund that is close to the date you expect to retire. For instance, if you hope to retire in 2040, your target dated fund should have the date 2040 on it.

The popularity of this kind of fund has soared for a number of excellent reasons. Aside from how intuitive these investments are proving to be for investors—which is an important aspect of making sure people are on target for retirement—these funds also tend to be very low cost (or at least should be). As of this writing, target dated mutual funds are approaching a trillion dollars in investments and now make up 20 percent of assets in 401(k) plans, which means you should have no trouble finding a good choice for yourself.

The four biggest providers of these funds are Vanguard, TIAA-CREF, Fidelity, and T. Rowe Price. If any of these companies runs your retirement plan, then you have some very solid target dated mutual funds to choose from. They will be professionally managed, totally diversified, and regularly rebalanced. It is truly a "set it and forget it" approach. And that's why they are working so well for investors.

THE BIGGEST MISTAKES YOU CAN MAKE WITH A TARGET DATED MUTUAL FUND— *DON'T MAKE THESE!*

Just because target dated mutual funds are "set it and forget it" doesn't mean it's impossible to make a mistake, however. The biggest blunder I see with target dated funds is when investors select more than one. You might assume that having multiple target dated funds will give you "extra diversification"—but, in fact, it just gives you a diversified mess.

This mistake sometimes comes about when investors aren't entirely sure when they are going to retire, which is understandable.

But even if you don't know exactly at what age or date you'd like to retire, you can probably make a good guess within five years of a reasonable target. Remember, it's always possible to switch to a later target dated fund if you have to keep working longer than you first anticipated. In addition, if you want to be conservative with your target dated investing, you can select a fund with a target date that is five years earlier than the date at which you'd like to retire. For example, a conservative investor who plans to retire in 2040 might select a 2035 target dated mutual fund, which will provide her with a more conservative approach.

Finally, you need to find out the fund's "glide path." This term refers to the continued investment strategy the fund takes upon reaching your retirement date. Some glide paths run right up to your retirement date and then stay static after that date, while others continue to work and adapt through your retirement date. Ideally, you want a target dated fund that runs through your predicted retirement date because hopefully you are going to live three to four decades or more after retirement. With that said, **it is critical that you review this type of fund closely once you get to within five years of retirement** and understand exactly how much risk the fund is taking, and what the balance is between stocks and bonds. I have unfortunately seen target dated funds that are too aggressive as the retirement date approaches. So always stay on top of what you invest in.

IT'S TIME TO DO YOUR OWN RESEARCH

You should also do your own research. Today, with the Internet, gathering information about fund performance is a snap. There are countless websites that offer financial information. To make it easier for you to find a good financial website, I've listed some of my favorites here so you can review everything from stocks to bonds to mutual funds and learn a lot about overall financial planning:

www.ishares.com. iShares is the largest provider of exchange-traded funds (ETFs) in the world. If your plan has ETFs, there's a good chance they were created by iShares. They currently offer more than 800 funds and manage over a trillion dollars in ETFs. iShares is owned by Blackrock, one of the largest asset managers in the world. You can learn all about ETFs at this website, as well as screen through them and build a sample portfolio.

www.mfea.com. The Mutual Fund Education Alliance is a great site with a lot of educational information on mutual funds. The site is designed to be a financial education center to help investors learn the basics about mutual fund investing. It includes investment tools, fund data, and links to resources and fund companies (that are members of the Alliance). Morningstar also provides the fund data on this site.

www.morningstar.com. Morningstar is the company that really started it all in terms of ranking mutual funds, and its website is probably the best of its kind. The Morningstar site offers unbiased commentary on funds with a straightforward rating system of "Gold," "Silver," and "Bronze." It also rates funds like movies, with a star system based on the funds' risks and returns. The website has loads of useful information for investors on trends and stocks. Go to the Morningstar homepage and click on "Funds." Then click on a section called "Fund Quickrank," which allows you to quickly screen funds based on their performance, their Morningstar ratings, or their volatility. Registration is required for this section, but it's free. To get full details, you will need to pay a subscription fee. You can also screen for stocks on this site.

www.wsj.com. *The Wall Street Journal* offers a useful screener for ETFs and funds that is free to the public but hard to find. (Google "etf screener Wall Street Journal" and you should find it). Subscribing to the *Journal* is a good idea for serious investors.

Yahoo Finance (https://finance.yahoo.com/screener/mutual fund/new). Yahoo Finance is probably the most popular financial site on the Web, and for good reason. This is a true full-service financial portal, offering stock and mutual fund analysis, portfolio tracking, message boards, research, and more. Try the Mutual Fund Screener tool at the URL given above. Clicking on the link for Top ETFs of Top Funds will take you to a screener where you can easily do a search based on categories and Morningstar ratings.

WHAT ABOUT INVESTING IN MY COMPANY'S STOCK?

If you are enrolled in a 401(k) plan, your employer may allow you to invest all or part of your retirement funds in your company's own stock. (This will be an option only if you work for a company whose stock is publicly traded.) As a loyal employee, you may feel this is definitely the way to go. But please be careful. While it's certainly true that investing in your company's stock can make you very rich if the company does well (we've all heard about the employees of Google, Facebook, and Amazon who became millionaires), it can also make you poor if the company stumbles. And even great companies occasionally stumble. On September 15, 2008, Lehman Brothers went bankrupt and the stock collapsed. Overnight, employees lost their jobs and saw a lifetime of savings in company stock disappear. People close to retirement age at Lehman who were heavily invested in company stock saw their nest eggs literally disappear in a matter of days. Here's what is scary—and I'm making this boldface and all caps so you really catch the point: **MANY OF YOU HAVE WAY TOO MUCH OF YOUR NEST EGG IN YOUR COMPANY STOCK AND YOU DON'T REALIZE IT!** *This works great, until it doesn't work.*

Not only do great companies sometimes stumble, but great economies sometimes slow, causing great stocks to crumble. So you want to be careful to limit the amount of your retirement money that you invest in any one company's stock—even if that company happens to be the one you work for. While investing in your company stock can make you rich when things go right, it can also make you poor overnight if things go horribly wrong.

I also strongly recommend that you do some research into your own company's stock, before you invest. The simplest way to do this is to go online and look for your company's "investor kit." Virtually all publicly traded companies offer these kits. They include articles about the company, a copy of its latest annual report, and what is known as its Form 10-K. The 10-K is a report that all public companies are required to file annually with the Securities and Exchange Commission (SEC). It provides detailed information on the company and its finances. Whether or not you're planning to buy stock in your company, I suggest that you read its 10-K.

Although the 10-K can look complicated, it's not really all that difficult to understand—and it can be incredibly informative. Indeed, reading through a 10-K will tell you everything from what your company does to how much its top executives are paid. It also details every possible thing the company thinks could go wrong that might adversely affect the price of its stock. This is really important information to know not just as a potential investor but as a current employee. You can also listen to the company's quarterly earnings conference call with Wall Street analysts or review the transcripts that are often available at SeekingAlpha.com. Finally, make sure to read the research reports on your company.

Now, you may be thinking, *An investor's kit? A 10-K? Research reports?! I wasn't a business major. What good is this stuff going to do me?*

Well, first of all, it will make you a much more knowledgeable employee. Most likely, the investor's relations kit will include press clippings about your company along with research reports from brokerage firms that follow your company's stock. The press clippings may tell you a lot about your company that you never knew, while the research reports can give you a good idea of what Wall

Street experts think of it. (These reports are written by professional securities analysts whose job it is to follow specific companies and make predictions about their future performance.) If, for some reason, your investor's kit doesn't contain any research reports, ask the investor relations department for a list of brokerage firms that "cover" your company's stock. Then call these firms and ask for a copy of their most recent report on your company. They should be happy to mail it to you at no cost.

Basically, what you want to find out from a research report is whether the analyst thinks the stock is a "good buy" and, if so, why. The 10-K, which is a detailed financial report that the SEC requires every publicly traded company to file each year, will provide you with an enormous number of facts and figures about your company's operating results, current problems, and future prospects.

But you should do more than just read reports. Look around at work. Are key employees buying the company's stock? Is your boss? Ask him or her. At good companies, the answer is usually a resounding yes. Finally, ask yourself how the company feels to you on a "gut" level. Is morale good? Are its customers happy? Does management seem to have a coherent strategy for the future?

Once you've absorbed all this, you can supplement your knowledge by going online and checking out one of the many websites that specialize in providing information about individual stocks.

There are too many to list here, but a useful roster would include the following:

www.barrons.com
www.finance.yahoo.com
www.fool.com
www.google.com/finance
www.marketwatch.com
www.morningstar.com
www.nasdaq.com

www.nyse.com
www.sec.gov
www.seekingalpha.com
www.thestreet.com
www.valueline.com

Five-Star Tip: If you discover that your company is not particularly well run and that no one is buying its stock because it's losing money, then changing your 401(k) investment strategy may turn out to be the least of your worries. Indeed, you might want to reconsider why you're working there. Maybe you should get your resume together and find yourself a new job before some sort of corporate restructuring is announced and you find yourself laid off. The devil is in the details, as they say, and it's often amazing how much you can truly learn by reading a publicly traded company's annual reports, insider trades, and research reports that cover your company.

RULE NO. 2
Take advantage of the free money your employer may give you!

As I shared earlier, in many cases, employers will supplement your retirement plan contributions with contributions of their own. These "matching" contributions, as they are called, usually start at 20 percent of what you've put in and sometimes go as high as 100 percent! For example, say you work for a company that matches 50 percent of your contributions. If you put away $5,000 a year for your retirement, your employer's 50 percent matching contribution will add $2,500 to your retirement fund. So in just one year you'll have put away $7,500, and that doesn't include any investment growth your fund may have enjoyed over the year.

What's particularly great about this is that you now have $7,500 socked away that didn't actually cost you $7,500. It didn't even cost you the $5,000 you contributed to your retirement plan. Why not? Because if you hadn't put this $5,000 into your pretax retirement account, you would have had to hand over about $1,500 of it to the government in the form of income taxes. This means that this $7,500 investment really costs you only $3,500! That adds up to a 100 percent return on your investment in the first year alone—and once again, that's without counting any investment growth. Say you enjoyed a 15 percent return for the year (which, okay, isn't necessarily a realistic assumption every year, but has definitely happened multiple times in recent years). Fifteen percent of $7,500 is $1,125, which brings your balance to $8,625. So from a measly $3,500 investment, you are up more than $5,000! And that's in just one year. See how this can get to be fun? Remember, again, to check the vesting schedule on these "matches," as they are not yours until they fully vest. Many companies have a four-year vesting schedule on matches.

> **Five-Star Tip:** Don't make the huge mistake of contributing only the percentage of your paycheck that your company will match. A lot of people think they are being smart when they do this. They are not. The reason to max out your retirement contributions is to build a secure financial future and avoid taxes! Whether your company matches is irrelevant. If your employer does happen to add some money to your contribution, that's icing on the cake. You still need to bake that cake, which means maxing out your contributions!

> **RULE NO. 3**
> **Don't borrow from your retirement plan.**

Many retirement plans allow you to borrow money from your account—that is, take money out without having to pay taxes or penalties—as long as you eventually return it with interest. This may sound like a good deal, but in reality, it can be a terrible trap. In short, don't do it. The money you are putting away for retirement is just that—money for your retirement.

People who borrow money from their plans to make down payments on homes, cover college costs, or—worst of all—pay off credit-card debt are only asking for trouble. Why? Because at some point they are going to have to pay the money back, and when that time comes, they may find they can't afford to. And then they are really in trouble.

I once had a client named Sally who quit her job shortly after filing sexual harassment charges against her boss. To add insult to injury, the moment she left the company, she received a letter demanding that she remove all her retirement savings from the company's 401(k) plan. (Because she was no longer an employee, the company had the right to do this.) That meant that she had to either transfer the money to a personal IRA account or withdraw it in cash (which would mean paying taxes on it and incurring the 10 percent federal penalty).

Normally, this wouldn't have presented a problem, but Sally was in a bind. A year earlier she had borrowed $15,000 from her 401(k) in order to settle some credit-card debt, and she wasn't yet in a position to pay the loan back. Unfortunately, as I explained to her, if she couldn't repay it before she left the 401(k) plan, the IRS would consider the loan a premature IRA distribution subject to taxes and penalties.

In desperation, Sally tried to borrow money from a bank, but it said no. She turned to her parents. They too were unable to help her. In the end, Sally had to pay income tax on the $15,000 she had borrowed, plus a 10 percent penalty. The total bill came to over $7,000. Lacking the cash, Sally ended up having to negotiate with the IRS, which eventually agreed to let her pay off her liability in installments. All of this was the result of borrowing money from a 401(k).

The point is, none of us knows what the future holds. Ideally, your 401(k) plan should be the last place you turn to for money. If you can, leave your retirement money alone until you are ready to retire.

RULE NO. 4
Consolidate your accounts.

Many people remember Grandma's advice about not putting all your eggs in one basket, but they often misunderstand it. Not putting your eggs in one basket means diversifying your risk—putting your money into different kinds of assets, such as different types of stocks, bonds, mutual funds, and other investment vehicles. It doesn't mean opening an IRA at a different bank or brokerage firm each year.

Every day I meet people who have four, five, or six—sometimes more than a dozen—different retirement accounts. The record back in the day when I was a financial advisor and taking clients personally was held by a client named Ben. Ben always had been what we call a CD shopper. Before he met me, every year he would literally spend days going from bank to bank to find the best rate on certificates of deposit for his new IRA. The trouble was, he was so focused on "buying" his next IRA that he never thought about the pitiful rates his old IRAs were earning. (Those "terrific" rates he got lasted only for a year; when his "premium" CDs matured, the bank would roll them over into new certificates that didn't pay nearly as much.) When I met with Ben he had over $160,000 in CDs in 18 different banks—earning an average of less than 2 percent a year! I showed him how much better off he would be consolidating all his CDs into one IRA account and then managing his money for a combination of growth and income.

The fact is, there is simply no way you can do a good job of managing your retirement accounts if they are spread all over the place. If that's what you've done, consider consolidating them into one IRA custodial account. Not only can you completely diversify your investments within a single IRA, but you'll also find it much easier to keep track of everything.

> ### RULE NO. 5
> **Be careful whom you list as the beneficiary of your retirement account.**

I find it terrifying how many well-intentioned people decide to create a living trust to protect their estates—and then either misunderstand their attorney's advice or are given bad advice.

Many lawyers instruct clients who've just established a living trust to make sure to put all their assets in it. As a result, people go out and reregister the beneficiary of the retirement accounts in their trust's name. Normally a big mistake. Never, ever, ever put your IRA in the name of a trust or make your beneficiary of the IRA a trust. When you do this, your spouse loses the ability to do what's called a spousal IRA rollover. A spousal IRA rollover allows a widow to take over her late husband's IRA and put it in her name, without having to pay any taxes on it until she actually starts taking the money out (presumably when she reaches retirement age). If the husband has transferred ownership of his IRA to a trust, the wife can't take it over in the event of his death; instead, the account goes to the trust and the proceeds become taxable. (If you are single, putting your IRA in the name of a trust similarly could limit the ability of your children or your siblings to enjoy the tax-deferred benefits of your retirement savings.)

For much the same reason, you shouldn't make a trust the beneficiary of any of your IRAs or 401(k) plans. Doing so can lead to catastrophe. Take the case of Diana, a recent widow who came up to me in a panic after I made this point to a class of mine. Diana had just lost her husband to cancer. In an effort to get their financial house in order before he died, she and her husband had consulted a discount brokerage firm, which referred them to a local attorney, who created a living trust for them. The attorney, she told me, had recommended that her husband make the trust the beneficiary of his 401(k) plan.

When I heard that I just about went white. Swallowing hard, I asked her how much money was in the plan.

She said her husband had accumulated close to a half million dollars.

"Well," I said, "then you have a potential $250,000 problem." That, I explained, was how much money she was likely to lose to estate and income taxes immediately as a result of the attorney's bad advice. But that wasn't all the lawyer's mistake would cost her. Diana was only 38, meaning she had more than 20 years to go before she reached retirement age. If you figured in how much less she probably would earn over the next two decades because she would no longer be able to defer taxes on the rest of her husband's 401(k) money, you'd come up with a total loss closer to $500,000. A very costly mistake.

Diana looked at me desperately and asked if there was anything she could do. I called her attorney and discovered that he had created more than 100 trusts that year—and given the same bad advice each time. He didn't even understand what he was doing wrong until I explained it to him!

Fortunately for Diana, there was a solution to her problem. We got her late husband's trust to decline his 401(k) money, as a result of which Diana was able to do a spousal IRA rollover the way it should be done.

The moral of the story is twofold: Be careful where you go for legal advice, and be careful whom you make the beneficiary of your retirement account. If you leave your retirement account to a trust, the proceeds may be taxable depending on the trust. What you and your spouse should do is leave your accounts to each other first and then to your children. As a spouse, whoever lives the longest will be able to do a spousal IRA rollover and then the children, when they inherit the IRA, can elect how they want to take the money out.

As long as we're on the subject of beneficiaries, if you or your spouse has been married before, you might want to make sure neither ex is listed as the beneficiary on any of the retirement accounts. I've seen this happen more than a half dozen times in the past five years—and not just on retirement accounts, but on insurance policies too!

In addition, you also should make sure you have a "contingent beneficiary" listed on your retirement account—that is, a second choice in case your primary beneficiary dies before (or at the same time) you do. For example, let's say you are married with children, and you and your husband are killed together in a car accident. If you had listed your kids as contingent beneficiaries on your IRA, they would automatically get control over your retirement money. (They could then either leave the money in the account for five years or arrange a yearly minimum distribution based on their life expectancy; in either case, the tax benefits of the IRA would be preserved.) If, on the other hand, you hadn't listed a contingent beneficiary, the courts might be forced to have your accounts distributed, which would mean subjecting them to tax. Please, take a few minutes **today** and review the beneficiaries and contingent beneficiaries of your retirement accounts.

RULE NO. 6
Always take your retirement money with you.

When you leave a company where you've been contributing to a 401(k) plan, don't leave your retirement money behind. Rather, immediately inform the benefits department that you want to do an IRA rollover. What this means is that your former employer will transfer your retirement funds either to a new custodial IRA that you have set up for yourself at some bank or brokerage firm or to the 401(k) plan at your new employer (assuming there is one and that it accepts money from other plans).

Leaving funds in an old 401(k) plan can become problematic and sometimes disastrous. In the event of your death, your beneficiary would have to go back to a company where you may not have worked in years in order to get your money. This process can take months. By contrast, if you've moved your money to an IRA, all your beneficiary has to do is take your death certificate to the brokerage firm or bank, and the IRA will be rolled over to the beneficiary's account—tax-free—usually within three days!

Another reason not to leave your money in a former employer's plan is that companies are constantly changing their 401(k) providers. If your old company changes plans, your money will have to be transferred to the new plan—and if for some reason the company is unable to find you (say, because you moved), you won't be able to tell it how you want your funds invested in the new plan. Lacking instructions, the company could wind up parking your money in a low-interest money-market fund, which could potentially cost you tens of thousands of dollars in lost earnings. Don't lose control of your money. Do an IRA rollover and take it with you when you go. Make sure you get professional help with this—I don't want you to create a tax nightmare by doing this incorrectly.

RULE NO. 7
Don't shortchange yourself.

Whatever else you do in your financial life, please take retirement planning seriously. I know I sound like I'm preaching here, but as I said before, there is really nothing you can do that will have more impact on your future financial security than maximizing your contributions to a retirement account and then making sure that money works really hard for you.

The fact is, if you are not currently maxing out your retirement contributions—whether to a company-sponsored 401(k) or 403(b) plan, to your own IRA, or to a retirement account for self-employed people—you are living beyond your means. This is not meant to be harsh; it is meant to be a wake-up call. Contributing to a retirement plan is not a luxury; it is a necessity! Please give yourself the opportunity to retire as early as you would like, with enough money to have all the fun you deserve.

BASKET THREE:
YOUR DREAM BASKET

Pretend for a moment you had a magic lamp with a genie inside. As we all know, genies are obliged to grant their masters (or mistresses) three wishes. So what would yours be? If you could have—or be—anything you wanted, what would you wish for?

That may seem like a childish question, but it's not. What it's really asking is something quite important—namely, what dreams of yours currently are going unfulfilled? Do you long to see the world? Quit your job? Start your own business? Devote yourself to some charitable organization?

It is one of the sadder facts of life that most people stop dreaming as they get older. The number one reason, I'm sorry to say, is money. For the most part, it takes money to make our dreams come true, and most of us simply don't have enough. Lacking the necessary resources, we find ourselves frustrated; eventually, we stop bothering to dream at all.

That's the bad news. The good news is, it doesn't have to be that way. You *can* make your dreams come true . . . and you won't need a magic lamp—or its modern-day equivalent, a winning lottery ticket—to do it. Nor will you be restricted to just three wishes.

To make your dreams a reality, you have to do only two things: identify what your dreams are and create a plan to finance them. That may sound pretty obvious, but you know what? Most people never do it.

Smart Women, however, aren't like most people. So let's get started . . .

RECAPTURE YOUR WIDE-EYED OPTIMISM

You know why so many people play the state lottery? It's because for the price of just $1, they get the opportunity to dream. Unfortunately, that's generally all a person gets. The reality is that you have a better chance of being hit by lightning than actually winning a lottery.

Even though most of us know that, we play anyway. That's how powerful our need to dream is. Dreams energize us. They add passion to our lives. It's hard to be depressed when you are excited about your future, and that's what dreams do: They make us believe that tomorrow is going to be better than today.

Think back for a moment and recall, if you can, what it was like when you were a kid. Can you remember a time in your life when you believed you could be anything and have anything you wanted? Do you remember what it felt like not to have to worry about bills and work and family responsibilities? Try to imagine that for a moment. Pretend you are a little girl who feels she can have or be anything she wants. What would it be? Who would you become?

Try to pursue these questions more deeply than you did in Step Three, when you were coming up with goals for yourself. We are not talking here about earning 10 percent more income or losing ten pounds. We are talking about *dreams*. Do you want to climb the pyramids of Egypt? Study painting in Paris? Open a shelter for battered women?

Remember, you are trying to be young and imaginative like you were when you were a kid, not stressed-out and conventional like you are now. (Just kidding!) Seriously, though, what do you want to see happen in your life? What's missing? Where do you want to go? Perhaps your dream is to own your own home. Or to take off from work for a whole month and not call the office once! Maybe you would like to write a book.

Whatever your dreams happen to be, I want you to write them down. On the following Dream Sheet, list your five top dreams. If you don't have the time to do this right now, then set up a time later to meet with yourself and create your dream list. That's right— make an appointment with yourself to reserve somewhere between 30 and 60 minutes in which you will write down the dreams that excite you. And don't make excuses. Your dreams are worth half an hour of your time.

MAKING YOUR DREAMS A REAL PART OF YOUR LIFE

Once you have written down your top five dreams, the next step is to spend a little time thinking about what it would take to make them a reality. How much money will be required? How long will it take you to save that much?

The more defined your dreams are, the easier it will be to estimate what it will cost to realize them. You definitely should spend a little time on this, for as I explained back in Step Three, the key to getting what you want in life is to be specific about it. Once you have a good idea of what it will take, you can determine how much you need to put away each month. By putting money away each month, you will feel your dream come closer to reality, and as it

DREAMS

Designing and Implementing the Fun Factor!

THERE ARE TWO PARTS TO THIS EXERCISE:
• Ten blanks for writing down your most important dreams
• A form in which you specify your five most important dreams over your lifetime

STEPS:
• On this page, below, fill in the ten blanks with as many dreams as possible that you want to accomplish during your lifetime.
• On the next page, specify:
  1. Five Most Important Dreams
  2. Make Specific, Measurable, and Provable (i.e.: How much will it cost?)
  3. Immediate Action in the Next 48 Hours
  4. Whom Will You Share Your Dreams With?
  5. What Values Do They Help You Accomplish?
  6. What Challenges Will You Face?
  7. Strategies to Overcome Anticipated Challenges

1.   6.

2.   7.

3.   8.

4.   9.

5.   10.

FIVE MOST IMPORTANT DREAMS	MAKE SPECIFIC, MEASURABLE, AND PROVABLE	IMMEDIATE ACTION IN THE NEXT 48 HOURS	WHOM WILL YOU SHARE YOUR DREAMS WITH?	WHAT VALUES DO THEY HELP YOU ACCOMPLISH?	WHAT CHALLENGES WILL YOU FACE?	STRATEGIES TO OVERCOME ANTICIPATED CHALLENGES
1						
2						
3						
4						
5						

does, you will find yourself getting more and more excited about your future.

WHAT IF I DON'T HAVE ANY SPECIFIC DREAMS RIGHT NOW?

I usually suggest to my clients that they should fund a dream basket whether they are able to come up with a list of dreams or not. After all, just because you don't have a specific dream right now doesn't mean you never will. And wouldn't it be nice to have some money already put aside when something comes along (as it inevitably will) that falls into a "dream" category?

Sometimes dreams are not what we expect. I once suggested to a young woman named Lisa that she start funding a dream basket even though she didn't have any specific dream in mind. Six months later, Lisa's dog Brandi got really sick. Without an operation that cost $1,500, Brandi would die. Lisa immediately turned to her dream basket for the money, and today Brandi is wagging her tail and doing whatever else happy dogs do. As Lisa explained to me later, "I had no idea what my dream was at the time I started putting money aside, but when Brandi got sick, I knew that my dream was to help her live. If I hadn't funded my dream basket, I would have lost Brandi. My dream basket kept her alive!"

HOW TO FUND YOUR DREAM BASKET

Your dream basket is the place where you put aside the money you will need to make your dreams (other than security or retirement) come true. You should fund it the same way you fund your retirement basket—that is, with a fixed percentage of your income that you automatically contribute every month. As I said earlier, making the process automatic is the best way I know to ensure that you actually stick to your savings plan. Set up a systematic investment plan, in which a set amount of money either is deducted directly from your paycheck or is transferred from your checking account the day after you are paid.

The size of your regular contribution should be determined by the likely cost of your dreams. As a rule of thumb, it probably should be at least 5 percent of your after-tax income (which is to say, a lot less than the 12 percent of pretax income that you should be putting into your retirement basket). While 5 percent of your after-tax income isn't a huge amount, it is certainly big enough to create a very powerful long-term savings vehicle. Needless to say, if your dreams happen to be of the particularly expensive variety, you will want to put away a larger percentage of your income. The key here is to realize that it's up to you; the more money you put away, the faster your dreams will become a reality.

The form in which you keep this money will depend on how long you expect it will be before you're ready to make your dream a reality. Some dreams require just a year or two of planning and saving; others may take half a lifetime. Over the next few pages, I will discuss a variety of different investment vehicles and explain which are right for what time frame.

In order to keep things simple (and there's certainly no point in making them more complicated than they need to be), you should think of your dreams in terms of how long it will likely take you to realize them. Specifically, you should categorize them as being either short-term, mid-term, or long-term dreams. Short-term dreams are those that can be accomplished within a year or two. (An example might be getting yourself in a position to be able to take a luxury vacation.) Mid-term dreams take a bit longer to fulfill—say, between two and five years. (A typical mid-term dream might be having the funds to put a down payment on a house.) Long-term dreams require even more time than that. Some (such as being able to quit your job so you can move to Tahiti and live on the beach) may take decades.

Obviously, you don't fund a short-term dream with a long-term investment strategy. Here are my recommendations for the best ways to construct your dream basket.

HOW EXACTLY SHOULD I INVEST MY DREAM-BASKET MONEY?

There are literally thousands of ways to invest. You can buy individual stocks and bonds. You can buy certificates of deposit. You can purchase commodities or preferred stocks. You can buy convertible bonds. You can acquire gold or silver, or art or stamps. You can buy Bitcoin (be really careful on that one).

The list goes on and on. Because there are so many investment choices, people often don't know what to do. As a result, they do nothing. When it comes to funding your dream basket, I don't want you to be so overwhelmed that you find yourself unable—or unwilling—to take immediate action. Nor do I want you to be held back by the amount of money you may be required to put up. So with these factors in mind, I'm going to suggest that you fund your dream basket by investing in mutual funds or exchange-traded mutual funds, which I will cover in greater detail in a few pages.

WHAT EXACTLY IS A MUTUAL FUND?

It both scares me and amazes me to hear the responses I get when I ask people at my classes and seminars what a mutual fund is. Over the years, I have found that there a number of people investing in mutual funds without knowing what they are. People say things like "It's a big stock," "It's a safe investment," "It's a special stock," "It's a bank product used to help people buy stocks," "It's a holding tank where you put stocks," and on and on.

So, for the record, let's get the real definition of a mutual fund, courtesy of Fidelity.com. The site defines mutual funds as "investments that pool your money together with other investors to purchase shares of a collection of stocks, bonds, or other securities, referred to as a portfolio, that might be difficult to recreate on your own. Mutual funds are typically overseen by a portfolio manager." This means that a mutual fund gives an investor the benefit of a diversified portfolio without having to make individual investment decisions on her own.

WHY INVESTING IN MUTUAL FUNDS MAKES SENSE

In my opinion, there are six key reasons why you should invest your dream-basket money in mutual funds.

1. They are easy to invest in.

You can start a systematic investment program with as little as $50 a month (and sometimes less) with a mutual fund. A financial advisor or the mutual-fund company itself can help you set this up, often at no cost.

2. They offer instant diversification.

Since mutual funds are portfolios that could include hundreds of stocks and bonds, you enjoy immediate diversification even if you are putting away as little as $50 per month.

3. They offer professional money management.

Professional money managers oversee mutual funds, which means they bring professional research skills, trading execution, expertise, and experience to the task of managing your funds.

4. They are cost-efficient.

The Morningstar rating service has found that the average internal mutual-fund management fee is about 0.57 percent of the assets managed—a cost that is down significantly since this book was originally written. As a matter of fact, owning a mutual fund has never been less expensive than it is today. The reality is that an individual investor would probably wind up paying a lot more than this if she tried on her own to build and manage a portfolio of individual stocks and bonds.

5. They are liquid and easy to monitor.

Mutual funds can be liquidated relatively easily. You can usually pull your money out of a mutual fund with less than five days' notice. You'll also find that most mutual funds are priced daily, and their prices are available online and in the newspaper, right next to the stock tables. This means that you can find out how your investment is doing every day if you want to.

6. They are boring.

Because of their diversification, mutual funds don't fluctuate in price as much as individual stocks or bonds. This might seem a little boring if your idea of investing comes from movies where sweaty traders shout "BUY!" and "SELL!" at each other—but as far as I'm concerned, in the investment world, boring is good.

Now that you understand why mutual funds are a good investment, it's time to consider which type makes the most sense for you. According to **Statista.com**, there are approximately 9,500 mutual funds to choose from (not including exchange-traded mutual funds). To make things simple, I'm going to suggest exactly what type of mutual-fund investment I personally would use to fund my dream basket. The only real variable is the time horizon—that is, how long you think it will take you to accumulate all the money you'll need to fund your particular dream.

FOR SHORT-TERM DREAMS (LESS THAN TWO YEARS)

It doesn't get simpler than this. As I write this, "cash is back" as rates move up. If you're saving to finance a short-term dream, such as going on a vacation or redoing the kitchen—anything you can achieve in two years or less—you need to keep your funds as safe and liquid as possible.

Money-market accounts. In my opinion, there is only one sensible investment that meets these criteria: Your money should go into a money-market account. I discussed money-market accounts previously in Step Five as a great alternative to regular bank checking accounts. In this case, you don't necessarily need the checking feature because you're not going to be using this money until you're ready to realize your dream.

A money-market account is a mutual fund that typically invests in very liquid, very safe, very short-term government securities. As I noted earlier, money-market accounts can be opened at most brokerage firms with relatively small initial deposits. Indeed, in many cases, if you set up an automatic investment plan, you can fund them with as little as $50 a month.

These accounts are not only incredibly safe, they are also quite stable. In recent years, they've generally offered an average annual interest rate around 1 percent (in the original version of this book they were 4 percent; as interest rates go up, these rates may someday return but don't hold your breath).

In many cases, you can find money-market accounts that pay as much as or more than a one- or two-year certificate of deposit. What's more, money-market accounts are liquid, which means you can pull your funds out at any time without ever having to pay a penalty fee. With rates as low as they are today, money markets are simply a safe place to put your money for the short-term dream.

Treasury bills. Also known as T-bills, these fixed-income securities are issued by the federal government and can be purchased either directly from the Treasury Department or through a bank or brokerage firm. Issued in increments of $10,000, T-bills mature in a year or less, and technically, they do not pay interest. What actually happens is that the T-bill is issued at a discount, which is then redeemed at full price (also known as the par value) upon reaching maturity. If you buy them through a broker, T-bills generally can be sold on a moment's notice simply by making a phone call, and you usually can collect your money within three days. There is no penalty for selling a T-bill this way before it matures, though you will have to pay a small commission.

> **Five-Star Tip:** As a result of modern telecommunications, it's now easier than ever to buy T-bills, notes, and bonds directly from the government. To find out about the Federal Reserve Board's Treasury Direct program, you can visit their website at **www .treasurydirect.gov**.

FOR MID-TERM DREAMS
(TWO TO FIVE YEARS)

Given the slightly longer time frame, liquidity should be less of an issue for mid-term dreams than for short-term ones. The same goes for safety. You've got a little more time to play with, so you can afford to take a bit more risk—which means you can expect a bit more reward. Not that you should take any big chances, mind you; the idea, after all, is to protect your money, not gamble with it. Short-term bond funds are a good option for ultraconservative investors who don't want to risk anything happening to their dream money. But anyone who wants to see a little more of a return and can handle a little more risk should consider what's known as a balanced fund.

Short-term bond funds are investments in short-term government bonds—usually Treasury bills with six-month to four-year maturity dates. These types of bond fund are very safe and relatively stable (meaning the price won't fluctuate much).

Balanced funds are mutual funds that invest in both stocks and bonds. Generally, about 60 to 70 percent of a balanced fund's assets will be invested in stocks, with the rest invested in bonds (usually Treasuries). As a well-diversified fund, this type of fund is less risky than a pure stock fund. You shouldn't expect a balanced fund to outperform the stock market—but it should come close to matching it. How close? On average, with a balanced fund, you will see about 75 percent of the returns you would get from a similar-sized investment in the stock market. In fact, the past ten years have seen balanced funds generate annualized returns of about 8 percent. Of course, these are not guaranteed returns; the returns are based on the market's returns, and past performance does not guarantee future performance.

Balanced funds are to stock funds what the tortoise is to the hare. Investing in the balanced fund will give you slow and steady progress to where you want to go, with no nail-biting. That's why they are by far my favorite "starter" investment. These are also good for long-term investment dreams.

FOR LONG-TERM DREAMS
(FOUR TO TEN YEARS)

When you are saving for dreams that will take you more than four years to reach, then it's time to consider putting your dream-basket money into investments that are more growth-oriented. With the longer time frame before you will need to access that dream money, you can afford to take more risk in order to get a bigger return. That's why I recommend that you invest in stock-based mutual funds for these sorts of dreams.

WHERE SHOULD I START?

As far as I'm concerned, the first place you should put your long-term dream-basket money is in an index fund. Index funds are simple, inexpensive, easy to set up, and they work. What more could you ask?

Index funds are stock mutual funds that mimic a specific index. In recent years, the most popular of these have been S&P 500 index funds. These funds invest in the 500 stocks that make up the Standard & Poor's index. Next to the Dow Jones Industrial Average (which consists of 30 or so "blue chip" stocks), the S&P 500 is one of the most commonly quoted stock-market indicators. That's because the performance of the S&P 500 pretty much matches the performance of the market as a whole.

The main reason index investing has become so popular is that it costs less than investing in other kinds of funds. The cost of an average index fund may be 80 percent less than that of an actively managed fund. What's more, index funds offer real tax advantages. Because index fund managers move in or out of particular stocks only when those stocks are added to or dropped from the index they're mimicking (something that happens relatively infrequently), there is barely any trading that results in taxable capital gains. In addition, while index funds may have lagged behind some actively managed funds in the go-go years of the late 1990s, historically they have tended to do better than most other funds. (Over the past 20 years or so, index funds have outperformed roughly 75 percent of the actively managed funds.)

If you want even broader exposure to the stock market than an S&P 500 index fund, you might consider a Wilshire 5000 index fund. As the number suggests, the Wilshire 5000 tracks the performance of 5,000 separate stocks and, as a result, represents one of the most diversified market gauges you can find.

Here is a list of some popular index funds. Remember, they all represent investments in the stock market—meaning there is risk involved. So read their prospectuses before you invest any money.

S&P 500 Index Funds

Fidelity Spartan 500 Index (symbol: FUSEX)
(800) 343-3548
www.fidelity.com
Minimum investment required for a regular account:
$2,500/for IRA: $2,500; Systematic Investment Plan: Must first meet minimum investment/$10 for additional investments.

Schwab S&P 500 Fund (symbol: SWPPX)
(866) 855-9102
www.schwab.com
Minimum investment required for a regular account:
$1/for IRA: $1; Systematic Investment Plan: $100 minimum for additional investments.

Vanguard Index 500 (symbol: VFINX)
(800) 992-8327
www.vanguard.com
Minimum investment required for a regular account:
$3,000/for IRA: $1,000; Systematic Investment Plan: No minimum required.

Wilshire 5000 Index Funds

Schwab Total Stock Market Index Fund (symbol: SWTSX)
(866) 855-9102
www.schwab.com
Minimum investment required for a regular account: $1; Systematic Investment Plan: Must first meet minimum investment/$100 minimum for additional investments.

Vanguard Total Stock Market (symbol: VSTMX)
(800) 992-8327
www.vanguard.com
Minimum investment required for a regular account:
$3,000/for IRA: $3,000; Systematic Investment Plan: No
minimum required.

EXCHANGE-TRADED FUNDS (ETFS)

At some time over the past 15 years, you have probably heard something about a new class of index funds known as exchange-traded funds. These funds have exploded in popularity since I first wrote this book, and they have made some major changes to the world of investing. There are more than 4,779 ETFs now, and the number is growing, according to Statista.com. In fact, there is now nearly $4 trillion in ETFs globally, according to research firm ETFGI.

At their core, ETFs are mutual funds that are traded like stocks, which means you can buy and sell ETFs during market hours in the same way that you can buy and sell common stock. Investors love these funds because they are so liquid, they are incredibly tax efficient, and they are low cost—with an expense ratio of about 0.20 percent (and sometimes less). To sweeten the pot, most ETFs sell for less than $100 a share, which offers an incredible ability to invest and diversify for very little money.

Some of the most popular ETFs are the S&P 500 Index Depositary Receipts (known as Spiders, because their trading symbol is SPY), iShares Core S&P 500 (trading symbol IVV), Vanguard Total Stock Market ETF (trading symbol VTI), the Dow Jones Industrial Average Model Depositary Shares (or Diamonds; trading symbol: DIA), the NASDAQ 100 Trust (known as Cubes, after its QQQ symbol), and the S&P MidCap 400 Depositary Receipts (symbol MDY).

ETFs can be purchased through virtually any brokerage firm or online trading company. For more details on this exciting new investment vehicle, go to **www.ishares.com** or visit **www.etf.com**.

MOVING BEYOND THE "GETTING STARTED" PHASE

When you are just getting started, balanced funds and index funds are a great way to get your feet wet. Over time, however, you should consider building a diversified portfolio of mutual funds.

BUILD YOUR PORTFOLIO AROUND "CORE" FUNDS

I'm a huge believer in building a portfolio that consists of what I call "core type" mutual funds. The key to successful investing is to keep the process relatively simple and straightforward. With this in mind, here are the five types of funds I believe you should consider when building a mutual fund portfolio. They are listed in the order of what I consider most conservative to most aggressive.

Target Dated Funds. Target dated funds aren't just for retirement, although I covered the concept of these funds in the retirement basket section on page 199. Go back to that page to review the details. These funds will do the necessary work of selecting the funds and assigning the asset allocation for you, making them like a more advanced balanced fund. That's why you could easily decide to use a target dated fund for your dreams. For example, if it's 2018 when you read this and your dream is going to take five years to fund, then you could pick a fund coming due in five years (2023) close to that date. If you use a target dated mutual fund or an asset allocation fund, then you don't need the funds I am listing next (because they will more than likely already be included in the fund).

Large-Capitalization Value Funds. A large-cap value fund invests in companies with large market capitalizations—that is, companies whose outstanding stock has a total market value of $10 billion or more. Companies of this magnitude tend to be more secure and established than most, and as a rule, they pay quarterly dividends to shareholders. The "value" part of the name reflects the basic strategy these kinds of funds pursue. Generally speaking, the manager of a value fund looks for high-yielding large-cap stocks that sell at low price-earnings multiples. (That's a fancy way of saying that these funds like to invest in solid companies whose stock is selling at bargain prices.) By investing in these types of stocks, you can often get consistent returns with relatively lower volatility. I'm a big fan of value investing.

Large-Capitalization Growth Funds. This type of fund invests in what are commonly referred to as "growth stocks." Large-cap funds typically look for stocks with a market value greater than $10 billion. Typically, growth stocks do not pay dividends because growth companies prefer to invest their profits in research, development, and expansion. Some great examples of large-cap growth companies are Apple, Microsoft, Facebook, Google, Oracle, Intel, and Amazon.com. These companies are huge, but they are not yet focusing on paying dividends because they are focused on powering their earnings into areas that they believe will grow the value of the company.

Medium-Capitalization Funds. Otherwise known as "mid-caps," these funds invest in medium-sized companies—that is, those with a market capitalization of $2 billion to $10 billion, such as Domino's Pizza, ResMed, and Packaging Corporation of America. The potential for great returns here is high, but so is the risk. As a result, even though you find a lot of volatility in this sector, I think most portfolios benefit from containing some exposure to mid-cap stocks.

Small-Capitalization Funds. It's getting harder to classify these funds because some small new company can go public these days with no earnings and overnight see its market capitalization suddenly spike to $1 billion or more. Typically, small-cap funds invest in companies with market caps that range from about $250 million

AVERAGE INVESTMENT PERFORMANCE		
For the Period: 10/1/89–12/31/17		
Portfolio/Investment	Strategy	Average Annual Return
DJ Industrial Average w/Dividends		10.86%
S&P 500 Index w/Dividends		9.80%
Morningstar Large Blend Funds	U.S. Large-Cap Core	8.42%
Morningstar Mid-Cap Blend Funds	U.S. Mid-Cap Core	10.01%
Morningstar Small Blend Funds	U.S. Small-Cap Core	10.24%
Morningstar Foreign Large Blend	International (Developed) Equities	3.98%
Morningstar Diversified Emerging Mkts.	Emerging Market Equities	7.49%
Morningstar World Large Stock	Global Equities	7.22%
Morningstar World Allocation	Global Stock/Bond Allocation	7.28%
Morningstar Intermediate-Term Bond	Intermediate-Term U.S. Bonds	5.50%
Morningstar Intermediate Government	Intermediate-Term U.S. Govt. Bonds	5.01%
Morningstar Corporate Bond	Investment-Grade U.S. Bonds	6.67%
Morningstar High-Yield Bond	High-Yield U.S. Bonds	6.88%
Morningstar Muni National Intermediate	Intermediate-Term U.S. Municipal Bonds	4.66%
Morningstar World Bond	Global Bonds	5.66%
Morningstar Money Market—Taxable	Money Markets	2.68%

Created by Sterling Capital
Source: Morningstar
The DJ Industrial Average and S&P 500 Index represent returns of passive indexes, while the "Morningstar" portfolios represent the average return of investment managers in the respective strategy.

to $3 billion. This reflects an ultra-aggressive approach, which can potentially produce great returns. Small-cap investing is a lot like betting on the hare instead of the tortoise. The younger you are— which is to say, the more time you have to recover from a potential disaster—the more you can afford to invest in this way. But be careful. I don't recommend putting more than 20 percent of your assets into this type of a fund.

International or Global Funds. As the name implies, these funds invest in stocks from foreign countries. While an international stock fund invests solely in foreign stocks, a global fund will usually have only about 60 percent of its assets invested abroad; the remaining 40 percent will be in domestic stocks. Remember, as big as it is, the United States represents only a small portion of the total world economy, and if you invest only in domestic stocks, you're missing out on a lot of opportunities.

WHO SAYS YOU CAN'T EARN 10 PERCENT ANYMORE?

One of the most common things I hear is that it's impossible to earn 10 percent in the stock market now. Really? Says who? I intentionally gave you the first chart to show you a long-term perspective of the market returns. Now let's look at the past eight years. You could have basically thrown a dart into the market and picked nearly any stock-based index fund and had double-digit returns. This is why when I wrote *Start Over, Finish Rich* my mantra was "Recessions make millionaires." Recessions always create the next generation of millionaires if you invest and buy things that are "on sale." As I write this, the market is up nearly 300 percent from the low in 2009. I have no idea when you will read this. The market could be going through a correction or continuing its bull market run up. What I know is this: The next time the market has a significant correction, don't believe people who tell you, "This time it's not going to recover—this time is different." The markets have always recovered. A correction is not fun to go through, but if you don't panic, you can live through it and thrive.

AVERAGE INVESTMENT PERFORMANCE		
For the Period: 3/9/09–12/31/17		
Portfolio/Investment	Strategy	Average Annual Return
DJ Industrial Average w/Dividends		19.15%
S&P 500 Index w/Dividends		19.23%
Morningstar Large Blend Funds	U.S. Large-Cap Core	17.21%
Morningstar Mid-Cap Blend Funds	U.S. Mid-Cap Core	18.30%
Morningstar Small Blend Funds	U.S. Small-Cap Core	19.00%
Morningstar Foreign Large Blend	International (Developed) Equities	11.98%
Morningstar Diversified Emerging Mkts.	Emerging Market Equitie	12.23%
Morningstar World Large Stock	Global Equities	14.81%
Morningstar World Allocation	Global Stock/Bond Allocation	9.25%
Morningstar Intermediate-Term Bond	Intermediate-Term U.S. Bonds	5.16%
Morningstar Intermediate Government	Intermediate-Term U.S. Govt. Bonds	2.77%
Morningstar Corporate Bond	Investment-Grade U.S. Bonds	7.72%
Morningstar High-Yield Bond	High-Yield U.S. Bonds	10.87%
Morningstar Muni National Intermediate	Intermediate-Term U.S. Municipal Bonds	3.97%
Morningstar World Bond	Global Bonds	4.71%
Morningstar Money Market—Taxable	Money Markets	0.09%

Created by Sterling Capital
Source: Morningstar
The DJ Industrial Average and S&P 500 Index represent returns of passive indexes, while the "Morningstar" portfolios represent the average return of investment managers in the respective strategy.

WITH 9,500 FUNDS TO CHOOSE FROM, HOW DO I KNOW WHICH ONE IS RIGHT FOR ME?

Let's face it, even mutual-fund investing has become pretty complicated in recent years. There are so many different funds (9,500 at last count)—not to mention the nearly 5,000 ETFs we previously discussed. So many ads screaming about performance. So many books, magazines, websites, television shows—all of them with their own suggestions on how to pick a mutual fund. It's enough to make a Smart Woman confused to the point of not taking action.

Here's the good news. Helping you build a diversified portfolio is exactly the kind of thing a good financial advisor can do for you on a fee basis. At the end of this chapter, I'll cover what you need to know to hire a financial advisor (so keep reading). For now, remember that a good advisor will do all of the following for you: discuss your goals and risk tolerance, help you build a professionally managed portfolio of funds, oversee your portfolio, and rebalance it as necessary. These days, many advisors use both actively managed mutual funds and ETFs, and many of them will do so for accounts starting at $25,000 (and sometimes less). In addition, you will be able to find a managed portfolio option at virtually every single major financial service firm.

It may seem complicated, but you've already learned more by reading this book than most people will ever learn about investing. You can do this. And you don't need to do it alone.

FOR REALLY LONG-TERM DREAMS (TEN YEARS OR MORE)

There are long-term dreams and then there are *really* long-term dreams. Say your dream is to build a second home in Hawaii, but you know it won't be possible until your kids are out of college, which is at least ten years away. Where should you put your dream-basket money in the meantime? Mutual funds can work incredibly effectively for these sorts of long-term dreams as well, and I could simply rest on the previous section on them. However, there are additional options for these sorts of really long-term dreams, and I want to make sure you're aware of them all, which is why I'm now going to go over annuities.

Annuities may or may not be the right product for you. But the fact of the matter is that annuities make a up a major part of the investment landscape—more than $220 billion was invested in annuities in 2016—so it's important to understand what they can offer. You might hear people bash annuities, but that is often because they are marketing a competitive product, such as a managed stock account. You can use annuities for both dream accounts and retirement investing. The two major types of annuities you might want to use for long-term dream investing are fixed indexed annuities and variable annuities.

Let's take a look and try to understand the basics of them.

WHAT IS AN ANNUITY?

When you buy an annuity, you enter into a contract with an insurance company. Under this contract, you pay a premium (that is, you invest) in exchange for a guaranteed payout option. These payout options vary from annuity to annuity, but the guaranteed payout can be yours for a specific term or for the remainder of your life. Annuities have two phases: During the first phase, you pay money into the annuity and the contract accumulates value and grows. The second phase begins when you start to withdraw money. This is called the distribution phase.

The important thing to understand about all annuities is that they are insurance contracts. This means that any guarantee you receive on behalf of an annuity is backed by the strength of the insurance company issuing the contract. **Do not buy an annuity until you are clear on the quality of the insurance company.**

FIXED INDEXED ANNUITIES

Often referred to as "FIAs," fixed indexed annuities are a tax-favored form of annuity, which means your money will grow tax-free until you're ready to take it out. In other words, your investment is "tax-deferred." FIAs dominate the annuity industry, and outsell variable annuities by a power of five to one. As of 2016, more than $117 billion went into FIAs as compared to only $25 billion in variable annuities.

So what's the big draw for FIAs? In short, they offer investors a "no downside" investment (as well as principal protection), which means you can't lose money if the market goes down, and you get to participate in the gains when the market goes up. There is a catch, however. Since your principal is protected, you don't participate in all of the market upside. Your return is tied to a predetermined index (such as the S&P 500), and you may only earn something like 50 percent of upside with a cap in any given year. All the specifics depend on the individual product you purchase, and the devil is in the details. This will also depend on the year you invest in it.

So what can you expect from an FIA? The FIA will start with an offer of a guaranteed rate. It will be a relatively low rate, but still potentially higher than what you can find with other products with guaranteed rates, such as CDs. So let's assume you find an FIA with a 3 percent rate. The insurer guarantees that you will never earn less than 3 percent annually. But in addition to the 3 percent guarantee, your product is also attached to a market index. In this example, let's say your FIA is tied to the S&P 500. If the S&P 500 goes up 10 percent, and your participation rate is 50 percent, then you'll earn

5 percent—not the 10 percent of the full market surge. What if the market goes down? In that case, you won't see a decline in your investment, as you'll still earn your guaranteed 3 percent.

You can use an FIA to later provide you with a guaranteed income for life if you elect to annuitize it, depending on the individual policy riders.

"What?!" you might exclaim. "David, this sounds too good to be true!" Yes, I know it does. It's all about the details. Don't worry, we will cover them right after we discuss variable annuities.

VARIABLE ANNUITIES

Variable annuities, like the fixed indexed versions, are insurance contracts. In this case, however, the insurer wraps an insurance policy around mutual funds—stocks, bonds, money-market funds, or a combination of your choice. These mutual funds are called "subaccounts," and the insurance policy, or "insurance wrapper" allows the money in the subaccount to grow tax-deferred, just as with fixed indexed annuities.

What makes variable annuities different from FIAs is the fact that your returns are based on the returns earned by your subaccount selection, and you generally cannot count on a fixed rate guarantee. There is also no protection from a potential market downturn. However, variable annuities do provide you with a full return on your investment. For instance, if you have a variable annuity with a subaccount invested in an S&P 500 index fund, and the S&P 500 goes up 15 percent in a year, you get to keep all 15 percent. There is no limit to your upside as there would be with an FIA.

THE UPSIDE AND DOWNSIDE OF ANNUITIES

I started off by saying that an annuity might or might not be right for you. The benefit of these insurance products is that they can offer you principal protection and tax deferral advantages—and in some cases, depending on how you structure your annuity, they can provide a guaranteed income for life and a long-term care benefit. What you get out of an annuity depends on the specific annuity product you purchase.

But you need to remember that nothing in life is free, including the principal protection and tax deferral benefits you receive from an annuity. So there are some potential drawbacks that could make an annuity less beneficial to your situation. In particular, let's talk about the tax-deferred growth you'll enjoy from both FIAs and variable annuities. It's great that your money grows tax-deferred— but Uncle Sam will want to see those taxes eventually. When you take profits out of your annuity, they will be taxed as ordinary income as opposed to long-term capital gain (this tax issue applies to taxable accounts, not retirement accounts). That's not great news because ordinary income can be taxed at a higher rate depending on your income and tax rate. This is something you need to consider carefully before investing in an annuity. The second potential drawback to annuities is the fact that your money will be locked up for a long time. You may not access your money before reaching age 59½ without paying a government penalty fee of 10 percent (as you would with an early withdrawal from an IRA). Third, you can expect lots of fees involved in getting the benefits and guarantees of the insurance. **You must review the fees in detail before you invest.** The fourth drawback is the fact that the annuity is only as strong as the insurance company backing it, which means you absolutely must check the insurer's ratings and strength before investing. Finally, know that you will likely face a surrender fee. This is what you must pay if you sell your annuity or take any distributions from it above a certain dollar level within a set time frame of the original purchase date. An average surrender fee time frame may range from 7 to 12 years, and the fees can cost upward of 7 to 10 percent, which decline over time. When you are in the market for an annuity, be sure to ask the person presenting it to you about all of the "internal fees" and "back-end" surrender fees or sales charges. You can often find annuities these days that offer level fee structures that eliminate these long-duration surrender charges, so be sure to ask your financial advisor or insurance professional about them if deferred sales charges concern you.

How do you determine which type of annuity might be right for you? It all depends on your situation. Neither type may suit your needs. I personally now prefer the fixed indexed annuity over the variable annuity. I'm happy to take only part of the upside of the index to protect myself when the market takes a downturn. Just as I would personally choose indexed universal life insurance above variable life insurance, I'd opt for an FIA over a variable annuity today.

But it's important to stay current on what's happening in the world of investing. The game of investing is always changing, with new products and new tax rules, which is why I wrote this update, and why you're reading it. You have to stay current on what is available. And by reading this update, you are.

THERE'S NOTHING WRONG WITH ASKING FOR HELP

We've covered an awful lot of ground in this chapter. Between all the recommendations I've made about how to fill your three baskets, I'm sure your head must be spinning. But remember—financial planning really isn't that complicated. For the most part, smart investing (which is the only kind of investing Smart Women do) is simply a matter of knowing what steps to take and in what order.

The fact is, becoming financially secure and being able to fund your dreams is a lot like opening a safe. Unless you know what numbers to turn and how, you'll never get inside. With the right combination, however, the world's strongest safe can be opened with very little effort. You now know the combination to your financial safe. Use the tools I have given you, in the right order, and your financial dreams will become a reality.

While I believe that every Smart Woman is capable of managing her finances on her own, if that is her goal, I still strongly suggest that before you start making investments, you consider getting some professional guidance. Now, hiring a professional to help you does not mean you are weak or lazy or lacking in confidence. It's like hiring a coach—and there's nothing wrong with hiring a coach. The most accomplished people in the world hire and work with coaches on a daily basis. Serena Williams, one of the greatest tennis players of all time, still works with a tennis coach. She doesn't say, "Oh, I know everything there is to know about tennis; I'm done learning." She uses a tennis coach to keep getting better. Michael Jordan, the greatest basketball player of all time, was devoted to his coach, the Bulls' Phil Jackson. Meryl Streep, the brilliant Oscar-winning actress, uses drama and dialect coaches.

Why do these people, all of whom are at the top of their respective games, still rely on coaches? Because they want to keep improving—and because a coach can give you something that is very difficult (if not impossible) to give yourself: accurate and objective feedback on how you're doing.

RICH PEOPLE HIRE FINANCIAL ADVISORS

Wealthy investors almost always employ financial advisors. This is not just my opinion; it is a fact. There are approximately 2 million households in the United States with a net worth of over $3 million, and the bulk of these families work with one or more financial advisors. What about the rest? According to the Certified Financial Planning Board, more than 40 percent of Americans choose to work with a financial advisor. This is up from 28 percent in 2010.

So consider hiring a financial coach. Not only will he or she make the job of managing your finances much easier, but if you hire a good one (which is the only kind you should consider), you probably will end up achieving better results than if you tried to do it on your own.

How do you find a good financial advisor? The interesting thing is that, while this may be one of the most important professionals you ever hire to help you in your lifetime, most investment books don't discuss how you should specifically go about hiring one. Having grown up and spent my entire life in the financial world, there are a couple of things I know for a fact. One is that if I were to leave the investment business, I would not continue to manage my own money. I'd hire someone to help me because every year the laws and conditions governing the financial arena change, and if I were not managing money full-time, I'd soon lose my edge and ability to manage my money well. As a result, I'd be forced to go out and do what you may need to do right now, which is to start interviewing prospective financial advisors.

Since the first edition of this book was published, I've heard from literally thousands of readers asking me to recommend a financial advisor for them. To help you do your own research, I've created the **10 Golden Rules for Hiring a Financial Pro**.

Based on my experience as a financial advisor, these are the rules I would use if I were going to go out and interview someone to help me manage my money. If you really apply these rules, I am confident you will be able to find a financial professional who can help you make smart decisions about your money. Most important, you'll be able to hire the best advisor possible and get the best attention possible.

The single most frustrating thing that happened to me personally following the original release of *Smart Women Finish Rich* is that we were bombarded with requests from women all over the country to manage their money. The reason this was so frustrating is that while I wanted to help everyone I simply couldn't handle all the requests.

Therefore, I've added to this list of Golden Rules a new rule to help you find a financial advisor in your own area. Rule number 10 now provides you with some of the best referral sources I could find to help you in your search for a financial advisor. My recommendation is that you consider hiring a local financial advisor, someone you can meet with face-to-face. Use these rules and the referral sources I listed. There are literally tens of thousands of great advisors out there and all you need to do is find one. And if by any chance you meet with someone that you're not totally comfortable with, simply keep looking. Remember, this is your money and, ultimately, even if you hire a financial coach, you are still in charge!

THE 10 GOLDEN RULES FOR HIRING A FINANCIAL PRO

RULE NO. 1
Check out a prospective advisor's background.

This is the first rule for a reason. Nothing else on this list matters if you don't take the time to thoroughly check out your prospective advisor's background. That's because no matter how successful he or she seems and no matter how highly recommended he or she is, if you don't check out your advisor's background, you are setting yourself up for trouble.

Not all advisors are created equal. You may encounter some who appear successful, but who are, in fact, nothing more than great salespeople. You might run into an advisor who impresses you with his sincerity and his mile-long list of educational attainments and career experience—only to find that he embellished his credentials and stretched the truth. You might be charmed by an advisor whom you later discover has formal ethics complaints filed against her. Some advisors out there even have criminal records.

The good news is that you can protect yourself from these sorts of "advisors." All it takes is a little research on your part.

To become licensed to sell securities, brokers and financial advisors are required to pass tests and register with the National Association of Securities Dealers. Because of these requirements, important information about licensed brokers and advisors is available to the public at the BrokerCheck site run by the Financial Industry Regulatory Authority at **www.brokercheck.org**. This site offers you all the information you need to know about a registered advisor's background, including education, work and business history, and licenses held and in which states. This website is now the best it has ever been as a quick resource to explore your advisor's complete history. Before you hire a financial advisor—in fact, before you even meet with one—visit the BrokerCheck site.

Possibly the most important information BrokerCheck provides is whether or not an advisor has any "disclosure events" on his or her record. A disclosure event is the term for an ethics complaint or criminal prosecution levied against an advisor—and needless to say, you probably don't want to hire an advisor who has such a disclosure event on his or her record. While BrokerCheck does not provide the nature of any particular disclosure event that may be on your advisor's record, it does allow you to request additional information by mail and will link you to the SEC website. You can also visit **www.investor.gov** and click on the Investment Adviser Public Disclosure section for more information.

Finally, you can check out the SEC website at **www.sec.gov**, where there is an entire section called "Protect Your Money—Check Out Brokers and Investment Advisors." This is a fantastic site that goes into great detail on everything you need to know, with direct links to additional resources to review your advisor's background if he or she is an investment advisor and not a registered broker. If your advisor is a registered investment advisor, make sure you check out his or her "Form ADV," which is a two-part required form that must be updated annually for advisors to stay current. You can also go to **www.adviserinfo.sec.gov** and look them up yourself. Individual investment representatives of an RIA are also listed here.

There are many good advisors out there. I'm giving you all this detail to protect you from falling prey to one who's not.

RULE NO. 2
Go to your first meeting prepared.

A real professional will insist that you come to your first meeting prepared. That means he or she will ask you to bring copies of your investment statements, net worth, current expense breakdowns, and your most recent tax returns—in short, the kind of information called for in the worksheets in Appendices 1 and 2 of this book. There are 500,000 people in this country who call themselves financial advisors. They are not all equally excellent. A professional who doesn't ask you to bring this sort of information is not the kind of professional you want to hire.

If you are not willing to take the time to get organized prior to your first meeting with a financial advisor, or if you are reluctant to show your personal financial documents to a professional, then you probably are not ready to work with one. That's not intended to be harsh; it's intended to be realistic. Some people are very uncomfortable showing their financial documents to anyone and have a deep-rooted problem with trust. A person like this will not be happy hiring a financial professional regardless of how good the advisor may be.

RULE NO. 3
Always ask about the advisor's investment philosophy.

Ask the financial advisor about his or her philosophy on financial planning and money management. He or she should be able to explain it quickly and in simple terms. A real professional should have this part of the process down to a science and be able to explain it both easily and comfortably. If yours can't do this, take your business elsewhere.

Here's why this is important: An advisor can articulate his or her investment philosophy, but a salesperson cannot. That's because a salesperson will spend most of your meeting telling you what you want to hear. For instance, he or she might say: "You like stock trading? That's perfect because I'm a specialist in stock trading." Or: "You're getting stock options? Stock options are what I focus on so I can definitely help you." Or: "So you want to buy an annuity? That's great because annuities are all I do."

These may sound like the kind of hokey tricks you'd hear from a high-pressure salesperson in a movie, but, believe me, they are still taught by old-school sales trainers and you may well encounter such responses. Someone who talks like this is not the kind of advisor you want. The advisor you want to work with will spend most of your first meeting reviewing your financial and personal situation and asking you lots of questions about your values, dreams, goals, financial worries, and plans and hopes for your future. The advisor you want to work with will not do a lot of talking—because talking usually means selling. You don't want someone who brags about performance. If ever you meet an advisor who starts promising you high returns, end the meeting, lose his or her business card, and never look back. Too many advisors these days use the remarkable returns of the recent bull market to position themselves as some kind of investing genius or guru. They don't know that you know the cardinal rule of investing:

Past performance is no guarantee
of future performance!

The advisor you can trust is the one who will give you realistic expectations. He or she will talk about "reality investing" and point out that although stocks (the S&P 500) have generated an average annual return of nearly 16 percent with reinvested dividends over the past nine years (this was written in early 2018), that does not mean the stock market will continue at a similar pace. An advisor worth his or her salt will discuss some realistic possibilities for returns and show you the full background of historical returns—not just a small snapshot of positive returns. Over 90 years, stocks have averaged just about 10 percent annually and diversified balance accounts have averaged just about 8 percent annually. While there have been incredible boom years and many, many average years, there have been plenty of years—that have even stretched into decades—in which stocks have not made money.

RULE NO. 4
Be prepared to pay for the advice you get.

The advice you receive from a professional financial advisor is generally not free. You might assume that this is an obvious statement, since a financial advisor is a professional offering a service that is worth money. But we live in a world wherein we've gotten used to finding so much for "free" (or at least offered at steep discounts) on the Internet that many people actually believe they can go into a financial professional's office and receive the benefit of his or her experience and knowledge for free. I'm sorry, but that's just not how it works.

In most cases, you will be offered a complimentary review meeting to go over your financial situation. Then if you want to move forward, and if the advisor feels like he or she can help you, at that point your advisor will offer to provide you with a detailed financial plan. Normally, you'll receive this plan in your second, follow-up appointment, at which point, if you move forward, you will pay for the advice offered. In some cases, your advisor may charge up front for the financial plan, whether or not you decide to move forward as a new client. Make sure you ask if there is a fee for the plan before your advisor draws it up.

So how do you pay for the advice you receive? While the financial services industry has been making some big changes regarding fee structures in recent years, you are likely to be offered one of two basic fee structures from most professional financial advisors.

COMMISSION-BASED ADVICE—BROKERS

With commission-based advice, your advisor will earn a fee each time he or she buys or sells an investment for you. This was the standard fee structure for the past century for the majority of stockbrokers (who are now known as financial advisors)—but this sort of commission-only advisor is quickly going the way of the dinosaur. That's because very few advisors are purely commission-based; instead, they are becoming what is known as fee-based advisors or fiduciaries. In some case, advisors become a "hybrid" or dually registered advisor, which means they earn both commissions and fees. We'll cover that next.

FEE-BASED ADVICE— REGISTERED INVESTMENT ADVISORS, A.K.A. "FIDUCIARIES"

Back when I wrote the first edition of this book, I said that I thought the industry was headed toward a fee-based model, and it turns out I was right. These days, RIAs—Registered Investment Advisors (also known as "fiduciary advisors"), who charge a flat fee on assets—are the model the industry has embraced. When you hire an RIA, your advisor is a fiduciary who charges you a fee on the assets he or she manages for you. For the advice received, you will pay an annual fee to cover all the services your financial advisor offers you, including all of your trades, meetings, proposals, and performance reports. In most cases, the fee will be a set proportion (usually between 1 and 2 percent) of the amount of money the advisor is managing for you. For instance, an investor with $100,000 to manage will pay her advisor $1,000 to $2,000 per year.

These days, every major brokerage firm and independent firm in the country has taken on the model of the fee-based payment structure. This means the price of fee-based advice is quickly coming down, since those firms provide competition that keeps prices lower. In addition, remember that the fee structure is almost always dependent on the amount of money under management. In other words, the more assets being managed, the lower the fee.

There are a number of advantages to this kind of fee structure. To start, there is no possible conflict of interest when you get fee-based advice. Your advisor's payment depends on the value of your assets, so it's in his or her best interest to see your assets grow as much as possible. In addition, fee-based advisors get paid only if their clients are serviced well and kept happy. If advisors invest their clients' money and then forget about them, the clients will leave and the fees will stop coming. All of this is why you'll find fee-based advisors are more service-oriented. Fee-based advisors know that their clients are more than just a one-time sale, since their businesses rely on long-term relationships. (By the way, if you hire a fee-based advisor, make sure you tell your tax accountant, because under some circumstances the fees you pay may be tax-deductible.)

HYBRID ADVISORS—
DUALLY REGISTERED ADVISORS

Dually registered advisors hold two important licenses: a license to sell securities through a brokerage firm and a license to provide advice as a registered investment advisor (RIA). A dually registered advisor will typically explain to new clients that he or she is an RIA who does fee-based planning. The advisor will put together a financial plan for you, including an investment portfolio. At that point, your advisor will build you a diversified portfolio of professionally managed funds (for example) and charge you a flat fee of, say, 1 to 2 percent on the assets managed (again, this is only an example). If you then need life insurance or you're interested in purchasing an annuity, your dually registered advisor can generally help you with that as well, since the agent will have a brokerage license for selling insurance products. Under that brokerage license, the advisor is paid a commission, which is unrelated to the flat fee you will pay for your assets under management.

The bulk of advisors today are actually dually registered. The key is to ask whether your advisor is one of them. It's confusing, and you should know which hat the advisor is wearing when he or she provides you with advice that you pay for.

WHAT TYPE OF ADVISOR
SHOULD I LOOK FOR?

I personally recommend that you first and foremost work with a fee-based Registered Investment Advisor (RIA) firm—a "fiduciary." The fiduciary responsibility is a legal requirement. It requires your advisor to put your interests first and disclose potential conflicts of interest. For instance, you don't want an advisor who recommends an investment to you because he or she would get a higher commission from it. Over the past few decades, the financial services industry (and particularly the large national firms) have really pushed their proprietary funds (their own products) in order to earn higher fees. Thankfully, this practice has been challenged and reduced in recent years as a result of lawsuits, but you need to remember how important it is to have an advisor who is independent and free of conflicts of interest. You want an advisor who is focused on what is best for you and who is completely transparent. This leads to a final important issue: If the advisor is a dually registered advisor—as in, he or she is both an RIA and a licensed broker—then you want to know that up front. You want the advisor to explain fully to you

---

THE RIGHT ADVISOR CAN BE WORTH OVER 3 PERCENT ANNUALLY

I'm often skeptical on specific data points around advice. Still, Vanguard is a very credible source, and this data comes from them. According to a Vanguard Research Report, the potential for an advisor to add value to a client relationship can be significant. In their words, it's about "3% annually." How?, you might ask.

- Lowering expense – cost-effective implementation = 45 basis points (0.45%) savings
- Rebalancing – your investments = 35 basis points (0.35%) savings
- Behavior coaching – helping you to not hurt yourself = 150 basis points (1.50%) savings
- Asset location – optimizing portfolio that minimizes taxes = 0 to 75 basis points (0.75%) savings.
- Spending strategy – the way you withdraw your money = 0 to 70 basis points (0.70%)

If you add these up it comes to 3.75 percent. Vanguard is very clear in the study that this is not an annualized projection. If you want to read the detailed report yourself, Google it. It is sourced below.

Source: Vanguard Research, *Putting a Value on Your Value: Quantifying Vanguard's Advisors Alpha.* Authors: Francis M. Kinnery, Colleen M. Jaconetti, Michael A. DiJoseph, and Yan Zilbering.

what that means. And you want that advisor to show you the fees and commissions he or she is earning.

WHAT ABOUT THE FIDUCIARY RULE?

You may remember reading about the Department of Labor's Fiduciary Rule, which was supposed to go into effect in 2017 and 2018 and fundamentally change the transparency and rules around the way financial advice is provided. Unfortunately, at the time of this update, the Fiduciary Rule is like the U.S. healthcare system: still surprisingly uncertain. The current administration has put this new regulation on hold, there are challenges in court, and it's unclear what is going to happen with the rule and how it will evolve.

The important thing for you is finding an advisor who offers you transparency and no conflicts of interest—whether or not there is legislation in effect that requires fiduciary responsibility. No matter what happens with the Fiduciary Rule on the federal level, you want a financial advisor you can trust, who is transparent, and who puts your interests first, not his or her own. **This isn't that complicated. From an advisor's standpoint, it's called "do the right thing, always, for your client."** The complicated part is finding that advisor. They're out there. The best way, for now, to achieve that transparency is to work with an RIA who's a fiduciary and uses these rules.

> **RULE NO. 5**
> **Become an "A" client.**

It is not enough simply to hire a good financial advisor. You want whomever you hire to pay attention to you—ideally, to consider you one of his or her most important clients. Most people think that in order to be important to a financial advisor, you need to have lots of money. Nothing could be further from the truth. I have had clients with assets that range from $1,000 to $100 million, and I can assure you that some of the smaller ones were just as important to me as the biggest ones.

The fact is, it's not just money that determines how much your financial advisor cares about you. It's how you treat your financial advisor that matters. As an example, early in my career I had a client, Francine, who opened an account with me with just $1,000. I put Francine's money into a stock that tripled in value, so all of a sudden she had $3,000. I also bought this stock for more than a half dozen other clients. Most of them made significantly more money than Francine, because they had more invested. Unlike any of them, however, after the stock took off, Francine showed up at my office one day with four bottles of wine as a gift for me and each of my assistants. Now, I don't know what the wine cost Francine. I don't even remember whether it was red or white. What I do remember is that this small gesture of hers was talked about in our office for weeks. We couldn't believe how special it was. I'm still talking (and now writing) about it years later.

So when your financial advisor makes you some money, or you're thrilled with the advisor's service and care, take a moment to say "thank you." Sure, it's his or her job to make you money and provide top-level service. But that's no reason not to show your appreciation. No matter the size of your portfolio, a small gesture like a simple thank-you note or a bottle of wine can transform you into an "A" client.

Another great way to say "thank you" to your advisor—and become as a result an "A" client—is to refer the advisor some new business (that is, to recommend that a friend hire your advisor). Not only will this show your advisor how much you appreciate what he or she has done for you, it may turn out to be just what your friend needs to get her financial life together.

And it's not just financial advisors who should get this sort of consideration. When Francine gave me that little gift, it made me realize that I had never once expressed my appreciation to any of the professionals on whom I depend: my attorney, my CPA, my doctor, my haircutter, the mechanic who looks after my car—the list goes on and on. So a few years ago I started sending them all thank-you notes and in some cases a gift basket at Christmas. The first time I did this, my doctor called me personally to say "thank you." Guess what? Even though my doctor is routinely booked up three months in advance, I never have to wait for an appointment anymore. I just seem to get right in. My car mechanic framed my thank-you letter and posted it on the wall of his waiting room. My CPA seemed to find more deductions the next year.

I'm not kidding. Because of my small gifts and notes, my relationship with all these professionals is now different. They remember me because I made a small gesture to say "thank you." Try it. Our parents were right: Saying "thank you" goes a long way.

> **RULE NO. 6**
> **A good financial advisor explains the risks associated with investing.**

It's easy to forget about risk when the stock market is going gangbusters, but that doesn't mean you should. A good advisor will spend time explaining and educating you about the risks associated with investing. When I was running The Bach Group, before we implemented an investment plan we showed our clients exactly how often in the past the market had dropped, how long it had stayed down, and, based on the history of the previous 45 years, what we believed the risks associated with our proposal to be.

This is incredibly important because many people today do not fully understand—nor are they being prepared for—the risks inherent in any stock-market investment. If you meet with an advisor who does not discuss the notion of risk with you and ask you specific questions to get a feeling for your comfort level, thank her for her time and continue with your search.

> **RULE NO. 7**
> **Go with your gut instinct.**

When you interview a financial advisor, ask yourself if you feel comfortable with this person. Is this the kind of person you want to open up to and work with for years to come? Do you feel deep down inside that this is someone you can trust? The answer should be a "gut level" yes. If it is not, continue your search. You have not yet found your trusted advisor.

> **RULE NO. 8**
> **Make sure your check goes to the custodian—not the advisor.**

What can you do to protect your money from a Bernie Madoff Ponzi scheme or other type of outright theft? The most basic and important method of protecting yourself from these sorts of situations is to never, ever write an investment contribution check directly to your financial advisor. Never! Your advisor should be working with a major brokerage firm, and if the advisor is a fiduciary, he or she will be using what's called a "third-party custodian." It is to the custodian that you should write checks in order to add money to your investments.

The largest brokerage firms that hold RIAs' assets for clients are *Fidelity, TD Ameritrade, Charles Schwab*, and *Pershing*. Here's what happens: After you write the check (or otherwise transfer the money), your assets will be held at the brokerage firm, and you sign a limited power of attorney that provides the advisor with the ability to manage your money. You never want to give any advisor the right to make withdrawals or write checks on your account. Never. Ever. Ever. All investors should assume this important security measure for themselves and their money. You need to take this seriously. Ask prospective advisors whom they custody with, and remember that the custodian is who you write the check to. Finally, remember to go online at these firms—and see that your money is there. I always say: *Trust but verify.*

RULE NO. 9
Keep in regular contact with your financial advisor.

If you haven't heard from your financial advisor by phone or by letter in the past 12 months (statements don't count), then you may have fallen into what we call the client abyss. Get out quick. Either go in immediately and reacquaint yourself with the professional with whom you are working or start interviewing for a new advisor. As a rule, your advisor should contact you at least twice a year, and you should sit down together to review your financial situation at least once every 12 months.

RULE NO. 10
If you can't get a referral, do your own research.

There are many great financial advisors out there who are fiduciaries and are client-centric. This is what you want. Following is a list to help you get your search started.

The Financial Planning Association (FPA)
(800) 322-4237
www.plannersearch.org
This site allows you to search by zip codes for the names of certified financial planners.

National Association of Personal Financial Advisors
(888) 333-6659
www.napfa.org
This site allows you to search by zip codes and offers links to fee-only advisors.

Checking Out an Advisor's Background

Financial Industry Regulatory Authority
(800) 289-9999
www.finra.org, go to *www.brokercheck.finra.org*
This is the self-regulatory organization for the financial services industry. Always start here.

Certified Financial Planner Board of Standards
(800) 487-1497
www.cfp.net
This group sets and enforces the standards advisors must meet in order to call themselves certified financial planners. Its site allows you to check the status of a CFP certificate.

National Association of Insurance Commissioners
(816) 783-8500
www.naic.org
This group is an organization of state insurance regulators. Through its online National Insurance Producer Registry (NIPR), you can find information on more than 2.5 million insurance agents and brokers, including their licensing status and disciplinary history.

IN CONCLUSION

These ten rules are meant to make your search for a lifelong financial guide easier. Don't let anything I have said scare you off from searching for one. There are many, many good and ethical professionals out there who can help you with your financial decisions.

Remember, it's now time for you to move on your decision. If you have decided that you do want professional help, make hiring an advisor a priority. Your ultimate goal should be to hire an individual or a team that you can see yourself working with for a long time—perhaps even the rest of your life. Therefore, the hiring process is something you should take very seriously. Ask people within your community, talk to friends and wealthy people you know and respect, and find out whom they are working with. Spend time, interview more than one professional, ask for references, and then follow up and call those references.

I promise you—it will be worth the effort.

LEARN THE 10 BIGGEST MISTAKES INVESTORS MAKE AND HOW TO AVOID THEM

When I was five, my friend Marvin and I thought it would be fun to see what was behind those electric sockets our mothers were always warning us not to touch. I think I was the one who found the screwdriver, but it was definitely Marvin who stuck it in the socket. Wham!

Before either of us had a chance to react, Marvin went flying backward across the room and all the power in the house went out. "Wow," I said, gaping at my friend, who was now lying in a heap against the opposite wall. "Was that fun?"

Poor little Marvin looked at me with a dazed expression, then burst into tears.

I can't remember what lame story we eventually concocted to cover up what we'd done, but I do recall clearly that the experience taught me two important things. The first was never to stick a screwdriver in a light socket. The second was that while it's important to learn from your own mistakes, it's probably a better idea (and certainly a much safer one) to learn from other people's.

I bring this up because both these lessons are important to remember when you're trying to decide how to invest all that money you should now be putting in your three baskets. The fact is, when it comes to investing, many of us act like five-year-olds sticking screwdrivers into electric sockets. That is, we experiment ignorantly—and invariably wind up making some horrendous mistake that sends us reeling across the room in financial shock.

Over the course of this chapter, we're going to focus on what I consider to be the ten most "shocking" mistakes that investors generally make. My hope is that as a result of studying other people's mistakes, you'll be able to avoid the painful and expensive experience of having to learn from your own.

> ### MISTAKE NO. 1
> ### Becoming an investor before you are organized and have specific goals in mind.

Back in Step Three, we talked about the importance of knowing exactly where you are today financially and what eventual destination you've got in mind before you go charging down the road to riches. Well, I hope you don't mind if I repeat myself a bit here. The fact is, going off half-cocked—that is, without having a clear idea of how you stand and where you want to go—may well be the most common (and most avoidable) mistake investors make.

There's no getting around it. Before you invest any of your money, you must invest some of your time. The rule is simple: *In order to become a successful investor, you first have to get your values and goals written down on paper and your finances organized.* You absolutely must do a family financial inventory and balance sheet and determine precisely your current net worth. You also must get a good handle on what you earn and what you spend. This is not a guessing game or a time for estimates. Remember, until you know where you stand financially, you should not invest in *anything*. As I noted earlier, use the worksheet in Appendix 2 to get a solid grip on where you stand today financially.

I can already hear you protesting: "Worksheets? Financial inventories? This stuff takes time. What if I miss out on a great investment opportunity while I'm busy getting my finances organized?"

Believe me, I know that doing the foundation work is not nearly as exciting as investing in a hot stock. No one goes to a cocktail party and brags about the fact that she spent the weekend cleaning her financial house. Rather, people like to talk about the hot new investment they just bought—and now with all those personal-finance websites, magazines, television shows, investor newsletters, and Twitter "experts," it's very easy to be tempted into investing without first getting your money in order and your investment goals down on paper.

Resist the temptation. You can't invest successfully without knowing where you are starting from and what your investment goals are. Only after you have figured out these things will you be able to evaluate intelligently the opportunities around you and figure out whether (and how) they might make sense for you.

MISTAKE NO. 2
Not taking credit-card debt seriously.

Credit-card debt can be incredibly destructive. If you're single, it can keep you from achieving your goals and make you miserable. If you're part of a couple, it can destroy your relationship. I don't care how much two people may love each other; if one of them is constantly spending the couple into debt, I can promise you that eventually the relationship will fall apart. If both parties are running up debts, it will simply end that much sooner.

Why do I say this? First of all, carrying credit-card debt is stressful. Knowing that you owe a company money and that you're being charged as much as 30 percent interest on the outstanding balance will make even the most laid-back person anxious. Second, the anxiety never goes away; it's there—all day, every day—until the debt is paid off. And not only does it hang over you like a cloud, it hits you smack-dab in the face every month when the bill shows up.

Don't wait to find out about your credit record!

Nothing is worse than finding out that you have credit problems just when you're about to make a major purchase—say, when you're ready to buy your first home.

This happened to one of my closest friends, a woman named Renee, who makes a good living as a computer executive. When she and her new husband, Alan, started to look for a house in San Francisco a few years ago, she called a mortgage broker to get preapproved for a loan. This, she figured, was a no-brainer. She'd already asked Alan if his credit was clean and he'd said of course it was.

So imagine her surprise a few days later when the broker called her back and asked if she was sitting down.

"What's wrong?" Renee asked the broker.

"Well," he said, "Alan has some credit problems. In fact, his credit rating is so bad that there's no way the two of you can qualify for a loan together."

Renee was stunned. "How can that be? My credit is perfect, isn't it?"

"Sure," the broker said, "but his isn't."

The problem was those nice companies that used to give away the free T-shirts and made it so easy for a student to get a credit card. With their encouragement, Alan had opened a couple of those accounts when he was in college, charged a few items, and then had forgotten about them. Unfortunately, those nice credit-card companies don't forget. Instead, they had placed nasty little "no payment" flags on his record. And even though the amounts in question were relatively small (less than $200 on two accounts), that was enough to ruin his credit rating—and along with it, any chance he and Renee had of getting a mortgage together.

This kind of situation is exactly why Congress passed the Credit CARD act in 2009, which prohibits credit-card issuers from setting up application booths on college campuses and bans them from issuing credit cards to anyone under the age of 21, unless they have an adult co-signer or can prove they have the income to repay the debt. Sadly for Alan, this important legislation was too late to help him avoid a terrible credit rating.

Fortunately for them, Renee's credit rating was strong enough to qualify them for a home loan on her own, and so they were still able to buy a house. Anyway, the point here is not to single out Alan, but to demonstrate how easy it is to be blindsided by a bad credit report. Even when you think you have your act together, you may not. The moral . . .

Find out your credit rating now!

Don't wait to be surprised. Go get a copy of all your credit reports from the three main credit reporting companies: Equifax, Experian, and TransUnion. It's easier than you think. In October 2001, the government passed the Fair Credit Reporting Act, which mandates that you have the legal right to a free copy of your credit report once every 12 months—which makes sense, because it's your information.

There is only one legitimate website to go to and get these reports for free: **www.annualcreditreport.com**. Lots of websites say "get your credit report/score for free," but they are imposter sites designed to start charging you for this information 30 days later, so be very careful if you use any site besides this. If you find mistakes you can then go directly to the three major credit bureaus.

Here's how to contact each of the three main credit-reporting companies directly:

Equifax
P.O. Box 740241
Atlanta, GA 30374
(872) 284-7942
www.equifax.com

Experian
P.O. Box 2002
Allen, TX 75013
(888) 567-8688
www.experian.com

TransUnion LLC
Consumer Disclosure Center
P.O. Box 1000
Chester, PA 19022
(800) 916-8800
(800) 888-4213 (if you have been declined credit)
www.transunion.com

Five-Star Tip: In September 2017, the credit-reporting agency Equifax reported that it had been hacked as of May of that year, and that as many as 145 million consumers' sensitive personal information was potentially exposed during the breach. Because of this hack, many consumers have chosen to use a strategy called "credit freezing" in order to protect themselves from identity theft. Credit freezing makes it impossible for anyone, including you, to take out new credit in your name. There is usually a small fee of between $3 and $10 to freeze your credit with each credit-reporting bureau—although in the wake of the hack, Equifax has waived that fee for all consumers who choose to freeze their credit with them. A credit freeze lasts indefinitely, and is only lifted when you pay another small fee to "thaw" the report anytime you are looking to actually purchase a car, qualify for a mortgage, or otherwise open a new line of credit. Prior to the Equifax breach, credit freezes were a little-used strategy—but they are a smart way of protecting your credit from data breaches and identity theft.

If you discover any inaccuracies or mistakes in any of your credit reports, get them fixed immediately. The procedures for doing so are relatively simple, and the individual companies will tell you what exactly what's required. Basically, if you tell a credit-reporting company that your file contains inaccurate information, the company must look into your claim (usually within 30 days) and present all the relevant evidence you submit to whomever provided it with the information you're disputing. If this does not resolve the dispute, you may add a brief statement to your credit file, a summary of which will be included in all future reports. Make sure you read up on the latest updates on the procedures for fixing mistakes on your credit file on the companies' websites, as things may have changed since the Equifax data breach of 2017.

If you discover that you've got some legitimate black marks on your credit reports (for example, some old unpaid bills that you've forgotten about), do whatever you can to correct the situation. In general, that means pay off those old debts, and don't let any new bills go past due.

Beware of companies that say they can "fix" a bad credit report or give you a new "clean" one overnight. There is nothing that will "fix" a bad credit report except the passage of time and a consistent record of responsible bill-paying, and you contacting the credit-report companies and working with them to get your credit record clean. Want more help? The largest nonprofit referral source for credit counseling is the National Foundation for Credit Counseling, reachable online at **www.nfcc.org** or by phone at (800) 388–2227.

YOU CAN'T LIVE RICH IF YOU'RE IN A RAT RACE

If you currently find yourself deeper in debt than you would like to be, you are not alone. According to the Federal Reserve, U.S. consumer debt (i.e., what people owe on credit cards, car loans, and other consumer loans) reached $3.82 trillion in December 2017—an all-time high!

Why do we spend so much money that we don't really have? Basically, it's because we get hooked into thinking about the price of things not in terms of their total cost but in terms of how much the monthly installments will be. This is a marketing gimmick that you find almost nowhere else but in the United States. From car payments to mortgage payments to credit-card payments, virtually every kind of price tag in this country is denominated in monthly payments.

Unfortunately, if you want to live happily ever after, you can't be living paycheck to paycheck or credit-card payment to credit-card payment. You can't live rich if you're stuck in the rat race of life working yourself silly to just pay off debt.

IF CREDIT-CARD DEBT IS A PROBLEM, HERE'S WHAT YOU MUST DO

1. **Cut up the cards.** As I mentioned in Step Four, the "Latte Factor" chapter, you (and your partner, if you have one)—need

to have a credit-card "haircut." It's not complicated. Just take a $2 pair of scissors and cut up every piece of plastic cash you have. From then on, do all your spending in cash. I dare you to waste $75 on a "must-have" sweater or $100 on a "killer" pair of shoes when you have to pay for them with "real" money. Even better, I'd really be surprised if you could easily go into an electronics store and buy a $1,000 phone with 50 twenty-dollar bills. Counting out 50 twenties will make you realize just how much that new phone really costs.

2. **Delete your credit-card information from your favorite online retailers.** When I first wrote this book, a credit-card "haircut" was enough to force shoppers to stop credit-card spending. However, these days it's beyond easy to spend money without even leaving your house (or your bed!) because all of your favorite online retailers remember your credit-card information for you. You can go from not knowing an item exists to purchasing it in under a couple of seconds with this "convenience." If you struggle with online shopping, take the time to remove all of your credit-card information from retail websites. It's amazing how much money you'll save when you actually have to think about your purchases instead of mindlessly clicking "buy."

3. **If you're married, stop fighting with each other.** The two of you are on the same team. Debt is a "we" problem, not a "you" problem. This is true in a moral sense for partners in any committed relationship, but for married couples it has a legal dimension as well. When you are married, you are jointly responsible for all your debts, regardless of who incurred them. Say your husband runs up $50,000 in credit-card debt, divorces you, and then files for bankruptcy. Guess who the creditors will come after? You, if you've got any assets. I've seen this happen more than once. What this means is that if either of you has a credit-card problem, you need to get help

together. Remember, your enemy is debt, not each other; you need to rally against it together.

4. **Get help.** Contact a reputable, nonprofit credit-counseling organization such as the National Foundation for Credit Counseling. Visit **www.nfcc.org** for details. (As I noted, stay away from outfits that promise to "fix" your credit problems—usually for a healthy fee.) Generally speaking, a credit-counseling organization can help you consolidate your debt, renegotiate interest rates, and get creditors to stop harassing you. Most important, they can help you identify just how you got into debt in the first place and help you get out much quicker.

MISTAKE NO. 3
Having a 30-year mortgage.

In my opinion, without question the biggest single scam perpetrated on the American public today is the 30-year mortgage. Say you purchase a home with a $300,000 mortgage that you pay off over a 30-year period. Say the interest rate is 4.5 percent a year and your monthly mortgage payment is $1,519.98. When all is said and done, you actually will have given the bank more than $547,200! That's almost twice the original loan amount. Why did you fork over all that extra money? The answer, of course, is that in addition to repaying the $300,000 principal, you were also obligated to pay the bank $247,200 in interest charges.

What's the alternative? Well, if you paid off the same mortgage in 15 years, the total cost of your home would come to just over $413,000. That's still a lot, but it is about $134,000 less than you would have paid with a 30-year mortgage. How difficult is it to pay off a home in 15 years instead of 30 years? Not very.

TAKE YOUR 30-YEAR MORTGAGE AND . . .
SAVE $40,000 OR MORE!

Let's say you already have a 30-year mortgage. In that case, I suggest you . . . keep it. That's right. Go ahead and keep the 30-year mortgage you've already got in place, and if you ever get a new mortgage, I'd suggest you get one with a 30-year term in that case, as well. The fact is, 30-year mortgages give you a ton of flexibility.

Right now, you're probably wondering if you accidentally skipped a page or two, or maybe you think I've gone nuts. Just a couple of paragraphs ago, I was telling you how terrible 30-year mortgages are, and here I am saying you should keep yours—and maybe even get a new one.

Don't worry, I'm not canceling out my own advice. There's a trick to keeping a 30-year mortgage from costing you: Take out a 30-year mortgage, but under no circumstances should you take the full 30 years to repay it. A 30-year payment schedule means wasting a lot of time and money on interest. Instead, it's much smarter to pay off your 30-year mortgage early.

Here's how you do it. Log on to your mortgage lender's website and review the amount of your last payment. Now add 10 percent to that number. That's how much you are going to send to the bank each month from now on. For instance, if your monthly mortgage payment was $1,000 last month, from now on you'll pay $1,100 per month. Contact the bank to let them know you are doing this and that you want the additional $100 per month to be applied to the principal (and not the interest).

Keep this up, and you'll be able to pay off your 30-year mortgage in about 25 years. Up your monthly payment by 20 percent, and you can retire that mortgage in about 22 years (depending on the type of the mortgage)! In short, this is a simple idea that can easily save you tens—if not hundreds—of thousands of dollars in interest over the lifetime of your mortgage. In the example I went over on the $300,000 mortgage at 4.5 percent with a monthly mortgage payment of $1,519.98 a month, just adding $152 a month EXTRA toward the principal would pay that mortgage off **five years sooner, saving you $48,121! Make two extra payments of $152, and you would save $79,622!** *Reread that.* That's like two months of your Latte Factor! Right? **Two months of coffee at home a year, and you've paid your home off eight years faster and saved $79,622.** Now tell me this book wasn't worth the 15 bucks or less you spent on it!

If you're at all confused by this, call your bank or mortgage company and tell them you want to pay off your mortgage earlier than the schedule calls for. Ask them exactly how much extra a month you would have to send them in order to pay off your mortgage in 15, 20, and 25 years. Make sure to ask if there are any penalties for paying off your mortgage earlier (chances are, the answer is no). Then ask them to send this information to you in writing. Most likely, they'll be happy to help you, and in any case, it shouldn't take them very long to do the calculations.

If you'd like to check my math, feel free to use the same calculator I did at **www.bankrate.com**. Their mortgage calculator is an excellent resource for better understanding the costs of your mortgage. I ran all these numbers there, and you can easily run yours too.

3 MORE TRICKS TO PAY OFF YOUR MORTGAGE EARLY

1. **Set up a biweekly mortgage.** I love this approach and wrote about it in detail in *The Automatic Millionaire*. I also discussed it on *Oprah*, and it blew people away (it still amazes me people don't know about this mortgage hack). The powerful idea is that rather than paying your mortgage once a month you split your mortgage payment in half and make two payments

a month. So in the previous example, you have a $300,000 mortgage with a 4.5 percent interest rate and your monthly payment is $1,519.98. Instead of making the payment of $1,519.98 once a month, you pay $759.99 every two weeks. **By doing this you will pay your home off in 25 years and one month and save $43,559.62.** It's not quite as good as the system I gave you before, BUT in the real world it works better. Why? Because most likely you are paid every two weeks, so it's much easier on your cash flow and family budget to pay your mortgage every two weeks. Secondly, with a biweekly mortgage it's all done for you—automatically! You don't need to write the checks, track it yourself, or even think about it.

The only trick to this, however, is how to set it up. You may or may not be able to do this one yourself. You need to reach out to your bank and see if they offer a biweekly payment plan. Many banks now do, although some banks charge a small fee (which I think is still worth it).

2. **Make one extra payment a year.** I'm sure you have heard of this one. Almost no one does it. But if you do it and you have the extra payment applied to pay down the principal (make sure the bank does this correctly), then you will pay your mortgage off five years sooner and save $43,044.

3. **Switch your 30-year to a 15-year mortgage.** With interest rates still near record low levels, this one is also really worth considering. Take the $300,000 mortgage example. A 30-year mortgage at 4.5 percent will have a monthly mortgage payment of $1,520. What if you switch it to a 15-year mortgage? Assuming the same rate of interest (it will actually be lower because with a 15-year loan you will get a discount, but let's leave it the same for this example). At 4.5 percent, your payment will now be $2,295. That's $775 more a month, which is a lot, I know. **It's precisely $26 a day more. BUT you will now pay off your home in 15 years and save $134,110!**

One thing to keep in mind: When you make these extra mortgage payments, **pay close attention to your monthly statements**. *Banks often don't credit mortgage accounts properly.* I've had it happen twice with my own mortgage. In one case, we had been making extra payments for eight months—without a penny of it ever being credited against our principal. When we finally noticed, the bank said it thought the extra payments were meant to cover future interest we might owe. Can you believe that? It took us three months to sort things out. The moral: Even if you're not making extra payments, watch your mortgage statement like a hawk!

WHAT ABOUT THE GREAT TAX WRITE-OFF I GET?

I know some of you are probably thinking that I've ignored one of the most important aspects of paying off a mortgage—the fact that mortgage interest is tax-deductible.

You probably think 30-year mortgages are great write-offs because some accountant or financial advisor or well-meaning friend told you they were. And that's not totally crazy. On average, for every $100,000 in mortgage interest you pay, your tax bill will be reduced by $28,500 (28.5 percent being the federal tax bracket of the average citizen). But so what? Since when is it worth spending an extra $100,000 in interest over the life of your mortgage in order to save $28,500 in tax payments?

More than likely, you bought your home because you needed a place to live, not because you needed a great tax write-off. The tax benefits of home ownership are nice, but they don't outweigh the amount you can save by paying off your mortgage early.

If you need another reason to consider speeding up your mortgage payments, think about this: The faster you pay off your home, the sooner you can retire.

Now, there are some experts who disagree with this philosophy. Indeed, one school of thought suggests that rather than trying to pay off a 30-year mortgage more quickly, you should take a 40-year mortgage and strive to never pay it off. Well, that sure sounds like a lot of fun. What woman wouldn't look forward to making mortgage payments for the rest of her life just so she can have a tax write-off?

Even crazier, some financial planners, real-estate gurus, and journalists spent the entire real estate boom saying that you should cash out whatever equity you had in your home and invest it in the stock market or more property. In my opinion, this advice is totally out of touch with reality, especially given the 2008 meltdown of the real estate market. People who treated their homes like wallets and took out every cent of equity were assuming that they would simply "appreciate their way out of any problems." But no boom market lasts forever, and many of those unfortunate folks, some of whom refinanced again and again with shady adjustable-rate loans, faced foreclosure. The reality is that you need a place to live in which you can feel safe and happy. You can't live in a mutual fund or in an insurance policy. I don't care how great the return is, you can't park your car in it. And despite what these experts would have you believe, there are going to be years when the stock market goes down and that "perfect" mutual fund actually appreciates less than your home.

Let's get back to basics. Most people dream of owning their own home. Most people also dream about being able to retire early so they can enjoy their lives and spend time with their loved ones. If you buy a home and pay it off early, you can accomplish both of these dreams. So pay off your mortgage sooner rather than later, and don't ever let some slick salesperson tell you that having money in your home is like having cash "in them thar" walls or under your mattress. Cash in a home is your ultimate equity and your ultimate security. In my opinion, the sooner you own your home free and clear, the better.

WHAT ABOUT PAYING OFF YOUR MORTGAGE RIGHT AWAY?

If you're fortunate enough to enjoy some huge windfall—say, a lump-sum inheritance or a big bonus at work—you may be tempted to take the money and pay off your mortgage in one fell swoop. But before you do anything like that, first get some professional financial advice. While I believe in paying off your mortgage more quickly than the bank would like, it doesn't always make sense to pay it off all at once. There are a lot of variables involved—such as how long you intend to stay in your house, how much money you have, and when you were planning on retiring—and the right course of action isn't always obvious.

One more bit of advice: Avoid "creative" financing like the plague. You've seen what those adjustable-rate, interest-only, and negative amortization loans have done to millions of borrowers who got caught up in buyer fever during the real-estate boom. In the recession, many of them lost their homes as prices plummeted. Creative or "subprime" loans can lead to huge increases in your mortgage payments and even leave you owing more on your home than when you bought it. If you don't have the credit to qualify for a decent fixed-rate mortgage or the cash for a down payment, don't buy a house. Take some of the other steps in this book to fix your credit and save money, and before long you'll be able to buy your dream home . . . and buy it smart. Also, as I write this update, the Federal Reserve has raised rates four times in the past year and it is expected to raise rates four more times in the next year. Don't be creative with your finances. Lock in your rates. You'll sleep better at night.

MISTAKE NO. 4
Waiting to buy a house.

I've gotten countless e-mails from single women—especially those in their twenties and thirties—wondering if they should buy a house or condo. Many ask if it makes sense to hold off on buying real estate until they meet Mr. Right (or Ms. Right) and get married or are ready to settle down.

The answer is unequivocally no! Don't wait. Do it now.

Why the hurry? It's simple. When you own your own home, you are building equity for yourself. When you rent, you are building someone else's equity. (In other words, by renting, you make someone else rich; by owning, you make yourself rich.)

More fundamentally, you should never put off taking a financial action (like buying a house) because of something that might happen later (like getting married). When it comes to your finances, you should always live in the now. If you are single and want your own home, why wait for some man or partner to come along? Go for it.

The number one reason people put off buying a home is that they think they can't afford it. More often than not, they're wrong. While you do need to save up for a down payment, this is an achievable goal for Smart Women.

Second, many people don't realize how much of a house they could get for the equivalent of their current rental payment. To put it really simply, for every $1,000 you pay in monthly rent, you can afford about $125,000 in a mortgage. Say your rent is currently $2,000 a month. For that kind of money, you could get a $250,000 mortgage. In most of the country, $250,000 can buy you a lot of house.

And here's something else to think about. You aren't really in the game of building wealth until you get in the real estate game.

Real estate is an escalator to wealth. You have to be on it to build wealth. Moreover, until you own your own home, you're at the mercy of others. I found this out the hard way. When I wrote this book originally, 30 days before my wedding, I was evicted from my apartment in San Francisco. (I was renting, and the owner decided to move his kid into my unit.)

It was horrible. Not only did it make me feel helpless, but because I had to scramble to find a new place for us to live, I ended up having to pay twice as much for an apartment half the size.

About a year later, we purchased a condo. It was 1998, and real estate prices were sky high. Friends told us we were crazy to buy. Since then, however, the market price of our condo has increased. We have a wonderful home that we own, we now get a tax deduction (because the IRS lets you write off part of your mortgage payments), and we've built real equity. My single biggest regret is that I didn't buy sooner. As I update this book, it is amazing to think how much wealth I have built by simply owning a home. When we moved to New York City from San Francisco, we thought we would be in this city for a few years. We rented the first year and then we bought. Thank goodness—as 16 years later we're still in New York and real estate prices have gone up 200 percent since the time we got here. And rents have nearly doubled. Thankfully, we own. Trust me, long term you want to be an owner not a renter.

Here are some great websites to help you get started on the road to buying a home.

www.aol.com/real-estate
www.homes.com
www.msn.com/en-us/money/realestate
www.myfdre.com
www.realtor.com
www.redfin.com

www.trulia.com
www.zillow.com

MISTAKE NO. 5
Putting off saving for retirement.

According to the Federal Reserve, 47 percent of Americans can't get their hands on $400 in case of an emergency. And again, according to a recent report by GoBankingRates, 42 percent of Americans have less than $10,000 saved for retirement—and are at risk of retiring completely broke. Included within that 42 percent is a disheartening 14 percent of Americans who have put aside *no money whatsoever* for retirement.

This failure rate is not only totally unacceptable, it's also totally unnecessary. The difference between a comfortable future and destitution is literally a matter of no more than a few dollars a month. The problem is, by failing to plan, most of us in effect plan to fail.

The problem is not complicated. The longer you wait to get started, the more you need to save. The following chart illustrates this quite dramatically. It shows the savings records of two women, Susan and Kim. Susan began saving for retirement at age 19. For eight years, she put $2,000 a year into an investment account; then, at age 26, she stopped, never putting in another dime. Kim, on the other hand, waited until she turned 27 to begin putting money away for retirement. Starting then, and continuing right up through the age of 65, Kim put $2,000 into an investment account every year. Who came out ahead? The following chart shows the answer, and I'll bet you'll find it surprising.

As we discussed in Step Five, the best way to get started saving for retirement is to arrange to have it done without your having to think about it—that is, to have your monthly contribution either

THE TIME VALUE OF MONEY

Invest Now Rather Than Later

	SUSAN Investing at Age 19 (10% Annual Return)		S		KIM Investing at Age 27 (10% Annual Return)	
AGE	INVESTMENT	TOTAL VALUE	E E	AGE	INVESTMENT	TOTAL VALUE
19	$2,000	2,200		19	0	0
20	2,000	4,620		20	0	0
21	2,000	7,282		21	0	0
22	2,000	10,210	T	22	0	0
23	2,000	13,431	H	23	0	0
24	2,000	16,974	E	24	0	0
25	2,000	20,871		25	0	0
26	2,000	25,158		26	0	0
27	0	27,674		27	$2,000	2,200
28	0	30,442		28	2,000	4,620
29	0	33,486		29	2,000	7,282
30	0	36,834	D	30	2,000	10,210
31	0	40,518	I	31	2,000	13,431
32	0	44,570	F	32	2,000	16,974
33	0	48,027	F	33	2,000	20,871
34	0	53,929	E	34	2,000	25,158
35	0	59,322	R	35	2,000	29,874
36	0	65,256	E	36	2,000	35,072
37	0	71,780	N	37	2,000	40,768
38	0	78,958	C	38	2,000	47,045
39	0	86,854	E	39	2,000	53,949
40	0	95,540		40	2,000	61,544
41	0	105,094		41	2,000	69,899
42	0	115,603		42	2,000	79,089
43	0	127,163		43	2,000	89,198
44	0	139,880		44	2,000	100,318
45	0	153,868		45	2,000	112,550
46	0	169,255		46	2,000	126,005
47	0	188,180		47	2,000	140,805
48	0	204,798		48	2,000	157,086
49	0	226,278		49	2,000	174,094
50	0	247,806		50	2,000	194,694
51	0	272,586		51	2,000	216,363
52	0	299,845		52	2,000	240,199
53	0	329,830		53	2,000	266,419
54	0	362,813		54	2,000	295,261
55	0	399,094		55	2,000	326,988
56	0	439,003		56	2,000	361,886
57	0	482,904		57	2,000	400,275
58	0	531,194		58	2,000	442,503
59	0	584,314		59	2,000	488,953
60	0	642,745		60	2,000	540,048
61	0	707,020		61	2,000	596,253
62	0	777,722		62	2,000	658,078
63	0	855,494		63	2,000	726,086
64	0	941,043		64	2,000	800,895
65	0	1,035,148		65	2,000	883,185

EARNINGS BEYOND INVESTMENT	EARNINGS BEYOND INVESTMENT
$1,019,148	$805,185

SUSAN EARNS	$1,019,148
KIM EARNS	$805,185
SUSAN EARNS MORE	$213,963

Susan invested one fifth the dollars but has 25% more to show
START INVESTING EARLY!

deducted directly from your paycheck or **automatically** transferred from your checking account each month. The benefits of this approach are enormous. First (and most important), you can't spend what you don't see in your checking account. Second, it spares you having to debate with yourself whether you *really* need to make a contribution this month. Third, contributing once or twice a month is a lot easier than writing a big check at the end of the year. The fact is, most people who wait until the end of the year to fund their retirement plans end up either not doing it or putting too little away.

Remember, the sooner you start saving for retirement, the sooner you will be able to finish rich and go play! For more information on how to make your financial life automatic and easy, you might check out my book *The Automatic Millionaire.* (It has also recently been updated.)

> ### MISTAKE NO. 6
> ### Speculating with your investment money.

Everyone who sets foot in a Las Vegas casino may feel like a potential winner, but show me a gambler and I will show you a future loser. That's because when it comes to gambling, the odds always favor the house. It's may be possible to get lucky, but people who gamble will eventually lose. Always.

This is just as true when it comes to investing. Of course, the investment world calls this activity "speculation" instead of gambling, but it basically means the same thing. Just like a gambler, a speculator is looking to make a fast buck. And just like gambling at a casino, you will see a speculator get lucky every once in a while. However, over time, nothing is worse for your financial security than speculating with your investment money. This should be obvious, but it's not; otherwise, millions of Americans wouldn't be speculating in the market every day.

Here are the most common ways to speculate—avoid them!

TRYING TO TIME THE MARKET

Trying to time the market DOES NOT WORK. The idea that you are going to figure out when to move from stocks, bonds, and other investments to cash and avoid the next market downturn is a myth. According to no less an expert than Nobel laureate William Sharpe, an investor would need to be correct about timing the market 82 percent of the time just to **match** the returns you will get if you follow a buy-and-hold strategy over a period of decades. If you are thinking that an 82 percent rate of correct market timing seems doable, try this on for size: Warren Buffett, who is by all accounts one of the world's foremost experts in the stock market, aims for accurate market timing only about two-thirds of the time.

Here's the plain truth: You cannot successfully time the market. At best, you may get lucky once. You may be able to go to cash right before the market goes down but then you'll be sitting in cash when the market quickly recovers and leaves you behind in the dust. Most people move to cash after the market corrects, and they DESTROY their retirement.

Investors who moved to cash in record amounts in 2009 then sat in cash and watched their retirement earn nothing after losing 50 percent. Then, to add insult to injury, the market turned around and went up for eight straight years. Ironically, many of these investors are now getting back into the market at the all-time high. Please seriously listen to me on this: You will not succeed in timing the market. What works when you invest in the market is **TIME IN THE MARKET, NOT TIMING THE MARKET.** Sorry, we're not done here because this issue is too important to blow by—and important enough to appear both here and in *Smart Couples Finish Rich*. I need to make sure you understand how big a mistake it is to try to time the market.

3 REASONS TIMING THE MARKET DOESN'T WORK

1. History shows timing the market doesn't work.

I show this chart in my seminars. Look at it closely. Read it twice. Let it sink in.

MISSING THE 30 BEST DAYS COULD CUT YOUR RETURN TO A LOSS

If you had invested a hypothetical $100,000 in the S&P 500 on December 31, 1997, by December 31, 2017, your $100,000 would have grown to $401,346, an average annual total return of 7.19%.

But suppose during that five-year period there were times when you decided to get out of the market and, as a result, you missed the market's 10 best single-day performances. In that case, your 7.19% return would have fallen to 3.53%. If you had missed the market's 30 best days, that 7.19% return would have dropped to –0.91%. Of course, past performance cannot guarantee comparable future results.

THE PENALTY FOR MISSING THE MARKET

Trying to time the market can be an inexact—and costly—exercise.
S&P 500 Index: December 31, 1997–December 31, 2017

Period of Investment	Average Annual Total Return	Growth of $100,000
Fully Invested	7.19%	$401,346
Miss the 10 Best Days	3.53%	$200,296
Miss the 30 Best Days	–0.91%	$83,315
Miss the 50 Best Days	–4.52%	$39,649

Source: Sterling Capital

2. Taxes cost you when you time the market.

The problem with moving from stocks and bonds to cash is that if you have profits, **you pay taxes** (assuming the money was in a taxable account). You're either going to pay ordinary income if it's a short-term gain or long-term capital gains tax if you've held the investment long enough to qualify. I think about this a lot with the markets at an all-time high right now. Here's the basic math. Let's say I have an investment that is up $10,000. If I sell it to avoid losing money when the market goes down, I'm personally going to pay at least 33 percent in taxes on long-term capital gains (that's the brutal reality of living in New York City; I will have state and city taxes on top of federal). That means the market has to drop 33 percent to equal my decision to sell the investment and protect my gains to be even. Well, markets rarely drop 33 percent. The tax math makes selling to protect my gains against a short-term correction pretty silly to even try.

3. Markets recover fast—and you can easily miss the recovery.

Stock markets experience declines—and these declines are normal. They're not fun, but they are normal. Over the past 50 years there have been 14 market corrections (a market that declines by more than 10 percent) and 11 bear markets (a decline of more than 20 percent). The average recovery took 107 days. That's basically three months. See the two great charts that follow. So why do investors bail out of markets consistently after declines? Because they believe it's going to get worse, not better. History shows that the markets ALWAYS RECOVER. **There has never, ever been a declining market that has not ultimately recovered.** Please remember this at the next downturn. If anything, when you see the next stock market decline ask yourself and your financial advisor whether that is the time to add to your investments. Are things on sale? They just might be. Most important, remember that it pays to stay invested. It's expensive to panic.

MARKET DECLINES HAVE ALWAYS RECOVERED

S&P 500 Corrections (Declines Greater Than 10% But Less Than 20%) 1965–2014

| Peak | | Trough | | Recovery | | Number of Days | |
Date	Adj Close	Date	Adj Close	Date	% Drop	Peak to Trough	Trough to Recovery
4/2/12	1419.04	6/1/12	1278.04	9/6/12	−9.94%	61	98
4/15/10	1211.67	7/2/10	1022.58	11/4/10	−15.61%	79	126
11/27/02	938.87	3/11/03	800.73	5/27/03	−14.71%	105	78
2/18/97	816.29	4/11/97	737.65	5/5/97	−9.63%	53	25
10/10/83	172.65	7/24/84	147.82	1/21/85	−14.38%	289	182
2/13/80	118.44	3/27/80	98.22	7/7/80	−17.07%	44	103
10/5/79	111.27	11/7/79	99.87	1/18/80	−10.25%	34	73
9/12/78	106.99	11/14/78	92.49	8/10/79	−13.55%	64	270
6/30/75	95.19	8/21/75	83.07	1/12/76	−12.73%	53	145
11/7/74	75.21	12/6/74	65.01	1/27/75	−13.56%	30	53
9/8/71	101.34	11/23/71	90.16	12/20/71	−11.03%	77	28
4/28/71	104.77	8/9/71	93.53	1/18/72	−10.73%	104	163
10/9/67	97.51	3/5/68	87.72	4/29/68	−10.04%	149	56
5/13/65	90.27	6/28/65	81.60	10/5/65	−9.60%	47	100
				Mean	−12.35%	85	107
				Min	−17.07%	30	25
				Max	−9.60%	289	270

Bear Markets and Corrections, 1965-2015

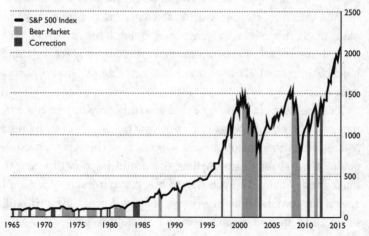

INVESTING IN COMPANIES THAT DON'T MAKE A PROFIT

You might think this would be obvious, but another very common way people lose money in the stock market is by investing in companies that don't make a profit. Buying stock means you are making an investment in a business. While some businesses run like well-oiled machines and make money year after year, others are poorly run (or maybe just brand new) and lose money. Wouldn't you prefer to invest money in a company that consistently makes money instead of one that doesn't? Of course you would. But despite this basic common-sense strategy, thousands of people buy stock every day in companies that have never shown a profit—or even produced a proven product. This happened in the late 1990s and early 2000s with Internet-related stocks. It seemed like companies could simply add the words "Internet" or "cyber-something" to their prospectuses, and the investing public would throw money at them. This Internet craze meant that some companies that were only in business for a year or two were worth billions of dollars on paper—despite consistently losing money. That's not sustainable. Eventually, of course, most of these "hot stocks" cooled off, and many of the investors who were sucked in by all the excitement lost their shirts. It's now happening with "cryptocurrency" or anything blockchain related. It's the same issue, new "thing." And it always ends badly.

There are people who argue that investing only in proven companies with solid earnings is a great way to miss out on the next Microsoft. I think this argument is nonsense. There is no need to get in on the absolute ground floor of a promising new company to make money from it. If you wait to buy into a new company until after it has compiled four or five years of steady profits, you will still be getting a great investment that will continue to grow.

Let's look at Microsoft itself. A super-cautious investor might have waited for the company to report profits for ten years in a row before she was willing to invest. She would have still made good money on the stock. Between 1995 (ten full years after the company first reported profits) and 2017, the price of Microsoft stock went from just under $4.50 per share to over $90 per share. That kind of growth is nothing to sneeze at, and it wouldn't require any risky investing.

So why take chances? Leave the risky businesses to the venture capitalists. As long as you are investing to secure your future, you should stick to solid companies with proven track records.

Five-Star Tip: The preceding section was written in 1998, before the technology boom really took off—and before it came crashing back to earth. For a long time after the first edition of this book was published early in 1999, I can't tell you how many people questioned my argument against investing in "dot-coms." Before the party ended, more than 500 such companies went public, feeding on our national appetite for get-rich-quick schemes. Companies like Webvan, Pets.com, and Etoys spent hundreds of millions of dollars on ads aimed at "building a brand"—only to find that if you don't make money, you can't stay in business. By now, we all know that the dot-com craze became a dot-com bust. But don't think it's all behind us. Every decade has its own dot-com craze, and the mistake is always the same. Investors get caught up in investing in what's hot, instead of in what's making money. Ultimately, they get their clocks cleaned. The rule is simple: no earnings, no investment. The dot-com of our time now will be the cryptocurrency craze. You watch—many of these "ICOs" (initial coin offerings) will be worthless. Billions will be lost. Or as Warren Buffett remarked about the crypto mania: "I expect it to end badly."

ACTIVELY TRADING YOUR ACCOUNT

One thing that makes women potentially better investors than men is that women generally are better at committing to the long term. When men buy stocks, they tend to get fidgety; they are constantly looking around, wondering if some better investment isn't waiting for them just around the corner. And while actively buying and selling investments may sound like a great way to stay on top of market developments, the fact is that there are only two winners when you trade frequently: the firm that executes your trades (because it earns a commission on every one of your transactions) and the IRS (because it gets to collect a piece of your profits every time you sell an investment for more than you bought it). There's no getting around it; under current tax laws, you simply cannot win over the long term by actively buying and selling stock in the short term.

Let's say you buy a stock at $10 a share and less than a year later you sell it at $12. You might think you made a 20 percent return, but you really didn't. First off, it probably cost you 25 cents a share to buy the stock and 25 cents a share to sell it. Right there, your $2 profit is cut to $1.50. Second, if you sell a stock at a profit within 12 months of when you bought it, you could end up paying as much as 40 percent of your earnings in short-term capital gains taxes. So there goes another 80 cents. Suddenly your 20 percent return has been reduced to around 7 percent. And that's assuming you actually did everything right and bought a stock that went up and then sold it at a profit.

The point is this: When it comes to investing in stocks, the key word is *investing*. You don't invest in a business by making a speculative stock purchase in the hope of a favorable short-term movement. You invest for the long term, with the goal of owning a particular company's stock for years. Trust me—this philosophy will make you significantly more money. At the very least, you'll end up paying far less in commissions and taxes.

THROWING GOOD MONEY AFTER BAD

I can't tell you how often I've seen people persuaded to put more money into an investment that has just suffered a significant drop in price—the so-called logic being that having fallen in price, the investment must now be a bargain.

This is known in the investment world as buying on dips. Often financial advisors will suggest that if you liked a stock at $20 a share, it must be an even better buy at $10. But just because the price of a stock has dropped, that doesn't mean it's now "on sale." That's true only if the company is well run and its stock happens to be down simply because of some short-term market gyration, rather than business problems that could prevent it from making money in the future.

I learned this the hard way. I once owned a stock that hit $65 a share and then started falling like a rock. When it reached $3, I said the stupidest thing I've ever said to myself: "Gosh, $3 sure seems cheap. If management can turn things around, it will be back to $10 in no time." With that in mind, I bought a thousand more shares— and watched the price go straight down the tubes to zero. And this was a company with a board of directors whose membership read like a "Who's Who" of American business.

The point of this expensive lesson was clear: When a stock price falls through the floor, and the company doesn't have a convincing explanation for the collapse (or a specific plan in place to correct the problem), don't add to your financial misery by doubling down. As investment guru Warren Buffett once put it: "The most important thing to do when you find yourself in a hole is to stop digging."

> ### MISTAKE NO. 7
> ### Building a portfolio that's not diversified.

If the dot-com bust and the last recession taught us anything about the stock market, it's that without a properly diversified portfolio, you can really get hurt financially!

Let this sink in for a moment. Greed makes people do really dumb things. Back when I was running The Bach Group, around 2000, I had some irate clients calling me wanting to know why all their money wasn't in technology stocks. These clients (almost all of them men) would call me and say, "David, why don't I own Yahoo? My friend bought it, and he's making a fortune."

Even worse, well-intentioned clients would call me and say they'd just heard some "expert" on the radio who insisted they had to own "the Nasdaq," whatever that was, so now they wanted to move all their money into it.

The worst part about all this was that most of these people were over 65! I actually lost a client, an 80-year-old woman, who was furious with me because I told her it was crazy to put half her assets into dot-com stocks. She told me I was an old fuddy-duddy.

There I was, 33 at the time, trying to protect an 80-year-old woman's nest egg, and I'm the fuddy-duddy.

Looking back, it would be funny if it wasn't so sad. The technology boom that supposedly made people instant millionaires in a matter of months (instead of the decades it's supposed to take) wound up going bust almost as fast as it went boom. And it was the "retail investors" (which is to say, you and me) who were the ones who got creamed . . . as usual. The winners were the institutional investors who bought shares of these risky companies at the initial offering price, sometimes as low as $10 a share, and then flipped them a few hours later for $90 a share. You and I didn't get that chance.

Still, some good did come out of it. It reminded us that there are no shortcuts. The only sure way to get rich is to do so slowly by building a well-diversified, rock-solid portfolio. As I noted earlier, you cannot time the market. Nor can you anticipate which sector of the market is going to be hot next week, next month, or next year.

Some people find this hard to accept. One of the worst things investors do is look at their portfolios at the end of a year and decide to sell stocks of theirs that didn't go up and buy ones that did.

In 1999, for example, value stocks and value mutual funds did horribly, either staying flat or going down. At the same time, growth stocks and growth funds went through the roof, shooting up as much as 40 percent that year. But if you had let hindsight be your guide and flipped out of value investments and into growth holdings at the end of 1999, you'd have gotten killed over the next 12 months

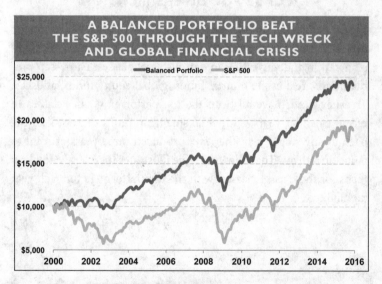

Source: Bloomberg, Based on $10,000 Starting Portfolio: 25% S&P 500, 25% S&P SmallCap 600, 25% Barclay's U.S. Aggregate Government/Corporate Bond Index, 25% Barclay's U.S. Government T-Bills Index, Rebalanced Annually.

as the Nasdaq tanked, falling more than 70 percent. And to make matters worse, while growth investments were collapsing, value stocks and funds were rising by more than 30 percent!

The chart on page 291 shows in simple terms exactly why you need to maintain a diversified portfolio. Trust me on this. You'll see lots of books in the stores written by "experts" who will tell you that one particular type of asset is fundamentally superior to all the others—and that, as a result, you should put all your money in it alone. In my opinion they are wrong. History has shown that no asset class will always outperform every other asset class. Because of human nature, strong asset classes inevitably become "overbought" (that is, overenthusiastic investors bid up prices too high). At that point, people panic and values plunge. So stay diversified.

A CASE FOR DIVERSIFICATION

In real estate, it's location, location, location. In asset allocation, it's diversification, diversification, diversification. A sound investment plan can include investing in various asset classes. Large-cap mutual funds, real estate mutual funds, global equity funds, and U.S. Treasury funds have all been the top-performing asset classes in recent calendar years, and while small-cap funds did not lead the pack in any single year, they still produced three years of solid to fantastic returns. The following table illustrates the average total returns for these asset classes, with the top performers for each year highlighted:

Year	Large-Cap Funds	Small-Cap Funds	Real-Estate Funds	World Equity Funds	General U.S. Treasury Funds
2005	7.05	4.55	12.16	13.54	1.77
2006	22.25	18.37	35.06	26.34	4.25
2007	11.81	−1.57	−15.69	11.17	6.83
2008	−36.85	−33.79	−37.73	−43.38	4.97
2009	37.21	27.17	27.99	31.78	3.82
2010	26.85	16.71	27.95	15.51	2.80
2011	−4.18	2.64	8.28	0.39	1.59
2012	16.35	15.26	19.70	17.51	1.25
2013	38.82	33.48	2.86	32.53	0.64
2014	13.05	4.89	28.03	−4.90	0.77
2015	5.67	−1.38	2.83	−0.81	0.45
2016	7.08	11.32	8.63	1.00	1.09
2017	27.65	21.78	4.83	9.45	0.31

Source: Invesco and Portfolio Visualizer

MISTAKE NO. 8
Paying too much in taxes.

The biggest enemy of your financial future is taxes. Yet when I review the financial situation of new clients, you'd be amazed how often it turns out that their previous advisors never did any tax planning for them.

When you are building an investment portfolio, it is absolutely imperative that you take into consideration your potential tax liability. The reason I spent so much time in Step Four and Step

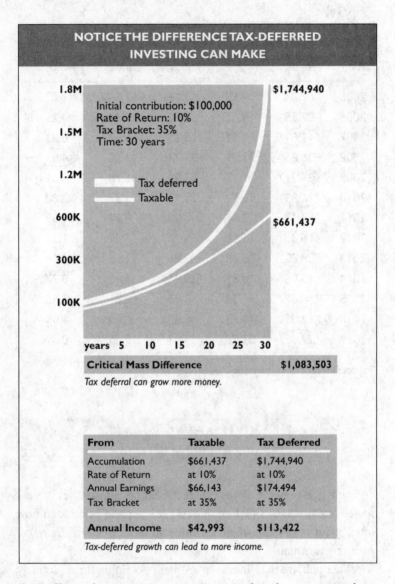

NOTICE THE DIFFERENCE TAX-DEFERRED INVESTING CAN MAKE

Initial contribution: $100,000
Rate of Return: 10%
Tax Bracket: 35%
Time: 30 years

Tax deferred
Taxable

$1,744,940
$661,437

| Critical Mass Difference | $1,083,503 |

Tax deferral can grow more money.

From	Taxable	Tax Deferred
Accumulation	$661,437	$1,744,940
Rate of Return	at 10%	at 10%
Annual Earnings	$66,143	$174,494
Tax Bracket	at 35%	at 35%
Annual Income	**$42,993**	**$113,422**

Tax-deferred growth can lead to more income.

Five talking about retirement accounts is that the money in them grows tax-deferred, which helps you to grow your nest egg much faster. The difference in not paying taxes on your investments over a 10- to 30-year period can be huge! It can mean the difference between financial pain or financial pleasure. The chart on page 292 shows how much faster your money will grow if it is invested in tax-deferred vehicles. Over a typical 30-year period, you could literally be talking about millions of additional dollars in your pocket!

As you can see, your money grows significantly faster when the profits are not drained away by taxes. Always seek to minimize your taxes when investing; ideally you should seek investments that grow tax-deferred.

MISTAKE NO. 9
Buying an investment that is illiquid.

An illiquid investment is one that you cannot sell immediately. To me, immediately means in less than five business days. If I can't sell it within five business days, I won't buy it. Why? Show me an investment you can't sell for a fixed period of time and I'll show you a potential problem.

Now, don't get me wrong. I'm not arguing against buying a home, or an investment such as a government bond that takes ten years to mature, or a mutual fund with an annual sales fee. All of these things may have a perfectly proper place in your investment portfolio. What I'm warning you against buying is something that is not salable for a specific period of time, no matter what. An example of the kind of illiquid investment I hate is a *limited partnership*—the two most dreaded words in the Smart Woman's financial vocabulary. When I bring up limited partnerships in my classes, I often hear moans and groans from a few of the older students. That tells me they have some experience with the subject.

Limited partnerships generally are set up to pool investors' money in order to purchase certain types of investments, typically real estate. The problem is that most limited partnerships are not salable—that is, not liquid—usually for as long as 10 to 15 years. "Don't worry about it," the salesperson typically tells a potential investor. "The money you're investing is for retirement and you won't need it for 20 years anyway." Sure, but what happens if an emergency arises and you've got to get your hands on your money early?

Now, I know some people will dispute me on this and insist that limited partnerships can make sense. Well, I'm sorry; I have seen too many account statements and heard too many firsthand stories from people who were burned by this kind of investment. As far as I'm concerned, limited partnerships are a bad idea for ordinary investors. They are not liquid, so don't buy them. Period. (If for some reason you come across a limited partnership that you feel you just have to be a part of, then my rule of thumb is don't put more than 10 percent of your investable assets into it. This way if you lose your whole investment, your financial world won't be completely devastated.)

Limited partnerships are hardly the only illiquid investment out there, so don't let down your guard. For example, there are investment companies (offering everything from collectable coins to second mortgages) that claim to make a "secondary market" in the investment they are selling. That's all well and good, but in many cases, they slip into the fine print a disclaimer saying they are not obligated to buy out your investment if you want to sell. *If that's the case, then what you're buying is not really a liquid investment.*

One of the worst cases I know of in this regard concerns a former client of mine named Barbara. Back in 1991, a devastating fire wiped out more than 2,800 homes in the hills above Berkeley, California. Barbara's home was one of them. Fortunately, she had adequate fire insurance. Her insurance company settled her claim for more than $500,000 and Barbara went about planning to rebuild her home.

Since construction wouldn't be ready to start for six months, Barbara put the money in a bank CD (a great place for short-term funds). A few weeks later a neighbor who was in a similar situation asked her what she'd done with her insurance money. When Barbara told him it was sitting in a CD earning 5 percent, the neighbor rolled his eyes. His insurance money, he claimed, was earning 15 percent.

That got Barbara's attention. The neighbor explained that a friend of his who invested in secondary mortgages had let him in on a deal. Barbara was impressed, and to make a long story short, she wound up giving her neighbor's friend half her insurance money—$250,000 in all—to invest in secondary mortgages. The friend's pitch was simple. The money would be safe because it would be backed by real estate. In any case, Barbara didn't need to worry because short-term investments in secondary mortgages were very easy to buy and sell. She would be paid 180 days' worth of interest up front and then get her principal back at the end of the 180 days. It sounded too good to be true.

It was. Barbara got her interest payment up front, but when the 180 days were up, she found herself waiting in vain for her $250,000 principal to be returned. When she went to ask her neighbor's friend what was going on, she discovered he was nowhere to be found. In a panic, Barbara ran to local courthouse to check the records on the property she supposedly had a second mortgage on. The property was in foreclosure—as a result of which Barbara's investment was unsellable.

Had Barbara used the rule of not investing in illiquid investments, she never would have had this problem. The fact is, secondary mortgages are almost never easily liquid because they are backed by real estate that would have to be sold for you to get your money back.

Liquid means that the public (that is, anyone you choose to sell to) can buy you out easily and quickly—ideally, in less than five business days. Examples of liquid investments include stocks, bonds, mutual funds, money markets, certificates of deposit, Treasury bills, and annuities. In fact, most investments are liquid. Just remember to ask the question: "If I absolutely had to, could I sell this and get my money within five business days?" If the answer is no, think hard before you put any money into the investment.

MISTAKE NO. 10
Giving up.

I once asked my grandmother if she had ever made any major mistakes investing. She told me that the first stock she ever bought went straight down and she lost everything she had invested. As she explained it, she had gotten a "tip" and just jumped in. She actually invested only a couple of hundred dollars, but at the time that represented a full year's worth of savings. She told me she felt sick and embarrassed, and was afraid to tell my grandfather.

"Well, what did you do?" I asked her.

"What could I do?" she replied with a smile. "The money was gone." Still, she realized one important thing: The problem was not the stock market; the problem was her inexperience with investing. "So I set out to become smart about investing and do it right the next time," she told me.

And that's just what she did. She read books (like the one you're reading now) as well as financial magazines and newsletters, she took classes, and in general she made an effort to get smart about investing. Did she invest perfectly from then on? Of course not. She made plenty of mistakes at first, but she learned from them, and over the years she built a million-dollar portfolio.

People often make a financial mistake, get bad advice, and then give up on their dream of financial security. *Don't let this happen to you.* You now know more than most people about how to avoid the most common mistakes that can be made with your investment dollars. Are there more pitfalls out there? Absolutely. Might you stumble into one of them? Possibly. But don't let that keep you from getting where you want to go. As you continue on your journey and acquire more knowledge of and control over your finances, you will start to be able to spot bad money decisions a mile away. It will be as if they have a huge sign on them reading "Kiss your money good-bye!"

Yes, you should be careful, but don't become overcautious. By learning to avoid the common pitfalls investors make, you can minimize your risk and put yourself on the road to financial security. But remember—*the biggest mistake you can make is not to become an investor.* And please remember that every single market correction and crash we have ever seen has been followed by a recovery.

RAISING SMART KIDS
TO FINISH RICH

Imagine for a moment how different your life would be if you had learned everything this book has just taught you about handling money when you were still a kid.

The fact is, you shouldn't have needed the material in this book. All this stuff should have been taught to you in school, along with math and reading and history. But for some reason, our educational system has decided that there is no room in the schools for lessons about money. Sure, there are some great creative teachers here and there who take it upon themselves to teach their students about handling their finances. But it's never been part of the mandatory curriculum.

To send a child off into the "real world" without teaching him or her how to be smart about money is to set that child up for failure.

With this in mind, I ask that you read this chapter whether or not you have kids—even if you're single and are convinced you'll never have a family. Why? Because teaching smart kids to finish rich is not about just teaching your own kids, it's about teaching *all* kids.

Perhaps you have a friend who has a child. Maybe you've got a niece or nephew. You could become their mentor.

Perhaps your kids are grown. Maybe you're a grandmother. Remember, as I related in the introduction, my entire life was shaped by the fact that my grandmother Rose Bach started teaching me at the age of seven that even a kid could become an investor. It was Grandma Bach who told me, "David, if you saved your birthday money and your weekly allowance, you could start buying stocks— and one day you could become a millionaire!" Grandma knew how to get my attention.

Unfortunately, most parents and grandparents don't do what she did. They don't teach their kids about money. As a result, their kids grow up financially illiterate. You can do something about that—we all can, and we all should.

OUR SCHOOL SYSTEM IS FAILING OUR CHILDREN FINANCIALLY

The national Council for Economic Education reports that a whopping 66 percent of high school students flunked a test of basic economic principles. Unfortunately, adults weren't much better informed, as 57 percent of the adults who took the test also failed it. What kinds of information did these students and adults not know? Two-thirds of all test-takers did not know that money does not hold its value in times of inflation, and two-thirds of the students who took the test were unaware that the stock market brings together people who want to buy stocks with those who want to sell them.

These results are frightening to me, and I expect they are for you too. However, shaking our heads won't do anything, since the situation won't change unless we change it. Think back to your school years. How many investing classes did you have? Did your teachers ever talk to you about retirement accounts, mortgages, stocks and bonds, or the miracle of compound interest? When I ask these questions in my seminars, invariably fewer than 1 person out of 20 answers in the affirmative. Often, the response is so poor that I'll tap the microphone and ask, "Is this thing working? Can you people hear me?" This usually gets a laugh . . . but no additional yeses.

Why is there such an education gap when it comes to finance? Why is it that our schools, which are supposed to prepare us for the real world, don't teach us anything about money? According to a 2016 study by PricewaterhouseCoopers (PwC), K–12 teachers in the United States don't feel comfortable providing a financial education to their students. The survey found that only 31 percent of teachers would describe themselves as "completely comfortable" teaching financial literacy, with another 51 percent feeling "moderately comfortable," and another 18 percent feeling "not comfortable at all."

In addition to this level of discomfort among our nation's teachers, PwC identifies four major barriers to including financial literacy in the classroom: Teachers lack appropriate curricula, qualifications, and take-home materials—and many teachers don't see financial education as a critical skill for college and career readiness.

This is not to pick on our nation's teachers. It's tough to teach what you don't know, and unless we get better at teaching financial literacy across the board, this problem could easily perpetuate itself. Meanwhile, it's left to parents to teach their kids about money. Unfortunately . . .

PARENTS ARE FAILING TOO!

Parents don't feel much more comfortable with financial literacy. According to a 2016 Consumer Financial Literacy Survey conducted by the National Foundation for Credit Counseling, 44 percent of American consumers would give themselves a grade of C or below on their knowledge of personal finance, and 41 percent of adults do not feel confident that they would be able to repay a $30,000 loan for education.

The conclusion to be drawn from this is clear: We have a system that is set up for failure. Our schools don't teach kids anything about money and parents are left to teach what they can—but since parents don't feel confident in their own financial knowledge, the cycle of financial illiteracy goes on and on.

THE GOOD NEWS . . . EDUCATION ABOUT MONEY CAN HELP!

Ultimately, what we need is a mandatory national financial literacy program—something similar to the Presidential Fitness Program the White House created back in the 1960s to teach our kids about the importance of being physically fit.

That program motivated millions of kids to get in shape. I know because I was one of those kids struggling on the pull-up bar in the third grade, unable to do a single chin-up. I remember being ashamed and humiliated by the experience of taking a national fitness test and failing. But it also motivated me.

It took me until the eighth grade, but I finally got that Presidential Fitness Badge. I felt proud that day, but more important, fitness became a way of life for me. To this day, I still work out four times a week.

If you agree with me that we need a national financial literacy program, you should make your voice heard. Let your representatives in Washington hear from you. (These days, it's easy to do online at **www.usa.gov**.) Tell your representatives you believe strongly that we need a mandatory national standard for financial education.

THE GOVERNMENT AND THE STATES ARE STARTING TO LISTEN . . .

Believe it or not, progress has been made in the past 20 years, since I wrote the first edition of this book. The Council for Economic Education releases a biannual study, the latest of which found that 20 states currently mandate that high school students take economics. Additionally, 16 states require standardized testing on economic concepts (this is the real key). According to CNBC, 45 states now include personal finance in their K–12 standards, up from 21 in 1998. Their reporting indicated that the more rigorous the standards, the better the results. The fact is that financial education works if it's mandatory. Studies show that students' credit scores are better and they have fewer late payments on credit after they take a course on money. The problem is that this financial education is not mandatory nationally, in all states. There is simply more work to be done, and we should start now at home.

THE RIGHT TIME TO TEACH THE KIDS IS NOW

You don't have to wait until your kids' schools teach them about money. That might not happen. So let's assume it's actually up to us. The question is, when is the right time to begin teaching your kids about money? Here's a test to help you determine the answer. Put a $1 bill in your left hand and a $100 bill in your right hand. Then ask your child which one he or she wants.

Children who are smart enough to know that the $100 bill is the one to go for are smart enough to start learning about money. So far, the youngest child I've heard of who could pass this test was a three-year-old. Try it out. You may find you have a future Warren Buffett on your hands.

COACHING SMART KIDS TO FINISH RICH

The most important thing to understand when it comes to teaching children about money is that all kids are not created equal. Obviously, yours is smarter than most, but every child should be allowed to go at his or her own pace.

In any case, here are eight simple steps you can take to get your children started on the journey to living and finishing rich.

STEP ONE
Explain where money comes from.

The first thing you need to explain to a young child about money is where it comes from. In our increasingly cashless society, many kids may not connect the fact that the plastic card you swipe at the grocery store, or the iPhone app you scan at a card reader, is spending money that looks like the cash they receive in birthday cards. When it comes to cash, kids may actually think money comes from a device that lives in a wall (what you and I would recognize as an ATM).

Perhaps the place to start is with the expression "Money doesn't grow on trees." We've all heard that phrase, you can tell your children, but do they know where money does come from?

Take out a dollar bill and some change, and explain how the United States Government manufactures currency. Then explain what it represents: how you earn it by working or investing, how you spend it to pay for the home you live in, the clothes you wear, and the food you eat. Have your child sit with you while you pay bills, and explain that the numbers on the screen correlate to dollar bills. This will help them recognize that just because you're not handling little green pieces of paper, you are still spending, saving, and investing money.

The older your children are, the more detailed you can and should be. If your kids are over the age of ten, don't hesitate to tell them in excruciating detail exactly what happens to your paycheck—how much goes to taxes and Social Security, to mortgage payments, to insurance, utilities, car payments, phone bills, and all the other necessities of life. Most children have no idea about their family finances. In fact, many parents find it easier to talk to their kids about sex than about money. This is why it's so important to invite your kids into your financial routines. Just as you can't expect your kids to learn to cook if they're barred from the kitchen during dinner prep, you can't expect them to learn how to handle money if they're kept out of your financial decisions.

Be honest with your kids . . . and be positive.

If your family is having money troubles, don't try to hide it. Your kids are probably aware of your problems anyway. But whatever you do, be positive. Explain that money is a really good thing when it is used respectfully, how it can help you lead a better life and help others, but that it is not a measure of your worth as a human being.

Many parents give the wrong message about money to their kids. Either they equate wealth with goodness or they say that people who have money are greedy. (Sometimes they deliver both these contradictory messages at the same time.) You want your kids to be attracted to money, not afraid of it. You want them to be comfortable with money.

> **STEP TWO**
> **Teach them the miracle of compound interest.**

Albert Einstein once said that the most miraculous phenomenon he knew was the miracle of compound interest. Many adults are still in the dark about this. You're not, so don't keep it a secret. Show your kids the charts on pages 120 and 122. Explain to them what can happen to a dollar when you invest it, instead of spend it.

HOW A DOLLAR A DAY CAN GROW UP TO BE $1 MILLION

Here's what happens if you save a dollar a day and then put it to work for you.

$1 a day at 10% = $1 million in 56 years
$1 a day at 15% = $1 million in 40 years
$1 a day at 20% = $1 million in 32 years

Makes you wonder, doesn't it, why we don't place more value on one-dollar bills. What if you really went crazy and saved $2 a day?

$2 a day at 10% = $1 million in 49 years
$2 a day at 15% = $1 million in 36 years
$2 a day at 20% = $1 million in 28 years

By the way, please don't start thinking like a skeptical adult and say, "Oh, but you can't find those kinds of returns." You can. Go to **www.morningstar.com** or **http://finance.yahoo.com** and do a search for mutual funds that have generated an average annual return of 10 percent or more over the past ten years. You'll find there are plenty.

In any case, the point here is not about investment returns. It's about the power of compound interest. Kids get excited by it. So do teenagers. When you show them what compounding does, they won't react the way many adults do and look for reasons why it can't work. To the contrary, they will realize that the dollar they've been wasting on a candy bar every day could make them rich! They will want to save and become investors. Which is your goal.

Five-Star Tip: Here's a real nugget on compound interest that is sure to catch your kid's attention. (It comes from J. J. Pritchard's book on finances for children, *Quest for the Pillars of Wealth*.) If, when he arrived in the New World in 1492, Christopher Columbus had deposited one dollar into a savings account that paid 5 percent a year in simple interest, each year he would earn 5 cents on his dollar—which is to say that by 2018, his one dollar would have grown to $27.30. However, if he had taken that same dollar and placed it in a bank account that paid 5 percent a year in compound interest, it would now be worth nearly $140 billion! That's the power of compounding.

STEP THREE
Make their weekly allowance a teaching tool.

One of the best ways to teach children about money is to give them an allowance. However, this does not mean simply handing over a specified amount of money with no strings attached. In my view, your child's weekly allowance should be based on three principles:

- They should earn it.
- They should value it.
- They should use it to help others.

Unfortunately, for many kids and their parents, allowances have become a rite of passage. The child hits a certain age and asks for an allowance. The parents then turn to their friends, take a survey on allowances, and settle on a dollar amount they feel comfortable with. They then proceed to dish out that amount every week to the child, who uses the money to buy candy, comic books, clothes, and other goodies that catch his or her fancy, fueling a vast army of consumers who as a group spend billions of dollars a year. Consider this . . .

IN 2017, TEENAGERS SPENT $264 BILLION

According to the site Statistic Brain, teenagers accounted for $264 billion in economic activity during 2017. Now, I know some of these kids had jobs, but an awful lot of them were using money that had been dished out to them by generous (and often guilt-ridden) parents.

I'm not saying we shouldn't give our kids money. But why not do it in a way that teaches them something about the nature of personal finance and money management? That's what the Rockefellers did, and they certainly knew something about money.

HANDLING THE ALLOWANCE QUESTION, ROCKEFELLER-STYLE

According to a snippet I read on the Internet from a book called *Kids and Cash* by Ken Davis and Tom Taylor, former vice president Nelson Rockefeller, who had earlier been the governor of New York (and the primary benefactor of New York City's famed Museum of Modern Art), once explained how his father, the legendary John D. Rockefeller, taught him about money. As Nelson Rockefeller told it, he and his five brothers were each given 25 cents a week. "If we wanted more money we had to work for it," he said. What's more, he added, "All of us had to keep a record of where our money went. We were required to give 10 percent to charity, save 10 percent, and then account for how we spent or saved the other 80 percent."

There is an amazingly powerful yet simple lesson from one of the wealthiest families in U.S. history. It comes down to this.

- To earn an allowance you have to work.
- 10 percent of your allowance goes to charity.
- 10 percent of your allowance goes to savings.

• 80 percent of your allowance can be spent but you have to track each expenditure.

If you think about it, that's pretty much what you've been learning in this book: Pay yourself first, watch your Latte Factor®, and give back to others. Think how much easier it would have been to make these strategies a part of your life if you had been introduced to them when you were a child, like the Rockefeller kids were.

I recall seeing an episode of Oprah Winfrey's TV show that included a segment featuring parents talking about how they taught their kids about money. One couple said they required their children to put part of their allowance into a family investment account that the kids ran themselves. Each month, they held a family investment meeting at which they discussed investment strategies and how their holdings were doing. That's a brilliant idea.

The point is that when it comes to giving out an allowance, you can just dole out the dough—or you can turn the exercise into a teaching tool that will have a massive, positive impact on your children's financial literacy.

WHAT IF WE'VE ALREADY BEEN GIVING OUR KIDS AN ALLOWANCE WITH NO RULES?

Be honest. Tell them that the rules have changed—that from now on, you intend to handle their allowance in a way that will teach them how to be future millionaires. They will get it. (And what are they going to do—go on strike?)

> **STEP FOUR**
> **Teach them about retirement accounts . . . now.**

The best time to open a retirement account is when you're a teenager! But how do you convince a teenager of that?

Actually, there is a way. Show your teenager the chart on page 310. The first column illustrates what would happen if a 14-year-old named Lucy were to open a retirement account and save $2,000 a year until she reaches 18—that is, depositing a total of $10,000. Even if Lucy never put in another dime after that, simply by letting the money grow in a tax-deferred retirement account (ideally, a Roth IRA) at 10 percent a year, she would wind up with more than $1 million in her account ($1,184,600, to be precise) by the time she was 65.

The other columns in the chart illustrate what happens if you don't start saving until you're older. One shows Susan, who starts at age 19; the other shows Kim, who waits until she's 27. Neither woman ever catches up to Lucy, even though both deposit significantly more money.

It's another demonstration of the miracle of compound interest, and it is extremely motivating!

HOW CAN A TEENAGER OPEN A RETIREMENT ACCOUNT?

Very easily. Any teenager with a part-time job can open a retirement account. All you've got to do is accompany your child to a bank or brokerage firm (or to the office of your financial advisor, if you've got one) to help with the paperwork. The key qualifications to open an IRA is that your child must have earned income and that the IRA deposit in any given year cannot exceed his or her income in that year.

Say your teenager works part-time bagging groceries and earns $1,000 over the course of a year. He or she could put as much as $1,000 into a Roth IRA. Now, don't worry. I haven't lost it completely. I know that very few teenagers are going to want to fund a retirement account with every dollar they earn. So here is what I suggest. Show your teenager this chart and explain that you want

THE TIME VALUE OF MONEY

Invest Now Rather Than Later

LUCY Investing at Age 14 (10% Annual Return)				SUSAN Investing at Age 19 (10% Annual Return)				KIM Investing at Age 27 (10% Annual Return)	
AGE	INVESTMENT	TOTAL VALUE		AGE	INVESTMENT	TOTAL VALUE		AGE	INVESTMENT	TOTAL VALUE
14	$2,000	$2,200	S	19	$2,000	2,200	S	19	0	0
15	2,000	4,620	E	20	2,000	4,620	E	20	0	0
16	2,000	7,282	E	21	2,000	7,282	E	21	0	0
17	2,000	10,210		22	2,000	10,210		22	0	0
18	2,000	13,431	T	23	2,000	13,431	T	23	0	0
19	0	14,774	H	24	2,000	16,974	H	24	0	0
20	0	16,252	E	25	2,000	20,871	E	25	0	0
21	0	17,877		26	2,000	25,158		26	0	0
22	0	19,665		27	0	27,674		27	$2,000	2,200
23	0	21,631	D	28	0	30,442	D	28	2,000	4,620
24	0	23,794	I	29	0	33,486	I	29	2,000	7,282
25	0	26,174	F	30	0	36,834	F	30	2,000	10,210
26	0	28,791	F	31	0	40,518	F	31	2,000	13,431
27	0	31,670	E	32	0	44,570	E	32	2,000	16,974
28	0	34,837	R	33	0	48,027	R	33	2,000	20,871
29	0	38,321	E	34	0	53,929	E	34	2,000	25,158
30	0	42,153	N	35	0	59,322	N	35	2,000	29,874
31	0	46,368	C	36	0	65,256	C	36	2,000	35,072
32	0	51,005	E	37	0	71,780	E	37	2,000	40,768
33	0	56,106		38	0	78,958		38	2,000	47,045
34	0	61,716		39	0	86,854		39	2,000	53,949
35	0	67,888		40	0	95,540		40	2,000	61,544
36	0	74,676		41	0	105,094		41	2,000	69,899
37	0	82,144		42	0	115,603		42	2,000	79,089
38	0	90,359		43	0	127,163		43	2,000	89,198
39	0	99,394		44	0	139,880		44	2,000	100,318
40	0	109,334		45	0	153,868		45	2,000	112,550
41	0	120,267		46	0	169,255		46	2,000	126,005
42	0	132,294		47	0	188,180		47	2,000	140,805
43	0	145,523		48	0	204,798		48	2,000	157,086
44	0	160,076		49	0	226,278		49	2,000	174,094
45	0	176,083		50	0	247,806		50	2,000	194,694
46	0	193,692		51	0	272,586		51	2,000	216,363
47	0	213,061		52	0	299,845		52	2,000	240,199
48	0	234,367		53	0	329,830		53	2,000	266,419
49	0	257,803		54	0	362,813		54	2,000	295,261
50	0	283,358		55	0	399,094		55	2,000	326,988
51	0	311,942		56	0	439,003		56	2,000	361,886
52	0	343,136		57	0	482,904		57	2,000	400,275
53	0	377,450		58	0	531,194		58	2,000	442,503
54	0	415,195		59	0	584,314		59	2,000	488,953
55	0	456,715		60	0	642,745		60	2,000	540,048
56	0	502,386		61	0	707,020		61	2,000	596,253
57	0	552,625		62	0	777,722		62	2,000	658,078
58	0	607,887		63	0	855,494		63	2,000	726,086
59	0	668,676		64	0	941,043		64	2,000	800,895
60	0	735,543		65	0	1,035,148		65	2,000	883,185
61	0	809,098								
62	0	890,007								
63	0	979,008								
64	0	1,076,909								
65	0	1,184,600								

Total invested = $10,000. | Total invested = $16,000. | Total Investment = $78,000.
Earnings beyond investment = $1,174,600. | Earnings beyond investment = $1,019,148. | Earnings beyond investment = $805,185.

| Lucy earns | $1,174,600 | Susan earns | $1,019,148 | Kim earns | $ 805,185 |

Lucy invested $68,000 less than Kim and has $369,415 more!
START INVESTING EARLY!

to help them get started on the right foot to finishing rich. Tell them that for every dollar they contribute to a Roth IRA, you'll contribute a dollar. If they put in $100, you will match it with another $100.

You see, the government doesn't care where the money used to fund a Roth IRA comes from. All it cares about is how much the account owner happens to have earned that year. I know some business owners who have put their kids on the payroll at a salary of $5,500 a year, which they then used to fund a Roth IRA. Of course, the kids have to report the $5,500 a year as income—but with the passage of the 2017 Tax Cuts and Jobs Act, a dependent child can have as much as $12,000 in income (whether earned or unearned) each year without owing any federal income tax as of the 2018 fiscal year.

As I see it, getting teenagers their own retirement accounts is both a smart financial strategy and a phenomenal teaching tool. By doing it, you accomplish two things. You teach your children about saving at a young age and you get them in the habit of "paying themselves first."

STEP FIVE
Teach them to think like owners instead of shoppers.

Earlier, I told you how my grandma Bach helped me make my first financial investment at age seven. Both my grandmother and my father changed my life by teaching me at a young age what it meant to buy stock in a publicly traded company.

The idea that there were things you could do with cash other than just spend it—that by investing you could turn a little money into a lot more—just blew me away. I remember asking my parents the first time we visited Disneyland, "Is this place for sale? Can we buy stock in this place?"

I couldn't believe it when they said yes. Don't get me wrong. I think mutual funds make great investments. But the experience doesn't match the feeling of owning a share of stock in a particular company. There is nothing quite like buying a Coke or logging on to Facebook and knowing that you own a piece of the company. Today, my two boys own companies like Shake Shack, Amazon, Disney, Snap—because these are the companies they are excited about.

With this in mind, teach your kids how to buy stock. Log on to an online brokerage firm and help them open an account. You'll have to open the account in both of your names, but it will be a great lesson. Then teach them how to look up stocks online and how to read the ticker on CNBC and the other financial services. (If you don't know yourself, you can find information on how to do so on your brokerage firm's website. It's not really that complicated.)

Something else you can do is buy one share of stock in a company your child knows and likes, and then ask the broker to have the stock certificate "issued out." This means the certificate will be sent directly to you, rather than being kept on file at the brokerage. If it's a cool company like Disney, the stock certificate will be gorgeous— nice enough to frame and hang in your kid's room. When his or her friends come over, your child can explain what it is and how he or she is becoming an investor. Pretty soon, your friends may be wanting to teach their kids about stocks too.

There is a company called **giveashare.com** that will do all of this for you. They will even have the stock certificate framed for you! If you want to do this as a gift, all you need is the child's name and Social Security number.

> **STEP SIX**
> **Teach them to use credit cards responsibly.**

THE CREDIT-CARD COMPANIES WANT
YOUR CHILDREN

Credit-card companies aren't stupid. They know that if they can get their cards into your children's hands, they will use them often, while making only the minimum monthly payments, thus staying in debt—and paying expensive finance charges—for years, if not decades.

For the companies, this is simply good business. Until they were forced to stop marketing to minors via the Credit CARD Act of 2009, credit-card companies were a fixture on college campuses in America. But even though issuing credit cards to anyone under the age of 21 is now harder for the companies, there are still myriad ways that young people can get into trouble with credit cards. They might just be slightly older when then fall into the credit-card trap.

YOU MUST TEACH YOUR KIDS NOW ...
BEFORE THE CREDIT-CARD COMPANIES
GET TO THEM

Sooner or later, your children are going to get credit cards and they are going to use them. Just how they use the cards will depend largely on how they were raised. If they've seen you constantly using credit cards, they will use credit cards constantly. If they've seen you run up bills you can't afford, they'll probably do the same.

Unless you start showing your kids the bills and explaining the stress that credit-card debt can cause, they will not realize the real implications of their purchasing decisions. I speak from personal experience. I grew up watching my parents use credit cards all the time. The only lesson I really learned was that you were supposed to pay your cards on time—a very important lesson, as it turned out, but hardly the only one I needed to learn. As a result, when I got to college, I was woefully unprepared to handle all the credit cards that were offered to me.

When I signed up at my new dorm room freshman year, I was greeted by representatives of three credit-card companies. They were giving away "free" clock radios, bike locks, and dictionaries. All you had to do was sign up for a card.

When my friends saw all the stuff I'd gotten, they all rushed downstairs to sign up too. Three weeks later, our mailboxes were stuffed with shiny new credit cards. Now picture this: You're 18 and you and everyone you know has instant access to "free money," courtesy of some brand-new plastic. What do you suppose we did? That's right—we went to town and partied.

By my sophomore year, I owed $5,000 in credit-card debt. When I confessed my plight to my parents, my father told me something I will never forget. "David," he said, "welcome to adulthood."

He went on to explain that the cards had my name on them, and that if I didn't pay the bills on time, I'd ruin my credit record and be scarred financially for years.

It was a splash of harsh reality that caused me to grow up fast. It took me a year to get out of that credit-card debt, but I did it. In the process, I learned a valuable lesson. Don't spend what you don't have. Today I use a debit card and an American Express card, and I never carry credit-card debt.

If only my parents had drilled it into my head earlier not to use credit cards and always to pay off the card in full each month. It would have saved me so much trouble and anguish.

Here's what you should teach your kids specifically about credit cards.

Explain what happens if you run up a credit-card balance and don't pay it off. Explain how brutal it is to have to keep paying 18 percent interest on purchases that have long since lost their shine. Share with them how if they don't pay their cards on time each and every month, they can literally damage their credit so badly that even years later they won't be able to get a mortgage to buy a house. All it takes is one little credit card with a $500 balance you forgot to pay off.

This is so important that, before your kids leave the nest, you absolutely have to have a "credit-card talk." In addition to emphasizing the importance of paying off their balances, make them understand that multiple credit cards are a disaster waiting to happen. All they really need is one card for use in case of emergencies. In no event should they have more than two.

Good luck with your talk. I know it won't be easy, but it will be worth it. You could wind up saving a child from future bankruptcy.

STEP SEVEN
Teach them to go for their dreams.

This last step has very little to do with money but a lot to do with life. I think one of the greatest gifts a parent or adult can give a child is the feeling that "this child is special." We need to literally douse our children with love—to keep reinforcing the feeling that they are special. You can't err by giving too much love or support. Nor do I believe that it's ever a mistake to tell children again and again that they are special and that if they try, they can accomplish anything they want. I think the biggest mistake we make with our kids is inadvertently teaching them not to try because they might fail. If anything, rather than discouraging failure, we should reward it.

A CHILD WHO FAILS TRYING SOMETHING NEW IS A CHILD WHO WILL LEARN FASTER

What's great about children when they are really young is that they have no fear. They aren't afraid of not looking good. They don't worry about not knowing how to do something. They just storm right ahead and try.

Unfortunately, society quickly changes this. Society teaches children as they grow older that failure is to be avoided. Our grading system at school reinforces this idea. Don't fail, the schools say. You must be good at all things. You must get good grades in all your subjects or you won't move ahead in life.

This idea that you need to be good at everything is absurd. The truth is that to be incredibly successful in life you may only need to be really good at one thing. In fact, this describes some of the most successful and richest and happiest people around. They've become so good at one particular thing that society rewards them for it, and refers to them as "stars."

BECOME A CHEERLEADER FOR YOUR CHILD

You can be a cheerleader for your kids and still enforce discipline. I had very strict parents, but they also cheered me on. They urged me to try new things and always "go for it." They encouraged me to take risks.

I don't think this kind of approach can ever be a mistake. The idea that we need to raise realistic kids is crazy. What's reality? Look at our world. New realities are created every day.

One of the most disappointing things about our schools and the way we raise our kids is that we don't spend more time teaching kids to take more risks. Instead, we teach them to play it safe. Be good, get good grades, get a good job, and eventually you can have a good retirement. That's the lesson society endorses.

But what if that lesson is totally out of date? What if the idea that getting good grades and then going to a good college and then getting a good job represents an outmoded plan? In fact, most of our schools today are based on a model created over a hundred years ago for an industrial society in a world totally different from the one into which most of us were born. Back then, you went to work, punched a clock, did what you were told, and eventually were handed a gold watch (maybe). There was hierarchy and a well-defined system within which to work.

Not anymore. Today, ideas created out of thin air can become billion-dollar enterprises. The people who get ahead are the ones who know how to communicate, how to think outside the box and persuade others. Unfortunately, many of our schools are still preparing our kids for the old system. Sit still. Be quiet. Do what you are told and we will give you good grades. Get good grades, get a good job, and get lifelong security.

I'm not suggesting that kids shouldn't get good grades and go to college. Of course they should. But it seems to me that our schools are creating worker bees at a time when society is rewarding entrepreneurs.

We need to raise our children to think bigger and more creatively than we did. So ask yourself right now, "What am I teaching my kids about life's challenges?" Are you raising your children to go for their dreams or simply to avoid failure?

STEP EIGHT
Encourage your kids to learn about money online.

It's likely your kids are already spending time online. Make sure they include financial education in with their social media, gaming, and entertainment time online. These are five great financial websites for kids:

DreamBigClub.org. This free site has been around since 2001, and it features Sammy Rabbit, who helps kids learn about money. The site has more than 200 activities for children, parents, and even teachers, and offers a ton of fantastic tools, curricula, books, coloring books, songs, and videos created to inspire young people to save, invest, and dream big. One of my favorite parts of this site is the original song called "S.A.V.E.," which they say was inspired by my book *The Automatic Millionaire* and has this fun lyric: "We're gonna make it habit, we're gonna make it automatic." To listen to it, click the Songs icon, then click "S.A.V.E." It's catchy!

FeedThePig.org. The American Institute of CPAs runs this fun site that offers cool tools, resources, articles, and tips for helping kids grow up to be financially stable adults. Your child can create a savings plan on this site, and connect to its companion site at **www.360financialliteracy.org**.

JumpStart.org. JumpStart is a nonprofit organization dedicated to training educators to teach money curricula in schools. This organization has been working for nearly two decades to help improve financial literacy, and I have personally met with them and volunteered to speak to hundreds of their teachers who have been trained. This website reflects just how amazing this organization is: On the site you'll find real content, tools, and resources to take on the task of teaching your kids about money at home and in the school systems. I highly recommend that you dig around on this site if you're interested in this issue.

Moneyasyougrow.org. This website connects you to a ton of resources that you can use to begin teaching your children about money. The Money As You Grow website is a government site that links you to a dedicated page on the Consumer Financial Protection Bureau website. You'll find resources that teach money lessons based on your children's ages, from young children to teens. There are downloadable worksheets and tools as well.

SesameStreet.org. For young children, Sesame Street's website has a section called "Finance for Kids," which you can find by searching the site. Once you're there, Elmo will help your kids learn more about the world of money with a number of fantastic lessons and other resources. Check out (and sing along to!) "The Jobs Song," which explains how people earn money.

Shark Tank. I highly recommend you watch this great television show with your kids. *Shark Tank* has become the go-to family show around the world. I have been watching this show now with my kids for years, and their sophistication level around entrepreneurialism and investing has grown exponentially. Just the other day, a company I'm an advisor to and investor in was sold in a very public way, and my fourteen-year-old son's first questions were "Dad, how much equity do you own? Were your options fully vested?"

WHAT ABOUT PAYING FOR COLLEGE?

While I have many concerns about how and what our schools teach our kids, I am still a strong proponent of education, teachers, and ultimately the value of a college education.

I just want your kids to know they have options. If you teach them the lessons you learn in this book, they can escape the rat race because they will know how to save, invest, and spend wisely.

This brings us to the most difficult financial challenge many parents face. How in the world are you going to pay for college?

COLLEGE IS EXPENSIVE . . . AND GETTING MORE SO EVERY YEAR

According to the College Board, the average cost (including tuition, room and board, books, and transportation) of attending a state college in the 2016–2017 academic year was $20,090 (in-state) and $35,370 (out-of-state). For private colleges and universities, the figure was $45,370. And that was just the average. The most expensive institutions—a group that includes Ivy League schools—carry price tags topping $60,000.

Any way you look at it, that's a lot of money. And it's getting worse every year. According to the experts, college costs are expected to continue rising at a 5 percent annual rate for the foreseeable future. So advance planning is important.

Fortunately, saving for college does not need to be overly difficult or complicated. There are currently four basic types of college-savings plans.

UGMA AND UTMA ACCOUNTS

The oldest type of college-funding mechanism is not designed specifically for college costs. Established in some states under what's known as the Uniform Gifts to Minors Act (UGMA) and in others under the Uniform Transfers to Minors Act (UTMA), these are simple trusts that are set up by parents for the benefit of their minor children. Typically, the account name will be something like "Jane Smith as custodian for Jane Smith, Jr."

What UGMA and UTMA accounts do is allow parents to transfer assets to a child without having to hire an attorney to set up a special trust. Normally, minors are not allowed to own assets like stocks or mutual funds or even bank accounts without a trust being established on their behalf. What makes these accounts popular is that they are easy to set up and manage. (Any bank or brokerage firm will happily take care of it.)

There is no limit on how much you can contribute to an UGMA or UTMA account, though anything over $15,000 a year may subject the child to federal gift taxes. While the assets in the account legally belong to the child, they are managed by whoever was named as the account's custodian (usually one of the parents).

The bad thing about UGMA and UTMA accounts is that when the child reaches the age of majority (either 18 or 21, depending on what you elect when you fill out the paperwork on the account), control of the account shifts from the custodian to the child. In other words, you can spend the better part of two decades saving for college for your adorable little boy, but if he grows up to be a monster who decides on his eighteenth birthday that he wants to use the money to buy a new Porsche and go to Europe with his girlfriend, there's nothing you can do about it. (Don't laugh; I've seen this happen.)

SECTION 529 PLANS

Section 529 plans are how people save for college today. What the 401(k) plan has become to retirement planning, the 529 plan has become for college savings. **You should take advantage of these now, before some politician comes along and tries to end them (which has been discussed).**

Since they were created in 1996, Section 529 plans have become the gold standard of college savings accounts. These plans are administered by individual states, so your state will probably have its own plan providers. But the tax code law that established the account is the same, so you get the same great benefits.

These plans come in two types. The prepaid tuition plan is useful if you already know that you want to send your child to a specific school in a specific state. But how many of us are in that position? That's why I like the college savings plan, which doesn't ask you to know anything about your child's college plans other than that he or she has one.

A 529 plan allows you to save a substantial amount of money (up to $400,000 in some states, although the average cap is around $300,000) toward each child's college education. As long as the money stays in the account, the money grows tax-free. You pay no taxes on dividends or capital gains. How great is that?

Even better, you don't pay taxes on the money when it's withdrawn to pay for approved college expenses like tuition, housing, and books. So while you may not get to deduct your 529 contributions on your income tax return like you can with an IRA, when college time rolls around the money comes without strings attached as long as you spend it on education. In addition, more than 30 states also offer either a full or partial deduction or credit for 529 plan contributions. So even though you don't get a federal tax break for your 529 contributions, you still might get a nice tax incentive from your state.

You remain in control of the account, too, unlike the UGMA and UTMA accounts, which hand control over to your kids when they turn 18 or 21.

A 529 plan also allows others to help you fund your kids' college costs. The government allows "third-party" contributions (e.g., by grandparents) of $14,000 per child in a single year—or a lump sum of $70,000 ($140,000 if it is a joint gift, e.g., from two grandparents) and the gift tax is then credited over five years. For kids with wealthy grandparents, this can make great sense from an estate-planning standpoint. That's what I call financial aid!

Finally, the 2017 Tax Cuts and Jobs Act included a pretty big change to 529 accounts. Prior to this legislation, money from a 529 account could only be used for qualified higher education expenses. Now, however, 529 plans may be used for up to $10,000 per year in K–12 expenses. This means it's easier for parents to save money for K–12 private school tuition or other expenses.

The best place to start investigating 529 plans for your family is **www.savingforcollege.com**, which offers an incredible library of relevant material. The first thing to do is look at the plans in your state, to make sure you don't miss your state tax deduction.

Websites for College Planning
www.college-insight.org
www.collegeboard.org
www.collegeresults.org
www.finaid.org
www.petersons.com

www.nasfaa.org
www.unigo.com

COVERDELL EDUCATION SAVINGS ACCOUNTS (ESA)

Formerly called an Educational IRA, this account, which was created in 2002, allows you to contribute up to $2,000 a year for each child toward college—or certain qualified K–12 expenses. The money grows tax deferred and when it is distributed for educational expenses (which must be done by the time the child reaches age 30) it comes out tax-free. Until the passage of the 2017 Tax Cuts and Jobs Act, Coverdell ESAs were the only tax-advantaged savings option for families who wanted to set money aside for K–12 private school tuition.

While these plans are better now that you can save more than the original $500 a year maximum contribution, they still are not, in my opinion, as great as the 529 plans. The $2,000 limit still is low and you give up control of the money. If your child doesn't go to school, the money is ultimately refunded to them, not you! And now that 529 accounts can serve the same function of helping families save money for private K–12 tuition, I would recommend that anyone with a Coverdell ESA roll over the account to a 529. You can do so with no tax consequences.

SOME FINAL WORDS OF ADVICE ON COLLEGE SAVINGS

Start a college savings account the year your child is born. If you do, you won't need to save more than $100 to $300 a month. On the other hand, if you wait until your kids are teenagers to start a college fund, which is what many parents do, the exercise becomes extremely challenging. It's not too late, but you have to play catch-up big-time.

In any case, while I am a huge proponent of parents establishing savings programs for their kids' college educations, I don't think such efforts should come at the expense of the parents' own financial futures.

Your security and retirement baskets come first. College funding comes second. I see too many parents sacrificing their financial security for the sake of their children's college education. That's a mistake. The greatest gift you can give your children is to ensure that you won't be a financial burden to them. If worse comes to worst, your kids can always get a part-time job when they're in high school and start putting aside their own money for college. There are also countless scholarships and loan programs for deserving students. Each year, literally billions of dollars in scholarships are available.

SCHOLARSHIP PROGRAMS

Visit the following websites for more information about scholarships and other college financial aid programs.

www.fafsa.ed.gov. FAFSA stands for Free Application for Federal Student Aid. Run by the U.S. Department of Education, it's arguably the most used, best website in the world for college scholarship information and is a great place to start your search.

www.collegeboard.com. From the folks who make students' lives miserable with those standardized tests, this website covers everything from taking the SATs to planning and paying for college.

www.fastweb.com. FastWeb enables students to create personal profiles to help them find scholarships that match their specific needs and qualifications. The site has a database of more than 1.4 million scholarships totaling more than $3.4 billion, and also offers articles, tips, and resources to help students improve their chances of winning a scholarship.

www.salliemae.com. Sallie Mae, the Student Loan Marketing Association, is the nation's leading provider of funds for education loans. In addition to being a great resource for federally guaranteed student loans, its website also includes a scholarship search engine, a lender locator, information about education loans, and lots of other good information about college planning, college savings, and debt management.

BECOME A MENTOR

I hope this chapter has motivated you to teach your kids about money—or, if you don't have any of your own, to mentor a child you care about. Here are some great sites to visit if you would like more information on mentoring and teaching kids.

The National Mentoring Partnership: **www.mentoring.org**
The Special Olympics: **www.specialolympics.org**
Big Brothers & Sisters of America: **www.bbbsa.org**
Friends of the Children: **www.friendsofthechildren.org**
Ability Online Support Network (in Canada):
  www.abilityonline.org
Make A Wish Foundation: **www.wish.org**

FOLLOW THE 12 COMMANDMENTS OF ATTRACTING GREATER WEALTH

So far on our journey to financial independence, we've concentrated primarily on how to make the most out of the financial resources you have—the best way, in other words, to slice up your financial pie. Now let's talk about how to bake a bigger pie.

The thing to keep in mind in this regard is that it's a mistake to separate your "money life" from your personal or professional life. It's not that your life should revolve around money. It's that your personal financial situation is inextricably linked to everything else that's important to you: your goals, your dreams, your health, your security, your freedom.

The fact is, the tools I hope you have acquired in the course of reading this book apply to much more than just money management. The good habits you should be developing as part of your journey to financial independence—things like focus and discipline and values-based behavior—can reinforce success in every aspect of your life. Indeed, as you change your financial behavior to match your values, you'll probably start noticing things happening in other areas of your life as well. At the very least, you're bound to become a lot more aware of the extent to which the choices you're making in your work life and personal life reflect (or *don't* reflect) your values. And that, in turn, will enable you to make more intelligent decisions about which professional and personal options make the most sense for you.

Remember, though, that it's not enough simply to understand intellectually the concepts we have discussed in this book. You have to apply what you've learned here. You have to go out and actually do it.

Now, that doesn't mean you have to climb Mount Everest. One of the most common misconceptions people have is the belief that in order to make massive changes in their lives, they have to do incredibly difficult and special things that require enormous effort and complicated skills. As a result of this misconception, most people get defeated—*they defeat themselves*—before they even get started. Don't let that happen to you! The point of this book is that you can make dramatic changes in your life—and ultimately help and support the people around you—just by using the simple tools I've provided.

But you have to use them.

GETTING PAID WHAT YOU'RE WORTH

One of the defining characteristics of a Smart Woman is that she is paid what she is worth. But getting paid what you are worth doesn't just happen to you; you have to act to ensure that you get what should be yours.

With this in mind, the last tool I'm going to give you now may be the most powerful one of all. That's because it possesses the ability to make it much easier for you to accomplish everything we've set out to do in the first seven steps of our journey. The tool I'm going to give you now will enable you to earn more money quickly.

Now, I know what you're thinking. Didn't I say that income didn't matter?

That's true; I did, and I still believe it. But as I said, the whole point of this book is that financial success is based on the cultivation of good habits—that to be financially secure and able to achieve your dreams, you need to have the right habits, tools, and beliefs. Now that you have them all, I want to make the process of getting where you want to go that much easier.

TAKING CONTROL OF YOUR CAREER ... AND YOUR LIFE

I am convinced that most people earn 10 to 30 percent less than they could be earning if they just took control over their careers. Think about this for a second. What if you could easily increase your paycheck by 10 to 30 percent over the next few months? Before you read this book, you might have thought about rewarding yourself with some new clothes or maybe even a new car. But now, with your new insight, think what truly amazing things you could do with your extra income: go back to school, travel the world, have enough to retire on by the time you're 55. Rather than making one-time purchases that satisfy instant cravings, you will be making an investment in yourself that's permanent. It is these lasting contributions to your life that reflect a real, substantive change in *you*.

Now, how do you increase your wealth so that you can make these critical investments?

You don't have to get this extra money just through a paycheck, of course. Whether you are climbing the ladder in a corporation, are self-employed, own your own business, or are managing an inheritance or alimony payments, there are certain behaviors and habits that will allow you to attract the wealth you deserve—as long as you decide to take control. These "rules"—which I call the 12 Commandments of Attracting Greater Wealth—aren't all about earning, however. One is even about giving it away! But, as you'll see, they are all about taking an active role in your life and making intelligent decisions rather than allowing fate to control you.

THE 12 COMMANDMENTS OF ATTRACTING GREATER WEALTH

Of all the stories I've heard over the years from women who have taken control of their lives, the most dramatic are about what happened when they went to work on improving their earning potential. That's because even a small increase in percentage terms—say, just 10 percent—can amount to thousands of dollars more a year in income.

Back in the introduction, I told you a story about a woman named Lauren whom I had coached on her personal finances and her career.

As a result of my coaching, Lauren was able to double her income in less than six months. Today, she earns a six-figure salary and is significantly happier than she used to be.

The same thing happened with Michelle. Although she had a great job that she loved, Michelle was frustrated because she wasn't being paid what she knew she was worth. Finally, she reached what I call "maximum frustration" and took action. The result: In less than three months, by applying the principles contained in this chapter, she got herself a new job that literally doubled her pay.

The best thing about Michelle's new job wasn't just the higher pay. It was that the new position allowed Michelle to grow as a person in a way that her old one hadn't. In just a year, she learned more about digital marketing and e-commerce than she had learned in five years on her previous job. The point is that by taking charge of your career, you can make sure that you're paid what you're worth—and by doing that, you can make sure you keep growing as a person!

The most important thing that happens when your income goes up is that your confidence goes up along with it. I'm not suggesting that your self-confidence should be based on your earnings. But I am a realist. If you think you are being underpaid, underappreciated, and underdeveloped in your current job, then you are being hurt as a human being—and that is unacceptable.

Chances are you are worth more than you are currently being paid. That's because you have abilities inside you that you haven't fully discovered yet, that are waiting to be brought out. By understanding and applying the following "commandments," you can bring these abilities out now.

COMMANDMENT 1
Don't accept less than you are worth.

When it comes to asking for a raise—whether you're dealing with a boss who signs your paycheck or a customer who has become used to paying a certain price for the product or service you provide—the biggest pitfall women face is their tendency to be "too nice."

Take my former client Lauren. She clearly had a serious case of "being too nice." Month after month, I listened to her complain about her 70-hour workweeks and the fact that she hadn't received a substantial raise in three years. Finally, after hearing one too many complaints, I asked Lauren why she thought she was worth more than the $65,000 a year her employer was paying her. She replied that there were people who did the same thing she did who were paid upward of $80,000 a year by a company that competed with hers.

"So why aren't you working for that company?" I asked her bluntly.

"Well, I like the people I work with," she said. "They're friends."

"Lauren," I explained, "friends are people you hang out with for free on the weekends. The people at your office are your coworkers and employers. Leave your job and you'll more than likely never hear from 90 percent of them again."

To make a long story short, I eventually persuaded Lauren to stop "being nice" and go talk to the competition. She did just that. A month later, they offered her more than $100,000 a year to come work for them. Her current boss (her good "friend") tried to get her to stay by offering her a big raise, but it was too little too late. Today, Lauren has new "friends" at her new job and earns almost twice what she was making a year ago.

The moral of Lauren's tale is simple.

YOU EARN WHAT YOU ACCEPT ... SO DECIDE NOW TO ACCEPT MORE!

Are you thinking right now about your current situation? Are you being "too nice" about how much you are currently earning? I suspect you are, since even highly paid and high-profile women are underpaid compared to their male counterparts.

Look at the actresses Jennifer Lawrence and Michelle Williams. In 2014, Lawrence discovered that she was paid less than her male costars for the film *American Hustle* only because of the Sony hack. Considering the fact that Lawrence was by far the biggest star in the movie, it was completely unreasonable that she should receive a smaller paycheck—and Lawrence herself wrote about how she was afraid of being perceived as "difficult" if she asked for what she was worth.

Just before I started this revision, news broke that Michelle

Williams received less than $1,000 to reshoot scenes in the film *All the Money in the World* (you can't make this stuff up!), while her costar Mark Wahlberg got a $1.5 million payout for the reshoots. Williams thought she was "taking one for the team," since the reshoots were necessary after the disgraced actor Kevin Spacey was ousted from the project. It didn't occur to her to ask for what she was worth when she thought everyone was supporting the cause of ending sexual harassment in the film industry. Talk about irony!

Having conducted thousands of Smart Women Finish Rich® seminars over the past twenty five years, I can tell you that one thing that really fires up the women who attend them is telling them it's time to stop being so nice when it comes to their earnings. You won't believe how many actually cheer when I say that. I remember a woman at a large seminar I did in Ohio who yelled out, "Dammit, you're right. I *am* too nice. I'm going back to my office to demand a raise today." The other women in the room broke up laughing, but the outburst led to a powerful and meaningful conversation.

What came out of this particular conversation was not unusual. "How many of you are underpaid right now and know it?" I asked the audience. More than three-quarters of them raised their hands. "So," I continued, "what is keeping you from asking for a raise?"

Here is some of what they said—and I promise you: It's typical of how most people answer this question.

I don't ask for a raise because . . .

- I'm afraid my boss will say no.
- I know I can't get it.
- My company only gives raises once a year.
- I'm not "up for a raise" until next year.
- We are cutting back so I'm lucky to have a job.
- I don't want to rock the boat.

- I don't want to look greedy.
- If I raise my prices, my customers will take their business elsewhere.

This is negative thinking. The fact is, you deserve every dollar you can get your hands on. There is nothing greedy about it. You deserve a raise, and you're capable of getting one. You just have to believe in yourself and start asking for it.

There is plenty of documented proof that a big reason women earn less than men is that women don't negotiate hard enough when they get a job offer. In their book *The Shadow Negotiation*, Deborah M. Kolb and Judith Williams report studying similar groups of men and women who were offered similar jobs. The women, they found, tended to accept the first offer a prospective employer made. By contrast, the men generally held out for a higher salary and better perks—and they usually got them.

Women entrepreneurs tend to do the same thing. Studies show that women who leave the corporate world to start their own consulting firms often price their services as much as 20 to 30 percent lower than their male counterparts.

Don't do this to yourself. The reality of the working world is that you almost never get more than you ask for. Ask for a little and you will get a little. So be less nice, more aggressive, and go get the paycheck you deserve. Starting today, stop selling yourself short—refuse to accept anything less than you are worth!

So how do you figure out what you are worth? Talking about your salary is often frowned upon both professionally and socially, which makes it tough for Smart Women to know how their paychecks stack up against others in the same field. Thankfully, there are a number of excellent online resources that can help a Smart Woman in any career field figure out the average salary for her position, location, and experience. If you're not sure whether your income is above or below average, try plugging your information into one of these Internet salary calculators:

www.glassdoor.com. In addition to a salary calculator and reports, this site offers company reviews from employees, benefits reviews, interview questions, and a job search database.

www.payscale.com. Search this site for a free salary report for one of more than 100,000 different job titles.

www.salary.com. The calculator on this site allows you to search for a salary estimate based on your job title and location, and compare it to similar jobs in your field.

Five-Star Tip: In addition to salary calculators online, another great way to determine if you are earning what you are worth is through a mastermind group. Such a group will consist of 5 to 20 other women working in your same field, with whom you can share advice, connections, resources, and support. A mastermind group is also an excellent place to ask about compensation so you can get a better sense of how much your work is worth. Your mastermind group can also help coach you through the process of asking for more money! You can create a mastermind group on your own by asking other women in your field if they would be interested in joining, or you can seek out an already established mastermind group to join. Here are some resources for finding mastermind groups in your area:

www.masterminds.org. On this site you'll find resources for starting your own mastermind group, as well as online groups that you may join. There are also a ton of articles and tips that will help you get the most out of your mastermind group.

www.meetup.com. This site offers you the opportunity to meet like-minded individuals in your area. Search for established mastermind groups or start your own with this site.

COMMANDMENT 2
Ask for a raise.

Has Commandment 1 got you fired up? I hope so. But now what? The answer is simple. It's time to ask for a raise . . . now. (If you are self-employed, then it's time to raise what you charge for your goods or services.) You need to think of your income as a living thing—which is to say that, like any other living thing, it is either growing or it is dying.

What is your income doing right now? Be honest. At a minimum, your goal should be to increase your income by 10 percent each and every year. Keep that up and your income will double just about every seven years.

Now, a 10 percent raise may sound like a lot, but it really isn't. If you ask for a 4 percent raise every six months, you'll effectively achieve your 10 percent goal every year, because the increases compound.

The nice thing about asking for a little raise on a regular basis is that it doesn't seem like such a big deal to your employer. An employer can rationalize letting you have a little extra money because the cost of replacing you (provided you are a great employee) is extremely expensive. In many cases, the cost of replacing a trained employee often totals as much as twice the departing employee's annual salary!

Put yourself in your boss's shoes. You have a great employee who comes in and asks for a 4 percent raise. If this employee is earning, say, $40,000 a year, the cost of the raise she wants will be $1,600 a year—or just $133 a month. Now compare that to the cost of posting a help-wanted ad on a job board, plus the lost time spent sifting through the applications and resumes that come in response, plus the cost of bringing candidates in for interviews. All of that work and time will cost you far more than $133 a month. And there's no guarantee you will be able to find a replacement quickly. And then there's the additional costs of downtime and training, meaning it could be months before the new employee is up to speed.

The bottom line is clear: It's not worth losing a good employee for the sake of a few dollars a month. If you add value on the job, this is how your boss will think about your request. It's something you should keep in mind when you ask for your raise.

The same logic applies if you are self-employed. Let's say you charge $35 an hour for your services. You have customers who have done business with you for years. If you raise your rates this week to $37 an hour, how likely is it that any of them will take their business elsewhere? Not very—not because of an extra $2 an hour. Face it, if you provide your customers with real value, it will be too much of a hassle for them to find a new "you."

Now, if you were to raise your rates every six months by a small amount—say, 5 percent—within a year, you'd have increased your annual earnings by 10 percent. This 10 percent increase could now go straight into your retirement basket and make you rich!

Many small businesses do exactly this sort of thing all the time, and you never even notice it. My dry cleaner raises its rates every six months like clockwork. Every six months, the cost of ironing a dress shirt goes up by 15 cents. What am I going to do—find a new dry cleaner I like as much as the old one just to save 15 cents a shirt? Of course not. And guess what? In this way, my dry cleaner has managed to double its prices over the past five years. And they haven't lost me as a customer. Because they do good work (they don't lose or ruin my clothes), I just accept that they are in the business of making money.

Remember that phrase: the business of making money. This is what a business does and this is what an employee should keep in mind. You are in the business of making money. So go get that raise.

COMMANDMENT 3
If you don't like your job, quit.

When all else fails, there is a lot to be said for quitting your job. If you are currently being underpaid, underappreciated, or underdeveloped in your career or business, I suggest you consider finding someplace else to work or something else to do.

This may sound extreme. In fact, this commandment is bound to offend some of you. That's understandable. If you know in your heart that you really should quit your job, but you're afraid to follow your instincts, your gut reaction is going to be "Who does David think he is to tell me to quit my job? He doesn't have my bills, lack of savings, overhead, kids, mortgage payment, college costs [insert additional excuses here]. Anyway, you can't quit a job just because you don't like it. The fact is, most people don't like their jobs. That's why they call it a job."

If I've offended you, I apologize. By now I hope you trust me enough to know my goal here is to coach you to action. I'm being brutally honest here because I don't want you to rationalize accepting a bad career or job. You deserve better. Too many people rationalize their whole lives. They lead lives of quiet desperation. It's brutal and, worse, it's all a lie.

Here's how the lie works. **People tell themselves it's okay:**

• To work at a job you don't love.
• To work with people you don't like.
• To work for a company you don't respect.
• To work for a company that doesn't respect you.
• To work for less than you are worth.
• To suffer at a boring job because you need it.
• To spend time doing something you are not really interested in because you are paid well.

- To go for security, even though it's killing your spirit.
- To give up on your dreams because you are an adult.
- To put your life's energies into something you don't feel passionate about.

Well, I say it is NOT okay.

It's a truly terrible mistake to DECIDE to spend your life doing something you don't love because you believe that someday you will have enough money saved to be able to do what you really want.

In my book, this is too much of a gamble. What if "someday" never comes? What if you work another 20 years at something you don't love? What if you give up the best years of your life for a paycheck, and then it turns out to be too late for your dreams?

Here's what I want you to ask yourself right now. Are you one of those people who is putting off your dreams in the hope that someday you'll have the resources necessary to have the career or life you really want? *Is this really okay for you?*

In a May 2018 interview on CNBC.com, Suzy Welch, the wife of former GE CEO Jack Welch and cofounder of the Jack Welch Management Institute, suggests that you should ask yourself, "When was the last time I did something at work for the first time?" Welch contends that if it's been a long time, then you should quit, even if you still like the job, because you've stopped growing—you're comfortable but are stuck in a "velvet coffin." Her advice is to "get out before the lid closes on you." That's a pretty vivid picture. Just know that it's okay to quit if you're not satisfied and have stopped growing in the job. Your life is too precious and too short to waste it.

In fact, Amazon takes this thought seriously enough that the company actually pays employees to quit! According to a 2018 CNBC article, the retail giant wants to make sure that all of its employees are truly committed to the company, so it offers full-time fulfillment center associates up to $5,000 to leave the company. The catch? Anyone who takes the payment can never work for Amazon again. The company doesn't actually want people to take the quitting bonus; it just wants them to take a moment each year to think about what they really want from their jobs—and this counterintuitive strategy really works. Very few people have taken Amazon up on this offer, and the annual opportunity to get paid to quit has enhanced employee engagement while keeping Amazon's turnover costs low.

If any of this rings true for you right now, if these ideas make you feel at all uncomfortable, then ask yourself this question: How would it really feel to quit your job? Imagine it. Might you ultimately feel better inside? Could this be a decision that's actually long overdue?

You'll know deep down inside if the answer is yes. If it is, the time has come to make a decision.

Make a plan to quit your job and give it a deadline. Decide now that you will quit your job in six months. Or maybe a year from now.

Whatever feels right, for your own sake, decide now. Create an "I Quit" date. Write it down and start planning your future today. Sure, you will feel nervous, but, believe me, you may feel more energized by this decision than any you have made in years, maybe decades.

COMMANDMENT 4
Start your own business.

Let's say you don't like your job. Who says you have to find yourself a new one? Did you know that most entrepreneurs today are women? Not only are more than 11.6 million companies owned by women, but according to the National Women's Organization of Business Owners, female-owned businesses today provide nearly 9 million jobs and generate $1.7 trillion in annual sales.

Female-owned businesses, particularly small ones that employ less than ten people, are also thriving at a rate higher than male-run businesses.

There are a lot reasons for this trend. Many women are fed up with corporate America and its invisible "glass ceiling." Others just want to be their own boss.

What about you? Each year, millions of Americans leave secure jobs to start their own businesses. Is it time for you to take the leap? Do you have an idea that you know would work if only you had the time? Do you have a dream of owning your own business?

If so, do what most entrepreneurs do. Start it on the side. Work extra hours, but get started. Maybe you'll need new job skills to make the transition. That's okay. The key is to figure out what you are passionate about that could earn you money.

Could you fail? Maybe. But maybe not. According to a recent report by success guru and bestselling author Brian Tracy, 74 percent of American millionaires made their riches by starting their own businesses. So think about it: What if you succeed beyond your wildest dreams? Here's my question to you . . .

What would you do if you knew you couldn't fail?

If the answer is "start my own business," then it's time to start doing some research.

> **Five-Star Tip:** Be very wary of companies and websites offering "home-based business opportunities." There are too many people out there looking to take advantage of well-intentioned entrepreneurs. I suggest you start your research with a terrific book that has become a classic on the subject of starting your own business. It's called *The E-Myth Revisited: Why Most Small Businesses Don't Work and What to Do About It*, by Michael E. Gerber.

I also recommend the following websites:

www.entrepreneur.com
www.fastcompany.com
www.hoovers.com
www.inc.com
www.nase.org
www.nawbo.org
www.sba.gov
www.smallbusiness.com

COMMANDMENT 5
Build your personal brand.

Whether you own your own business or work for someone else, you want to stand out. You want to be known as the type of woman who rises above the competition. In short, you want to show everyone that you are someone other people can count on.

What does it take to accomplish this? Fortunately, not a whole lot. All it takes is creating your personal brand—one that focuses on being a consummate professional.

One of the amazing things about the business world is that it is filled with people who are satisfied with being mediocre. As depressing as that may sound, it's also great news for Smart Women, because it means you don't have to do all that much to stand out. In fact, here's all it takes to make more money, earn the respect of your colleagues, and become known for your personal brand of professionalism:

1. Show up early.
2. Have a plan and implement it.
3. Always do what you say you will do.

4. Take total responsibility.
5. Have an attitude of gratitude.

These five things may not seem like much, but the fact is, most people don't bother to do them, either personally or professionally. Simply being a woman who shows up early with a plan, always follows through on what she promises, and takes responsibility will put you ahead of the pack in any workplace. Do these things, and your personal brand at work will represent competence and hard work.

An attitude of gratitude has been added since the first edition to this book because it's the most important business and life lesson I have learned in 25 years. You can't fail in life when you constantly appreciate what you have and come from a place of gratitude. An attitude of gratitude also makes you stronger. These five things may seem "cliché," but you might be stunned to discover how lavishly the world rewards such simple, professional behavior. Remember—simple is good; simple works!

Finally, online brand management matters a lot today. Maintaining a personal website on YOU—a personal brand site you can regularly update—is better than a business card and resume. Also, a strong and up-to-date profile on LinkedIn can make an enormous difference in your career and your life. You never know who may be trying to connect with you, and making sure your online professional network sees the best and most current version of your work can mean the difference between an opportunity and missing out.

In addition, Smart Women in the twenty-first century need to remember that any online social media presence is part of their overall brand. Whether you are on Facebook, Twitter, Instagram, Tumblr, or YouTube, it's important to see your activity on those platforms as part of your professional identity. Not only does that mean it's a good idea to use strong privacy settings on anything that is truly personal, but you should also remember that inactive accounts can look unprofessional. Go ahead and lean into whichever social media you are most active on—and delete those that have gathered cobwebs.

> ### COMMANDMENT 6
> ## Keep your overhead under control.

Nothing will trap you faster in a job or career than needing the income. I know it should be obvious, but for many of us it's not—until it's too late. Society is designed to get you to spend every penny you make and then some. The more you make, the more you are led to believe you should spend.

This is especially true as you become more successful. Advertisers want us to believe that when we succeed, we owe it to ourselves to buy their most expensive products. Open any magazine, listen to the radio, or watch TV and there they are: the beautiful people enjoying the good life—that is, the good life you get when you make lots of money and spend it on the advertisers' products.

In truth, most of us can't afford what they are selling. Lease a new BMW for $550 a month and you've just committed yourself to $6,600 a year in car payments. Add in taxes, gas, insurance, and registration, and that commitment has now grown to nearly $8,600 a year. And this is for a middle-of-the-road BMW. We're not talking about the big-time success (and expense) that requires you to lease the top-of-the-line BMW.

Now let's do the math. If you earn $50,000 a year after taxes, your take-home pay will be about $35,000. That means that 25 percent of your take-home pay is earmarked for car expenses! Sounds crazy, doesn't it? Yet there are hundreds of thousands of people out there driving fancy cars they can't afford. Why? Because they have focused on the "low" monthly payments.

WATCH OUT FOR
"LOW MONTHLY PAYMENTS"

The car industry created the concept of seducing customers by making luxury items available for "low monthly payments." Now nearly everything is sold on that basis. You can furnish your whole house and not pay a penny for 18 months. After that, it's just a matter of some low monthly payments. We Americans are being "low monthly payment-ed" to death. People underestimate how these little things add up.

The fact is, we all need less than we think. Keep your overhead under control. Don't let it rise just because your income has gone up. If your overhead matches (or, worse, exceeds) your income, you can end up stuck in a job you don't want, doing things with your life you'd rather not be doing.

> **COMMANDMENT 7**
> **Work each day as if you were going
> on vacation tomorrow.**

Remember the last time you went on vacation? Remember how much you got done right before you left? That last week at work and at home got you really organized, didn't it? You knew you had a lot to do, so you made a list of goals—a to-do list—to get it all done. You were in what we call pre-vacation mode.

We all can relate to this. For most of us, the last several days before a vacation are some of the most productive days of the year.

I learned the power of this concept from the legendary motivational coach Zig Ziglar. Zig believes that the way to handle your life and your career is to live every day as if you were going on a cruise tomorrow.

It's one of those things that makes perfect sense when you think about it. Except that most of us never do.

For many employees, a typical workday is something like this: Get to the office on time around 9 a.m. (never early). Get online. Check Facebook, Twitter, Instagram, your blog feeds. Have coffee, check in with friends. Around 10 a.m. start to review your e-mail and respond. Fiddle around until 11 a.m. Work hard for a half hour because it's almost lunchtime. Get ready for lunch. Go to lunch. Get back at 1 p.m., tired from the big meal. Return some e-mail or maybe even some calls, go to a few useless meetings, answer some more e-mail, get ready to go home. Around 4 p.m., start winding down and prepare for another busy day at work tomorrow.

Exaggerated? Maybe, but it's more true than not. Even those people who say they are so busy that they work 60 to 80 hours a week are often kidding themselves.

Now, think about how much work you get done just before you go on vacation. That's a real workday. Okay, maybe you don't want to work that hard every day. I can accept that. But here's my suggestion. Get to the office early, work really hard for six to eight hours— and go home!

You might be thinking, *Wait a minute, David. There is no way I can do that. I've got a job where I have to punch the clock. I can't just go home early.* Fine, consider getting a new job. Find yourself the kind of career where you get rewarded for results instead of duration. There are millions of such results-based jobs out there.

Or maybe you have a career that you love that is simply inflexible when it comes to schedules. I recognize that leaving an hour early is often a nonstarter for doctors, dentists, teachers, nurses, call-center employees, retail managers, and the like. But you can still figure out the best way to be productive with your work time, even if your job can't let you leave early. While this advice may not get you more free time if you work an inflexible schedule, it will still help get you noticed and advance your career.

The truth is that most of us can get very rich being very

productive for no more than six to eight hours a day. Who wouldn't work hard if they knew that the reward included getting to have a life too?

Realizing this changed my life. When I go to my office these days, it's to work. It's to get the job done, achieve results, and go home. It's not to socialize. I'm not antisocial or rude, but I don't have time for chitchat. I come to work to work, and as soon as I am finished, I get out of the office. I have a life out of the office.

The point of business is to have a life, not the other way around. So start working like you are about to go on vacation—and then go on one. You deserve it!

> **Five-Star Tip:** If you are not currently in a position to change your career, be honest with yourself. How much more productive can you really be at work? What would happen to your career if you "picked it up" a notch? What would happen if you came in to work an hour early every day just for 90 days and worked every day as if you were about to go on vacation? The truth is that your career would get a huge boost—and you would get noticed in a very positive way. Another truth is that when others (especially bosses) notice that you're getting to work early and are really working hard, they tend to be more open-minded about letting you leave early. Try it—the results may surprise you . . . pleasantly. I've now got friends who are working Monday through Thursday for ten hard hours, but then they take Friday off completely. That's also a great approach.

COMMANDMENT 8
Focus on what makes you unique.

We are all blessed with special talents that make us unique. Some people discover their talent at a young age and from then on focus their lives on honing it until they are rewarded by society. We call the most successful of these people "stars" or "pros."

But I'm not just talking about sports or movie stars. Stars exist in every realm. There are star salespeople and star parents and star teachers and so on. The questions you need to ask yourself are: What makes you uniquely valuable? What is it that you have to offer? One of the saddest things I see as I get older are people I love who have given up on their dreams. When I see friends working at jobs I know they aren't passionate about, I realize they have forgotten what it is that makes them unique.

A few years back, a good friend of mine took a suit-and-tie job. Now, this is a guy who loves being outdoors and doing things with other people. But he had looked around at what his friends were doing and, feeling left behind, he took the path he saw others following.

Unfortunately, he was not uniquely valuable at a suit-and-tie job. In fact, he was uniquely bad at it. So instead of moving up, he went nowhere fast. In the process, he became increasingly unhappy. It took him years to figure out that he had taken a path to a destination he didn't really want.

What about you? Are you spending time at work doing something you are uniquely good at? Do you know what you are uniquely good at?

Here are a few life-changing questions you should ask yourself today.

- What is it that I am really good at?
- What do I enjoy so much that I would do it for free if I had $20 million?
- What would I stop doing tomorrow if I had $20 million?
- What would I do differently with my life if I only had three years to live?
- What do others regularly tell me I am good at?

If you answer these questions honestly, the exercise can change your life. I know because it changed mine. This book and my seminars exist because in 1996 I had a heart-to-heart talk with myself in which I asked those questions. The answers surprised me.

The first thing I realized was that if I had three years left to live, I wouldn't spend it being a financial advisor. I realized I would want to write the book that you are holding in your hand today because I wanted to help thousands of people before I died.

The second thing I realized was that the one thing I really loved doing was coaching others. I love to speak on the topic of money, and if I had $20 million, I would still want to speak, write, and coach others about money.

This realization got me off my duff and forced me to focus on what I really wanted to do with my life. Ultimately, I realized that my unique talent wasn't just working as a personal financial advisor but exercising my ability to be a financial coach to thousands (and, hopefully, someday millions). *It amazes me, as I update this book, that my dream to help millions came true. It took two decades but they flew by, and it was worth it.*

So how do you apply this to your own life? Here's what I recommend. Answer the above questions today. Write down your answers in longhand. (Don't type them; studies show that writing things in longhand embeds them in your subconscious faster and more deeply.) If you have trouble answering the questions, get help from your friends. Ask them what they think you're really good at, what they think makes you unique. Also ask your coworkers, customers, and (if you have one) your boss.

By doing this exercise, you will learn a great deal about yourself. You may find that you have a job at which you are uniquely talented—in other words, that you are already pursuing your life's passion. If so, what you need to do now is really buckle down and spend as much time as possible on it (and, as our next commandment says, delegate your weaknesses).

If it turns out you are not spending the majority of your time on your unique ability or talents, hopefully the realization will leave you motivated like I was to "get going."

I can tell you from firsthand experience that once you discover and start working on what you're uniquely talented at, your passion will take you to a place in life you can't even imagine right now. And chances are that your income will grow in a major, long-term way as result!

For more information about exploring your unique talents, visit **www.strategiccoach.com**. Dan Sullivan, the creator of Strategic Coach, has trained thousands of entrepreneurs to focus on their "Unique Ability." I highly recommend his book *The Laws of Lifetime Growth*.

COMMANDMENT 9
Delegate the tasks you shouldn't be doing.

First thing tomorrow, you should delegate one task you currently perform that you know you shouldn't be doing.

Here's a simple example. If you are a career woman who works or owns your own company, you should NOT be doing your own laundry, your family's laundry, or any cleaning at home. Forget it. I am telling you right now that your time and passion are too valuable to spend doing things you can delegate to a cleaning service or laundry service for less than $10 an hour.

If you earn $45,000 a year, you are making around $22.50 an hour. That's what your time is worth. So why waste it doing anything you can pay someone less than that to do? You are much better off spending an extra hour at work and really focusing on growing your business or career than you are doing menial chores around the house.

I am constantly amazed at how many women get excited by this idea when I share it with them. Women who are making more than $50,000 a year constantly come up to me at seminars, saying things like, "I spend the whole day Sunday doing the laundry and cleaning, which I hate, but I just never felt right hiring a cleaning service."

I am here to tell you that if it's economically feasible for you to outsource something you hate doing, then you should outsource it! If you hate cooking, stop doing it. If you hate cleaning, stop doing it. Delegate those jobs. Spend the extra time with your family or on your passion and grow your income so you can get more out of life. Don't let the unrealistic pressures to do it all and have it all keep you from lightening your load.

The same goes for the way you handle tasks in the office. I meet women who have high-level careers, yet they still answer their own phones, do their own filing, and type their own letters.

Stop doing that. Stop doing anything you can pay someone else to do for less than your time is worth. If you stop wasting time doing things others can help you with, you can then focus on the things that will get you results at work and make you more money!

Specifically, you can focus on what makes you unique. Many people spend half their time at work doing things that are "process oriented" rather than "result focused." The reality is that we get paid for results, not process.

What if you have the job that someone else is delegating to? What if you are the assistant being delegated the letter typing, the telephone answering, the coffee making? In that case, make sure your boss agrees that this is what you are really supposed to be doing. What does your boss regard as your unique ability? Are there ways in which your boss thinks you can do more to help him or her?

Often, what your boss really wants from you is something other than what you spend the majority of your time at work doing. If this happens to be the case, explain to your boss what you are actually being forced to spend time on. It's entirely possible that he or she would help you get these tasks off your plate.

If you're the boss, try this with your staff. You may be amazed at their responses.

Nothing will increase your productivity faster than delegating the nonessential tasks you currently perform yourself.

There are a number of resources online that can help you find the right person to delegate your hated tasks to:

www.fiverr.com. Freelancers of all stripes advertise on this site for your business. Whether you need help around the house or the office, you can find a freelancer here.

www.taskrabbit.com. This site connects you with service providers as wide ranging as cleaners, errand runners, handymen, yard workers, deliverypeople, office administrators, and personal assistants.

www.upwork.com. Post the kind of job you need to have done on Upwork, and the site will quickly match you with the right kind of freelancers for your needs.

COMMANDMENT 10
Get up early.

When I started writing the first edition of this book in 1997, I had a huge challenge on my hands. I had promised the publisher I'd deliver a full-length manuscript by a set date. But where would I find the time to write it? I had a full-time job to which I devoted an average of 10 to 12 hours a day, often six days a week, and I hadn't yet learned the power of Commandment 7 or Commandment 9.

I knew I had to come up with more time. But I faced the same challenge you face: There are only 24 hours in a day. Finally, I came to terms with what I knew I needed to do. I decided I would get up no later than 5:30 every morning and start writing. At first this was brutal. I would drag myself out of bed, brew myself some coffee, and struggle to stay awake at the computer. But then something unexpected happened. As the weeks and months passed, I began to love my early mornings. There was no one to bother me, no distractions or interruptions. It almost felt as if I were on a vacation, because the time was my own and it was so quiet and peaceful, and I was working on my passion.

Eventually, I fell into a comfortable rhythm, in which I rose at 5:30 and worked uninterrupted until 7:30. In this way, I could give myself two straight hours of writing time and still make it to the office before almost everyone else.

Doing the math, I discovered these two extra hours in the morning amounted to 14 hours a week, or 56 hours a month. That's 672 hours a year. Do you have any idea how much you can accomplish in 672 hours? You can go for your dreams "on the side," you can get your body in shape, you can organize your finances, you can clean out your house and garage, you can start a business on the side, you can change the world. The power of two extra hours a day is enormous. And it's yours for the taking.

Is it easy to do? In the beginning at least, it's not. But you adjust in a matter of weeks. For starters, you begin going to bed earlier. I'm now usually in bed by 9 p.m. I used to stay up until 11 o'clock or midnight. What have I given up? Two to three hours a night of useless online surfing, or channel surfing—which is to say, very little. These days, even when I'm not working on a book, I still get up early. I meditate, write in my journal, work out, or read the paper with a cup of coffee. I get time to think and time to begin my day in the most powerful way imaginable.

This book is filled with ideas and exercises that are meant to change your life. The only reason they won't work for you is if you don't go to work on them. The number one reason most people have for not committing the time and effort to taking the kinds of actions I suggest is that they are too busy. Well, what if you were to get up one hour earlier every day for a year and spend the extra time using this book as a tool to make your life better? I promise you, your future will be greater than you could have ever imagined.

> **Five-Star Tip:** Want to copy my morning routine? It's pretty epic! I start with 20 minutes of meditation. (I personally do Transcendental Meditation and can't recommend it enough. You can visit **www.tm.org** for details.) Then I do my "attitude of gratitude" practice, where I use an app called the Five Minute Journal. On this app (which I love), I write down three things I am grateful for and three things I am looking forward to each morning. Then I exercise. And then I get ready with the kids and take my younger son to school. Even after all that, I'm still in the office a half hour to an hour before most people in my building. How do I do all of this? By getting up before 5:30 a.m. most mornings.

COMMANDMENT 11
Find a purpose greater than yourself.

Recently, I've heard many stories about wonderful schoolteachers assigning their students to write their own epitaphs or eulogies. It's a powerful idea. What would you want people to say about you after you're gone? What *will* they say about you?

How we live our lives now determines how others will remember us. Will they say we left the world a better place? I know for a fact that not a single one of my friends or family members cares how much money I currently have in the bank. When I die, they are not going to say, "Isn't it great that David had such a big retirement account. Isn't it great that he lived in such a nice home and had such a nice car?"

Not that nice things aren't worth having, but they aren't what I want to be remembered for. What I hope is that when I die my friends and family will say that I touched their lives—that I made their lives better by being their friend, that I added value to their lives.

I find that the more I focus my energy on coaching others and helping strangers, the more abundant my life becomes. The greatest gift I get from writing a book like this one is that it allows me in a small way to help many strangers, and in time I hope these strangers will come to consider me a friend.

There are so many ways to help others. Have you ever wanted to give something back to your community but didn't feel you had the time to spare? Or maybe you weren't sure exactly how to go about it? Well, perhaps it's time you finally did something. You can make the time.

The circle of life is truly amazing. Give to others and others will give back to you. Love others and you can feel that love come right back to you. Hold back your time, your energy, your wealth, and your love, and you ultimately lose it.

If you would like to start giving something back, check out these websites for more information.

> **www.americaspromise.org**
> **www.campfire.org**
> **www.charities.org**
> **www.give.org**
> **www.idealist.org**
> **www.mentoring.org**
> **www.networkforgood.org**
> **www.nvoad.org**
> **www.volunteermatch.org**
> **www.ymca.net**

COMMANDMENT 12
Be grateful.

While I was trying to finish this chapter, I hit a brick wall. I knew there had to be one more commandment—the clincher—that would pull everything together. I just couldn't find the right words.

For two days, I suffered from writer's block, unable to figure out what the final commandment should be. It was so frustrating that on Sunday morning, when I knew I had to finish the chapter, I didn't want to get out of bed. Then, while sitting there feeling sorry for myself, I decided to read a magazine. The magazine was *O* (Oprah Winfrey's magazine). I started reading an article in *O* about how to recover after a relationship breaks up.

The article had nothing to do with my life and nothing to do with what we're talking about here, but embedded in it was something that struck a chord with me. It was a section entitled "BE GRATEFUL." Now, that's not exactly an original thought. In fact, when I was writing the first edition of *Smart Women Finish Rich*, I initially wanted to include a commandment to that effect in this chapter. The idea was to paraphrase what Sir John Templeton, the billionaire investor, said when Tony Robbins asked him to single out what he regarded as the most important lesson for people interested in pursuing wealth and happiness. "Learn to live with an attitude of gratitude," Templeton replied. I loved that advice and, as I say, I wanted to include it in the book. In the end, though, it was edited out of my manuscript—not original enough, someone said.

Well, original or not, there I was, updating this book and reading this magazine, and the concept "BE GRATEFUL" hit me like a ton of bricks.

As a result, I got out of bed, took a shower, and started thinking about everything in the world that I had to be grateful for. In the end, I decided that rather than work on my book that day, I would make a list—a list of 50 things I felt grateful for. All at once, I went from being tired and depressed to motivated and passionate to feeling lucky to be alive.

How does this relate to you? Well, it hit me that no matter how motivated you are and no matter how much this book has inspired you to take action, there are going to be times when you get frustrated. There are going to be times when things won't go smoothly. You may ask for a raise and not get it (at least not on the first try). You may start buying stocks for your retirement account and the market will go down. You may decide to buy a home and then find out you can't afford the kind of house you want in the neighborhood you want.

Stuff happens. Stuff has always happened. You can't let that throw you, for no matter how much stuff may get in your way, nothing determines your future more than your own internal drive to succeed in life and your willingness to take action.

The question is, What can you do to keep yourself motivated when the world seems determined to block your efforts to live and finish rich? As I see it, the answer is simple: You can be grateful. Be grateful for everything you have in your life that is gloriously right, starting with the fact that you happen to be alive.

Of course, just because the answer is simple doesn't mean doing it is easy. The fact is, when the going gets tough, our grateful muscles disappear fast. To protect yourself against that possibility, here's what I want you to do with this last commandment. It doesn't cost anything and it won't take much time, but it might just change your entire outlook on life.

What I want you to do is take a piece of paper and write down 50 things you are grateful for. Simply write down everything that comes to mind. Now, since many of the things you write down are bound to be about other people whom you love or appreciate, I suggest you share your list with your friends and loved ones. After you've done that, put this list in your purse, wallet, phone, or day planner. Or use an app like the one I use—the *Five Minute Journal* app or book—and write down your gratitude daily. This conscious gratitude practice, along with meditation, has changed my life. The next time you feel down, tired, or stressed because things aren't working out exactly the way you'd hoped they would, take out your list and BE GRATEFUL. Remember, there's only one you and the simple fact that you exist makes this world a better place.

TAKE THE TIME TO SMELL THE ROSES

We have now reached the end of our journey together—though your individual journey to financial security and independence is just beginning. I want to close this book with a reminder of something I myself am often guilty of neglecting. In our efforts to build a secure future and protect our financial destiny, we should never forget that the greatest asset we have is life. Unfortunately, life is of limited duration and not guaranteed. There is no insurance we can buy that will give us back our life or make it possible for us to bring back those we love.

My point is that you shouldn't get so consumed with your financial journey that you don't spend enough time sharing moments with the people you love. As you take control over your finances and your career, please remember to let those you really care about know how much they mean to you. Not only will it make you feel better, but you will add more value to them spiritually than you will ever know.

Now that you've learned what it takes to become financially secure and reach your dreams, my final wish for you is that you enjoy the journey. The *Smart Women Finish Rich* process is not about pain or sacrifice. You don't have to give up the fun part of life to become a woman in total control of her financial future. You can become financially secure, reach your dreams, and still be a woman who has time to smell the roses.

LIVE YOUR LIFE WITH NO REGRETS

Shortly before she passed away, I asked Grandma Bach if she had any regrets in life. She said the only ones she had involved not things she did but the risks she didn't take. With that in mind, I'd like to suggest the following: If you believe you are going to be alive five years from now (and I hope you do), then there are really only two potential outcomes. You will either be five years older and have achieved your dreams (or at least be well on the way toward achieving them) because you have used the tools in this book and gone for it, or you will just be five years older.

As you go about your life, ask yourself regularly: Am I *making things happen* or am I watching things happen? Life is not a dress rehearsal. You get in life exactly what you go for. I say the heck with being a spectator. Go for it and jump in.

The choice is yours. Take the tools in this book and start now to begin your personal journey to the new woman you want to be in five years—more financially secure than you are now, more successful in your career, happier, even healthier. And remember—if you encounter a few setbacks along the way, don't let them deter you. You're not supposed to get everything right the first time. (And think about this: Mistakes and failures are just market research for your future successes!)

As you grow and take greater control of your life, please know that my thoughts and prayers will be with you. This journey we call life is an incredible gift, and I hope that in some small way this book has touched you for the better. I want you to know that I both respect you and admire your desire to be smart and live and finish rich—and that I look forward to meeting you someday . . . along the journey.

8 NEW TAX CHANGES YOU NEED TO KNOW ABOUT FOR 2018 AND BEYOND

In December 2017, just before I started work on this update, Congress passed the Tax Cuts and Jobs Act, which was the most comprehensive and substantial tax reform our country has seen since the tax cuts enacted under President George W. Bush in 2001 and 2003. This new legislation will affect nearly every taxpayer, and some Smart Women reading this book may have already noticed a difference in their paychecks since the law went into effect as of January 1, 2018.

There is a lot that Smart Women may like within the new tax rules. For most taxpayers, there will be more money left in each paycheck after Uncle Sam takes his cut. However, the new tax rules are incredibly complex, and all the strategies for dealing with these changes have not yet emerged. In addition, the Tax Cuts and Jobs

Act includes a sunset provision, meaning some of the changes we are seeing right now will be retired after the 2025 tax year.

Though covering all of the details of this new legislation is beyond the scope of this chapter, I did want to give you a primer on the aspects of the new law that are most likely to affect your taxes. Here are some of the changes coming to your taxes courtesy of the Tax Cuts and Jobs Act:

I. FEDERAL INCOME TAX BRACKETS HAVE CHANGED

Your income tax bracket determines what percentage you pay on the highest portion of your income. One of the goals of the new tax legislation was to reduce the number of tax brackets from seven to four, as well as reduce tax rates overall. While Congress was unable to pare down the number of brackets to four, they did succeed in providing lower tax rates for many filers and reducing the highest tax bracket from 39.6 percent to 37 percent. The following charts show how the new law has changed the income tax brackets.

2017 FEDERAL INCOME TAX BRACKETS		
Tax Rate	Single Filer	Married, Filing Jointly
10%	$0–$9,325	$0–$18,650
15%	$9,326–$37,950	$18,651–$75,900
25%	$37,951–$91,900	$75,901–$153,100
28%	$91,901–$191,650	$153,101–$233,350
33%	$191,651–$416,700	$233,351–$416,700
35%	$416,701–$418,400	$416,701–$470,700
39.6%	$418,401 and above	$470,701 and above

2018 FEDERAL INCOME TAX BRACKETS		
Tax Rate	Single Filer	Married, Filing Jointly
10%	$0–$9,525	$0–$19,050
12%	$9,526–$38,700	$19,051–$77,400
22%	$38,701–$82,500	$77,401–$165,000
24%	$82,501–$157,500	$165,001–$315,000
32%	$157,501–$200,000	$315,001–$400,000
35%	$200,001–$500,000	$400,001–$600,000
37%	$500,001 and above	$600,001 and above

The dollar amounts per tax bracket will change annually to reflect inflation, but these new rates will be in effect at least until tax year 2025.

2. STANDARD DEDUCTION AND PERSONAL EXEMPTIONS HAVE CHANGED

The IRS grants all taxpayers a standard deduction on their taxes, as a method for them to avoid itemizing their deductions. In addition, until the passage of the Tax Cuts and Jobs Act, taxpayers also had the option of claiming personal exemptions on their taxes in order to lower their taxable income. One of the goals of the new legislation was to consolidate the standard deduction and personal exemptions to create a single, larger standard deduction. As of 2017, the standard deduction was $6,350 for individual taxpayers, and $12,700 for married couples filing jointly. In addition, taxpayers could receive a $4,050 personal exemption—which meant that married couples could claim $8,100 as personal exemptions. With the new law, personal exemptions have been eliminated, and the standard deduction has been increased to $12,000 for individual taxpayers and $24,000 for married couples.

For many Smart Women, the new standard deduction will help to decrease their taxable income. However, for some families, the elimination of the personal exemptions could mean a smaller deduction. That's because, as of 2017, taxpayers could apply the $4,050 personal exemption to each family member. This means a family of four in 2017 could have deducted four personal exemptions for a total of $16,200 ($4,050 × 4 = $16,200), in addition to the standard $12,700 deduction for a married couple filing jointly—for a total deduction of $28,900. That same family in 2018 will only be able to claim the standard deduction of $24,000. However, though families may see a smaller deduction because of the elimination of the personal exemption, the changes to the child tax credit may more than make up for the difference.

3. THE CHILD TAX CREDIT HAS INCREASED

This tax credit is intended to help parents offset the costs of raising children. A tax credit is different from a deduction in that instead of reducing your taxable income, it reduces the amount of tax you owe by a specific dollar amount. This means that tax credits have the same value for everyone who can claim them.

With the changes in the tax law, the Child Tax Credit has now risen from its 2017 level of $1,000 per child under age 17 to $2,000 per child under 17. Of that $2,000 credit, $1,400 is refundable, meaning taxpayers whose tax liability is more than zeroed out by the credit may receive a refund of up to $1,400. The Child Tax Credit phases out for taxpayers above a certain income threshold. That threshold has gone up from $110,000 to $400,000 for married couples filing jointly, and from $75,000 to $200,000 for single filers.

In addition, there is a new nonrefundable $500 credit for dependents who are not qualifying children. These could include children over the age of 17 who are still claimed as your dependents, or potentially even dependent parents whom you are caring for in your home. This dependent credit also phases out at $200,000 for single filers and at $400,000 for married couples.

4. THERE ARE CHANGES TO THE ALTERNATIVE MINIMUM TAX

The Alternative Minimum Tax (AMT) is a tax rule that aims to ensure that high-income Americans pay a fair share of taxes, no matter how many deductions they itemize. Under this rule, high-income taxpayers have to calculate their taxes twice over: once under the standard tax rules and once under the AMT system. The AMT has been around for a very long time, but it was not indexed for inflation, so it was applying to more and more people over the years who were middle-income earners rather than high-income earners.

With the new tax law, the AMT has been permanently indexed to inflation to make sure that it is only applied to the high-earning taxpayers the law intended to affect. As of 2018, the exemption amount for the AMT rose from $54,300 to $70,300 for individuals, and from $84,500 to $109,400 for married couples.

5. THE SAVER'S CREDIT

This great little tax credit is one that many people don't know about, but it can help you reduce your tax burden and increase your retirement savings at the same time. This credit gives a break to middle- and lower-income taxpayers when they put money aside in a 401(k), 403(b), 457 plan, SIMPLE IRA, or SEP-IRA. Depending on your adjusted gross income and tax filing status, you may claim 50 percent, 20 percent, or 10 percent of the first $2,000 you contribute during the year to one of these retirement accounts. This means you may receive a (nonrefundable) credit of $1,000, $400, or $200 on your taxes.

The Saver's Credit is available only to taxpayers below certain adjusted gross income (AGI) thresholds: Single filers must have an AGI of $31,500 or less, and married couples must have an AGI of $63,000 or less.

6. THE END OF THE ACA TAX PENALTY

The new tax law also repealed the tax penalty associated with the Affordable Care Act. Uninsured Americans will no longer face a tax penalty if they do not get insurance. Although other aspects of the new tax law went into effect as of January 1, 2018, this particular rule does not go into effect until tax year 2019, so taxpayers without health insurance in 2018 may still be assessed the tax penalty for that year.

7. CONTRIBUTION LIMITS FOR RETIREMENT SAVINGS HAVE INCREASED

For 2018, contribution limits for retirement accounts that include 401(k), 403(b), most 457 plans, and Thrift Savings Plans increased to a maximum contribution rate of $18,500 if you are under age 50, and $24,500 if you are over age 50. This is a $500 increase from the 2017 limit. For individuals who want to consider a Roth IRA, the income phaseout has been raised to $120,000 to $135,000. For married couples who file jointly, the range of phaseouts is increased to $189,000 to $199,000. Please refer to **www.irs.gov** for updates.

8. MORTGAGE INTEREST DEDUCTIONS HAVE DECREASED

The deduction on new mortgage interest payments is capped at $750,000 as of 2018. This rule applies to mortgages taken out after December 15, 2017. If you have an old mortgage from prior to December 15, 2017, you are still able to deduct the interest on mortgage loan balances up to $1,000,000 and up to $100,000 on home equity loans.

You did it. YOU FINISHED the book. Congratulations. Keep this little book somewhere you can find it when you need help with your money. This can and should be a book you can return to for years to come—until the next update. If you would like more Live Rich goodness, stop by my website at **www.davidbach.com**—I send out a free newsletter when I'm inspired called *3 Minute Sunday*, and you can sign up for it there.

Now go love your life and live rich!

ACKNOWLEDGMENTS

My Grandmother Bach once told me that the key to having a fulfilling life was to understand that life's greatest fruit was always at the end of the branch and that you had to be willing to fall out of the tree to get it. The key, I was told, was to have people around you who could catch you should you fall. I have been blessed to have an incredible group of people around me as I go about taking risks to grab the fruit of life. Only because of these people who have supported me am I where I am today.

First and foremost, to the readers of the original edition of *Smart Women Finish Rich,* thank you, thank you, thank you. I will be forever grateful for having heard from so many of you about how it changed your life. It is your letters and e-mails that made the process of revising and updating the book so motivating. The knowledge that I have reached so many of you has made all the travel, hard work, and tight deadlines worth it. It is you who inspire me to want to help even more. I hope this new, 20th Anniversary edition of *Smart Women Finish Rich* answers your questions and meets your expectations.

Thank you also to the thousands of financial advisors nationwide who over the last decade have taught my Smart Women Finish Rich seminars and my Smart Couples Finish Rich seminars. Thank you for bringing my message to so many people in your local communities. To my incredible team at *AE Wealth Management* and all the advisors who are now teaching *Smart Women, Smart Retirement*™ and *Smart Couples, Smart Retirement*™ seminars—thank you for all you are doing to help retirees around the country live their best life and enjoy a true "return on retirement." To my partners Cody Foster and David Callanan, thank you for believing in this cause, and to Josh Jones for championing the seminars to success. As we approach $4 billion in assets in our new RIA it's truly amazing how far we have come as a team in such a short period. Seriously, well done, Team AE!

Smart Women Finish Rich would never have happened if I hadn't found a superstar agent. To Jan Miller, my "go-to gal," I will be forever grateful for our friendship and your belief in me and my vision. You make things happen, and I love it! To Jan's right hand, Ivonne Ortega, my internal champion, thank you for believing in what I do, and to Lacy Lynch, thank you for your marketing expertise. A special thank-you to Shannon Miser-Marven, who helped us push the original book to completion. To Allan Mayer, my collaborator on this project—as well as on *Smart Couples Finish Rich* and so many of my books—thank you, thank you, thank you for making these books what they are. From the beginning to the end, you have been a true professional and a delight to work with. Additionally, I would like to thank Emily Guy Birken for your editorial assistance on this update. You made it so much easier and I am grateful to you—well done. Finally, I want to give an enormous thank-you to my truly remarkable team at North Market Street Graphics. We have now done three book updates together in less than two years, a massive feat. Ginny Carroll, Vicky Dawes, Lainey Wolfe, Stewart Smith, and Madeline Brubaker—thank you. Without you and your team this book update would not have been possible.

To Vicki St. George, thank you for being the angel who tapped me on the shoulder at "Date with Destiny" and told me you could help me make my dream come true. It is because of your help on my book proposal that I was able to have my pick of agents. I will be forever grateful to you and your partner, Karen Risch, at Just Write for being the first experts to believe in and see my vision.

To my incredible team at Broadway Books, I loved you guys from the minute I met you.

To my original editor, Suzanne Oaks, thank you for believing in this project. It ultimately changed my life. To Kris Puopolo, you have edited and guided me now on five books and helped to shape my career—thank you for continuing this journey with me to help others live a great life. To David Drake, my publicist, we have now worked together for over a decade and on nine books—you are truly the superstar of superstars. THANK YOU for helping me bring my message to millions each year. To my new team at Currency Books—Roger Scholl, Tina Constable, Campbell Wharton, Jennifer Carrow: Thank you for your commitment to this updated edition. And to my new PR team at Jconnelly: We've been reaching millions with the *Smart Couples Finish Rich* update and now we're about to help millions more.

To my many original mentors, I owe both thanks and recognition. To my teacher and mentor Anthony Robbins, your friendship, teaching, and seminars have shaped my life since 1990, and for that I am eternally grateful. To Bill Bachrach, your book *Values-Based Financial Planning*, your TAC program, and your friendship have changed my life forever. Thank you for teaching me how to help others tap into their values about money. To Dan Sullivan, your "Strategic Coach" program already has had a major impact on both my life and my teachings. Thank you for showing me the power of focus and simplicity.

To my personal coach, Shirley Anderson, "Bravo, bravo, bravo." I applaud your greatness in coaching and I feel blessed to have found you. Thanks for helping me to see the light and follow my passion and life's dream of coaching millions to live and finish rich.

To my old friend Jeff Odiorne, who suggested over dinner, "Why don't you just take a day off work each week and write your book?" God, that was obvious. Thanks for coming up with it! To my close friends who have both listened to me talk about this book and supported me emotionally throughout the process, I thank you for your love and friendship.

To my many clients and students, with whom I have grown and from whom I have learned along the way, thank you for allowing me to make a wonderful living doing something I love.

To my incredible mother, Bobbi Bach, thank you for raising me to believe I could accomplish anything. You gave me the greatest gift a mother could give, the gift of love, security, and confidence. Thank you for the lunch where you told me to "spread my wings and fly"—that was the push I needed and the greatest love a son could ask for.

To my father, Marty Bach, I never realized how much work it took to get to the level of success you have achieved. Now I do. You always have been there for me, and I love you for it. Thank you for brainwashing me into the investment business and supporting me in everything I've done. This book would not have been possible without the support of you and mom.

To my successful sister, Emily Bach, you epitomize today's Smart Woman who is living smart and finishing rich. I am very proud of you. I knew the transition of my leaving my financial planning business and your running The Bach Group would go flawlessly.

And finally to my remarkable family. To my first amazing wife, Michelle, who cheered me on more than 21 years ago to do this book, and your incredible husband, Gene, and daughter, Charlotte—we make an amazing modern family. To my sons, Jack and James Bach, being your father is the greatest joy of my life. My mom once told me, "You will never know how much I love you until you have kids of your own," and she was right. Thank you for being the best two sons a dad could ask for. My heart bursts with love, joy, and pride as I watch you grow and become young men. To my wife, Alatia, you truly make everything better. I pinch myself sometimes when I think about how lucky I am and our family is to have found you. You were sprinkled with so much "special dust," and I am grateful every day to share in it. Thank you for saying "yes" when I asked you to come start your life with me. You made my life complete.

I love you all with all my heart.

David Louis Bach
New York, 2018

WHERE DOES THE
MONEY *REALLY* GO?

One of the most important parts of getting your financial life together is having a solid grasp on exactly what your current cash flow is. To do this, use the worksheet below.

First, determine how much you earn ...

Your Income

Wages, salary, tips, commissions, self-employment
income $_____

Dividends from stocks, bonds, mutual funds, savings
accounts, CDs, etc. $_____

Income from rental property $_____

Income from trust accounts (usually death benefits
from an estate) $_____

Alimony, child support, Social Security widow's benefits	$_____
Social Security benefits	$_____
Other income	$_____
TOTAL MONTHLY INCOME	$_____

Second, determine what you spend

Your Expenses

Taxes

Federal income taxes	$_____
State income taxes	$_____
FICA (Social Security taxes)	$_____
Property taxes	$_____
TOTAL TAXES	$_____

Housing

Mortgage payments or rent on primary residence	$_____
Mortgage payment on rental or income property	$_____
Utilities	$_____
Homeowners or renters insurance	$_____
Repairs or home maintenance	$_____
Cleaning service	$_____
Television cable	$_____
Home phone	$_____
Landscaping and pool service	$_____
Monthly Internet service	$_____
Condo or association dues	$_____
TOTAL HOUSING	$_____

Auto

Car loan or lease $_____

Gas $_____

Car insurance $_____

Car phone $_____

Repairs or service $_____

Parking $_____

Bridge tolls $_____

TOTAL AUTO $_____

Insurance

Life insurance $_____

Disability insurance $_____

Long-term-care insurance $_____

Liability insurance (umbrella policy) $_____

TOTAL INSURANCE $_____

Food

Groceries $_____

Food outside of home $_____

TOTAL FOOD $_____

Personal Care

Clothing $_____

Cleaning/drycleaning $_____

Cosmetics $_____

Health club dues and/or personal trainer $_____

Entertainment $_____

Country club dues	$ _____
Association memberships	$ _____
Vacations	$ _____
Hobbies	$ _____
Education	$ _____
Magazines	$ _____
Gifts	$ _____
TOTAL PERSONAL CARE	$ _____

Medical

Health-care insurance	$ _____
Prescriptions and monthly medicines	$ _____
Doctor or dentist expenses	$ _____
TOTAL MEDICAL	$ _____

Miscellaneous

Credit-card expenses	$ _____
Loan payments	$ _____
Alimony or child support	$ _____
Anything you can think of that I missed!	$ _____
TOTAL MISCELLANEOUS EXPENSES	$ _____
TOTAL MONTHLY EXPENSES	$ _____

Murphy's Law Factor

Take the total expenses and increase by 10 percent	$ _____
TOTAL INCOME	$ _____
Minus total monthly expenses	$ _____
Net cash flow (available for savings or investments)	$ _____

FINISHRICH
INVENTORY
PLANNER™

STEP ONE: FAMILY INFORMATION

Client Name_____

Date of Birth_____ Age_____ Nickname_____

Spouse's Name _____

Date of Birth_____ Age_____ Nickname_____

Mailing Address_____

City_____State___Zip_____Home Phone _____

Work Phone _____Fax _____E-mail _____

Spouse's Work Phone _____Fax _____E-mail _____

SS#_____ Spouse's SS#_____

Employer_____

Job Title_____

Spouse's Employer_____

Spouse's Job Title_____

Are you retired? Yes ____Date Retired_____No____Planned Retirement Date_____

Is your spouse retired? Yes____Date Retired_____No___Planned Retirement Date_____

Marital Status: Single____Married____Divorced____Separated____ Widowed_____

Children

Name	Date of Birth	SS#
1.		
2.		
3.		
4.		
5.		

Dependents

Do you have any family members that are financially dependent upon you or could be in the future? *(i.e. parents, grandparents, adult children, etc.)* Yes ___ No___

Name   1._____ Age _____
Relationship_____
Name   2._____ Age _____
Relationship_____
Name   3._____ Age _____
Relationship_____
Name   4._____ Age _____
Relationship_____
Name   5._____ Age _____
Relationship_____

STEP TWO: PERSONAL INVESTMENTS (DO NOT INCLUDE RETIREMENT ACCOUNTS HERE)

Cash Reserves

List amount in banks, savings & loans, and credit unions

Name of Bank Institution	Type of Account	Current Balance	Interest Rate
Example: Bank of America	*Checking/Savings/Money Market*	*$10,000.00*	*2%*
1.			
2.			
3.			
4.			
5.			

Fixed Income

List fixed-income investments

Example: C.D., Treasury Bills, Notes, Bonds, Tax-Free Bonds, Series EE Savings Bonds	Dollar Amount	Current %	Maturity Date
1.			
2.			
3.			
4.			
5.			

Stocks

Name of Company	No. of Shares	Price Purchased	Approx. Market Value	Date Purchased
1.				
2.				
3.				
4.				
5.				

Do you have stock certificates in a security deposit box? Yes _____ No _____

Mutual Funds and/or Brokerage Accounts

Name of Brokerage Firm/ Mutual Fund	No. of Shares	Cost Basis	Approx. Market Value	Date Purchased
1.				
2.				
3.				
4.				
5.				
6.				

Annuities

Company	Annuitant/Owner	Interest Rate	Approx. Market Value	Date Purchased
1.				
2.				
3.				

Other Assets (i.e., business ownership, etc.)   Approximate Market Value

1. _____ $ _____

2. _____ $ _____

3. _____ $ _____

STEP THREE: RETIREMENT ACCOUNTS

Are you participating in an Employer Sponsored Retirement Plan?
(These include Tax-Deferred Retirement Plans such as 401(k) Plans and 457 Plans) Yes _____ No _____

Company where your money is	Type of Plan	Approximate Value	% You Contribute

You:

1. _____ $ _____

2. _____ $ _____

3. _____ $ _____

Spouse:

1. _____ $ _____

2. _____ $ _____

3. _____ $ _____

Do you have money sitting in a company plan you no longer work for?

Yes _____ No _____ Balance _____ When did you leave the company? _____

Spouse:

Yes _____ No _____ Balance _____ When did you leave the company? _____

Self-Directed Retirement Plans

Are you participating in a retirement plan? *(These include IRAs, Roth IRAs, SEP-IRAs, SAR-SEP IRAs, and SIMPLE plans)*

Name of institution where your money is   Type of Plan   Approximate Value

You:

1._____ _____ _____

2._____ _____ _____

3._____ _____ _____

4._____ _____ _____

5._____ _____ _____

Spouse:

1._____ _____ _____

2._____ _____ _____

3._____ _____ _____

4._____ _____ _____

5._____ _____ _____

STEP FOUR: REAL ESTATE

Do you rent or own your own home?

Own _____ / Monthly mortgage is _____ Rent _____ / Monthly rent is _____

Approximate value of primary home $ _____ Mortgage balance $ _____

= Equity in home_____Length of loan ___Interest rate of loan ___Is loan fixed or variable?____

Do you own a second home?

Approximate value of second home $ _____ Mortgage balance $ _____

= Equity in home_____Length of loan ___Interest rate of loan ___Is loan fixed or variable?____

Any other real estate owned?

Approximate value $ _____ Mortgage balance $ _____

= Equity in home_____Length of loan ___Interest rate of loan ___Is loan fixed or variable?____

STEP FIVE: ESTATE PLANNING

Do you have a will or living trust in place? Yes _____ No ___ Date it was last reviewed_____

Who helped you create it? Attorney's name_____

Address_____

Phone _____ Fax _____

Is your home held in the trust or is it held in joint or community property? _____

Risk Management/Insurance

Do you have a protection plan in place for your family? Yes _____ No _____

Type of Insurance

Life Insurance Company   (i.e., Whole Life, Term, Variable, etc.)   Death Benefit   Cash Value   Annual Premium

1._____ _____ _____ _____ _____

2._____ _____ _____ _____ _____

3._____ _____ _____ _____ _____

Tax Planning

Do you have your taxes professionally prepared? Yes _____ No _____

Name of accountant/CPA _____

Address _____

Phone _____ Fax _____

What was your last year's taxable income?_____Estimated tax bracket?_____%

STEP SIX: CASH FLOW

Income

Your Est. Monthly Income _____ Estimated Annual Income _____

Spouse's Est. Monthly Income _____ Estimated Annual Income_____

Rental Property Income: Monthly _____ Annually_____

Other Income (i.e., partnerships, Social Security, pensions, dividend checks, etc.)

	Type of Income	Monthly	Annually
1.			
2.			
3.			

Expenses

Monthly Estimated Expenses $_____Annual Estimated Expenses $_____

What do you earn a month after taxes? $ _____

What do you estimate you spend?   - $ _____

Net Cash Flow   = $ _____

STEP SEVEN: NET WORTH

Total Assets $ _____

Total Liabilities   - $ _____

Estimated Net Worth   = $ _____

You can download a PDF of the FinishRich Inventory Planner™ at **www.davidbach.com/scfr**.

HOW TO REACH US

. . . go to *DavidBach.com*

If you would like more information about *Smart Women Finish Rich* or other programs we have developed, please contact us at **www.DavidBach.com**. There you will find information on:

- My free online *Sunday* newsletter (goes out on Sundays when I write it)
- How to attend a Smart Couples, Smart Retirement™ and/or Smart Women, Smart Retirement™ Seminar
- How to hire David Bach to speak at your next event
- For financial advisors: How to become licensed to teach FinishRich™ Seminars
- *And lots of other cool stuff for you to live and finish rich*

To everyone who has written and e-mailed me . . . THANK YOU from the bottom of my heart . . . I am incredibly grateful and humbled by the amount of letters and e-mails I have received thus far. If this book has made a significant impact on you, please know that I would like to hear about your successes!

Maybe your personal story (if you give us permission) will become part of a future edition. To share success stories, e-mail us at success@finishrich.com. I can't promise a reply, but I can promise I will read it. Also visit me at facebook.com/davidbach.

Lastly, I am no longer taking financial-planning clients and, due to legal liabilities, I unfortunately cannot answer personal financial questions. If you have specific financial questions, I strongly recommend meeting with a professional.

INDEX

ABOUT THE AUTHOR

David Bach has helped millions of people around the world take action to live and finish rich. He is one of the most popular and prolific financial authors of our time, with eleven consecutive national bestsellers, nine *New York Times* bestsellers, including two consecutive #1 *New York Times* bestsellers, *Start Late, Finish Rich* and *The Automatic Millionaire,* as well as the national and international bestsellers *Smart Couples Finish Rich; Smart Women Finish Rich; Debt Free For Life; Start Over, Finish Rich; Fight for Your Money; Go Green, Live Rich; The Automatic Millionaire Homeowner; The Finish Rich Workbook;* and *The Automatic Millionaire Workbook.* Bach carries the unique distinction of having had four of his books appear simultaneously on the *Wall Street Journal, Businessweek,* and *USA Today* bestseller lists. In all, his Finish Rich books have been published in more than nineteen languages, with more than 7 million copies in print worldwide.

Bach's breakout book, *The Automatic Millionaire,* was the #1 business book of 2004, according to *Businessweek.* It spent thirty-one weeks on the *New York Times* bestseller list and was simultaneously number one on the bestseller lists of the *New York Times, Businessweek, USA Today,* and the *Wall Street Journal.* With more than 1.5 million copies sold, this simple and powerful book has been translated into fifteen languages and has inspired thousands around the world to save money automatically.

Bach is regularly featured in the media. He has been a regular contributor to NBC's *Today*, appearing on the show over one hundred times. He appeared six times on *The Oprah Winfrey Show* to share his strategies for living and finishing rich and has made regular appearances on NBC's *Weekend Today* show, CNN's *Larry King Live*, ABC's *Live with Regis and Kelly*, *The View*, CBS's *Early Show*, ABC News, Fox News, Fox Business, PBS, and CNBC. He has been profiled in many major publications, including the *New York Times*, *Businessweek*, *USA Today*, *People*, *Reader's Digest*, *Time*, *Financial Times*, the *Washington Post*, the *Wall Street Journal*, the *Los Angeles Times*, the *San Francisco Chronicle*, *Working Woman*, *Glamour*, *Family Circle*, and *Redbook*. He has been a contributor to *Redbook* magazine, *Smart Money* magazine, Yahoo! Finance, AOL Money, and Oprah.com.

David Bach is the creator of the Finish Rich® Seminar series, which highlights his quick and easy-to-follow financial strategies. More than half a million people have learned how to take financial action to live a life in line with their values by attending his Smart Couples, Smart Retirement™, Smart Women Finish Rich®, Smart Couples Finish Rich®, and Find the Money seminars, which have been taught in more than 2,000 cities throughout North America by thousands of financial advisors.

An internationally renowned motivational and financial speaker, Bach regularly presents seminars for and delivers keynote addresses to the world's leading financial service firms, Fortune 500 companies, universities, and national conferences. He is the founder and chairman of FinishRich Media, a company dedicated to revolutionizing the way people learn about money. Prior to founding FinishRich Media, he was a senior vice president of Morgan Stanley and a partner of The Bach Group, which during his tenure (1993 to 2001) managed more than half a billion dollars for individual investors. He was the vice chairman of a nationally recognized RIA with $15 billion under management from 2014 to 2015. Bach is the cofounder and current Director of Investor Education of *AE Wealth Management*, one of the country's fastest-growing RIAs with more than $4 billion in assets on its platform (as of June 2018).

David Bach lives in New York with his family. Please visit his website at **www.davidbach.com**.